INNOVATIONS IN DESIGN

AHMEDABAD BUS RAPID TRANSIT SYSTEM

URBAN TRANSPORT INDIA SERIES

INNOVATIONS IN DESIGN

AHMEDABAD BUS RAPID TRANSIT SYSTEM

I. P. Gautam
H. M. Shivanand Swamy
Abhijit Lokre
Vijay Arya

with contributions by
Shefali Borikar-Shurpali and
Sandeep Paul

Centre of Excellence in Urban Transport | CEPT University

MAPIN PUBLISHING

First published in India in 2014 by
Mapin Publishing Pvt. Ltd

in association with

Centre of Excellence in Urban Transport,
CEPT University
Kasturbhai Lalbhai Campus, University Road,
Navarangpura,
Ahmedabad 380 009 • www.cept.ac.in

Simultaneously published in the
United States of America in 2014 by
Grantha Corporation
E: mapin@mapinpub.com

Distributed in North America by
Antique Collectors' Club
T: 1 800 252 5231 • F: 413 529 0862
E: info@antiquecc.com
www.antiquecollectorsclub.com

Distributed in United Kingdom and Europe by
Gazelle Book Services Ltd.
T: 44 1524-68765 • F: 44 1524-63232
E: sales@gazellebooks.co.uk
www.gazellebookservices.co.uk

Distributed in Southeast Asia by
Paragon Asia Co. Ltd, Bangkok
T: 66 2877 7755 • F: 66 2468 9636
E: info@paragonasia.com

Areca Books
Penang, Malaysia
T: 604 2610307 • F: 604 2633970
E: arecabooks@gmail.com

Distributed in the Rest of the World by
Mapin Publishing Pvt. Ltd
706 Kaivanna, Panchvati, Ellisbridge
Ahmedabad 380006 INDIA
T: +91 79 40 228228 • F: +91 79 40 228201
E: mapin@mapinpub.com | www.mapinpub.com

Research and Text
I. P. Gautam, H. M. Shivanand Swamy, Abhijit Lokre and Vijay Arya
with contributions by Shefali Borikar-Shurpali and Sandeep Paul

Photograph credits
Centre of Excellence in Urban Transport, CEPT University, except those listed below:
Cyrus Mobedji: Front cover, pp. 22, 143, 144 (top), 150 (top), 152–153,
Nicolas Charier: pp. 43, 68–69, 72, 112 (top-right), 147 (top), 155, 160–161, 175 (below), 179 (top), 180, 187, 188–189, 190

This document has been prepared by BRTS design team, Centre of Excellence in Urban Transport (CoE–UT), CEPT University. It documents the design process of Ahmedabad BRTS project. The views and opinions expressed in this document are the authors' own experiences throughout the journey of the project from conceptualization till implementation. The research, analysis and conclusions drawn by the authors have been verified to the extent possible. Any lapse may be brought to our attention for incorporation in future printings. The images, drawings, diagrams are creations of BRTS Design Cell, CoE–UT, CEPT University, unless otherwise credited. Reproduction permissions for graphics in this document have been given exclusively to CoE–UT and will require their permission prior to any sort of reproduction.

ISBN: 978-81-89995-93-5 (Mapin)
ISBN: 978-1-935677-48-2 (Grantha)
LCCN: 2014949291

Copyediting: Vivek Khadpekar
Proofreading: Neha Manke and Ankona Das / Mapin Editorial
Design: Gopal Limbad / Mapin Design Studio
Printed and bound by Parksons Graphics, India

Front Cover: The BRTS bus station near Gujarat University campus
Pages 2–3: An evening at Kankaria Lake BRT station. This is a bus and pedestrian-only zone.
Page 5: A barrier-free design
Pages 10–11: BRTS corridors attract diverse activities that make attractive destinations.
Back cover: The Kankaria carnival sees extensive use of the BRTS.

Foreword

India is urbanising rapidly. Over the last decade, with strong government support, many of our cities have undertaken path-breaking initiatives in resolving issues associated with urban transport, and specifically mass transit systems. The Bus Rapid Transit System (BRTS) is now acknowledged as a key mode to help large-scale mobility of people. It is also recognised for its ability to allocate road space equitably. This is in consonance with our National Urban Transport Policy.

I am happy to say that India now has eighteen cities at various stages of progress in their BRTS journey. The Ministry of Urban Development (MoUD) is extending sustained support to these cities, not only through capital funding for infrastructure and rolling stock but also through capacity building. The four Centres of Excellence in Urban Transport that were established in 2009 four years ago at IIT Delhi, CEPT University Ahmedabad, IIT Chennai and NIT Warangal, are doing excellent work.

MoUD has seen and supported the evolution of Ahmedabad's BRT system since its inception in 2005. We have seen how the Ahmedabad Municipal Corporation and CEPT University have worked in partnership at all stages of the project and continue to do so even today. In fact, one of the many things that make this a success story has been the partnership between these two organisations.

The present book on the Design Evolution of Ahmedabad's BRTS will prove very useful to all cities in India that are engaged in developing BRT systems. The name Janmarg itself is interesting—a *marg* or street meant for people. This book shares the Janmarg experience. It does not seek to prescribe a particular design or method, but to trace the evolution of the rationale underlying some critical decisions, the necessity to go beyond conventional design and to adapt to local situations. I am sure other cities will benefit from this book, and that it will be a valuable resource for researchers and academics as well as students.

Lastly, about the authors: the excellent contribution of Prof. Shivanand Swamy and his team at the Centre of Excellence in Urban Transport at CEPT University, and their passion for and dedication to their work is exemplary. I have had the opportunity of observing the contribution of Shri I. P. Gautam who, as the Municipal Commissioner of Ahmedabad, guided the BRTS project and worked closely with CEPT University. I wish them all the very best and look forward to their sharing many more stories about Janmarg.

Dr. Sudhir Krishna, IAS
Secretary, Ministry of Urban Development, Government of India
10th May 2014

Preface

The story of the design evolution of Ahmedabad's BRT system is still an ongoing one. As the system evolves, not only in Ahmedabad but in other Indian cities, people have many questions. Does this kind of system really work? Are our roads wide enough to accommodate BRTS? Is all the investment made by government really worthwhile? Planners and designers also grapple with crucial questions. Is it a good idea to segregate lanes in the centre than at the sides? Where should the bus stations be located? How do I deal with narrow roads?

Janmarg in Ahmedabad also explored many options before finalizing its design. It was flexible in changing design elements even during implementation stage. It was and still is seen as a long term infrastructure provision. Every element was discussed, debated, and experimented with before a final decision. Many of these experiments led to innovations and best practices.

Since its inauguration in 2009, Janmarg has been accepted as the first 'complete' BRTS in India. It has influenced planning and design choices in other cities in India and abroad. This book traces the design journey of Janmarg, the alternatives that were considered, the rationale underlying the choices made, the innovations it fostered and the lessons for the future—for Ahmedabad and for other cities. With more and more cities looking at BRT systems as mass transit options, Ahmedabad attempts to demonstrate what is possible in the existing paradigm of increased congestion, narrow streets and increasing focus on technical and engineering solutions to urban transport.

I. P. Gautam | H. M. Shivanand Swamy | Abhijit Lokre | Vijay Arya

14th May 2014

Acknowledgement

The birth of Janmarg as an idea was conceived and given shape in the year 2005 by the Government of Gujarat as part of an integrated transit strategy for Ahmedabad. Shri Narendra Modi, Honourable Chief Minister of the state and as Chairman of Gujarat Infrastructure Development Board, approved the project and oversaw all the developments throughout the project development phase. The interventions of Gujarat Government at appropriate time not only made Janmarg come into being but also made it a world-class system. The authors of this publication, who also worked on the project in various capacities, would like to express gratitude for the opportunity and the guidance received from him.

Smt. Anandiben Patel is another champion for this project. In her role as Urban Development Minister, she ensured that contentious issues were resolved in time and the project moved forward. We would also like to acknowledge the support the project received from Shri Nitinbhai Patel during his tenure as the Urban Development Minister of the state.

Former Mayor of Ahmedabad, Shri Asit Vora, both as standing Committee Chairman and subsequently as the Mayor, gave wholehearted support to the project and ensured smooth interface with citizens. The present Mayor Smt. Meenaxiben Patel and standing committee Chairman Shri Bhupendra Patel have continued their support to the project.

We would particularly like to acknowledge the support received from Dr. Anil Baijal, Dr. O.P. Agarwal, Dr. M. Ramachandran, Shri S.K. Lohia, Ms. Manjula Subramanium, Shri Kailashnathan, Shri S.R. Rao, Shri Paneervel, Shri Anil Mukim, Shri K. Srinivas, Ms. D. Thara, Shri G.R. Aloria, IAS, Shri Jayant Parimal, and Dr. R.N. Vakil, who have contributed significantly to the project at various times in the project cycle.

Dr. G.P. Mohapatra, who took over as the Municipal Commissioner, Ahmedabad, and Chairman, Janmarg, ensured that the momentum did not subside. His tenure has seen a doubling of the network and clear action plans for sustaining the gains made so far.

We also acknowledge the support from international organisations such as Embarq, ITDP, GIZ and CAI Asia. Their inputs at critical stages of the project have benefited it.

And at the end, we thank the citizens of Ahmedabad, who have wholeheartedly accepted Janmarg as a way of life. Their acceptance has made the project what it is today.

I. P. Gautam | H. M. Shivanand Swamy | Abhijit Lokre | Vijay Arya

14th May 2014

Contents

Foreword 6
Preface 7
Acknowledgement 8
Legends 12
Acronyms 12

Background

What is BRTS? 14
System Types 15
About Janmarg 19
Planning for Janmarg 21

BRTS Design

Basic Layout 23
- BRT Lanes: Side or Median? 24
- Bus Station: Kerb or Median? 26
- Bus Station: Location 28

Cross Sections 29
- Phase I: Right of way 32
  - 60 m 32
  - 45 m 36
  - 40 m 40
  - 36 m 46
  - 30 m 50
  - 24 m 52
- Phase I: Innovations 56
  - Overtaking Lanes 56
  - Adapting Design for Special Situations 58
  - Grade Separating for Pedestrians 60
  - Splitting the Flyovers 66
  - Accommodating HT Lines 72
- Phase II: Right of way 76
  - 60 m 76
  - 40 m 80
  - 36 m 84
  - 30 m 86
- Phase II: Innovations 90
  - Elevating BRTS 90
  - At-Grade Turnaround 93

Junction Design 99
- Four-arm junction with Two-way BRTS 102
- Four-arm junction with Flyover 104
- Four-arm junction with Square about and Two-way BRTS 106
- Four-arm junction with Square about and Bus Priority 109

Placemaking 111
- Street Design 114
- Public Space Design 120
- Access to Bus Station 123

Street Design Elements 125
- Benches 127
- Bollards 128
- Railings 130
- Kerb Cuts 132
- Raised Pedestrian Crossing at Bus Stations 134
- Parking Module and Tree-pit Cover 135
- Tree-pit Cover Details 136

Transit Infrastructure System 139
- Bus Stations 143
- Interchanges 168
- Workshops 176

Ideas for Future 181
- Drivers' Facility 182
- Interchange with Terminal 184
- Elevated Turnaround 186

Conclusion 191
Bibliography 192
About the Authors 194
About Centre of Excellence in Urban Transport 196
BRTS Team 197
BRTS route map, Ahmedabad 198

Legends

BL	BUS LANE
BS	BUS STATION
M	MEDIAN
PP	PEDESTRIAN PATHWAY
CT	CYCLE TRACK
CW	CARRIAGE WAY
SL	SERVICE LANE
P	PARKING
S	SEPARATOR
HS	HAWKERS' SPACE
	BRTS BUS
	PEDESTRIAN CROSSING
	EXISTING TREES
	PROPOSED TREES
	PARK
	BOLLARDS
	STREET LIGHTS
	PAVEMENT LIGHTS
	HIGH MAST LIGHT
	PROPERTY ENTRANCES

Acronyms

AEC	Ahmedabad Electricity Company
AJL	Ahmedabad Janmarg Limited
AMC	Ahmedabad Municipal Corporation
AMTS	Ahmedabad Municipal Transport Service
BRTS	Bus Rapid Transit System
BSNL	Bharat Sanchar Nigam Limited
CBD	Central Business District
CEPT	Centre for Environmental Planning and Technology
CNG	Compressed Natural Gas
CoE–UT	Centre of Excellence in Urban Transport
CS	Cross Section
FRL	Finished Road Level
GPS	Global Positioning System
GSRTC	Gujarat State Road Transport Corporation
HT	High Tension
IIM	Indian Institute of Management
IPTS	Integrated Public Transit System
ITS	Intelligent Transportation Systems
km	Kilometre
m	Metre
Min	Minimum
MS	Mild Steel
NH	National Highway
NHAI	National Highways Authority of India
O-D	Origin-Destination
ONGC	Oil and Natural Gas Company
PRL	Physical Research laboratory
RFID	Radio Frequency Identification Device
RoW	Right of Way
ROB	Rail Overbridge
RTO	Regional Transport Office
SS	Stainless Steel
ST	State Transport
sq.	Square
TAZ	Traffic Analysis Zone

Background

What is BRTS?

One of the biggest questions that cities face today is how to deal with the immense movement of people and goods. Of these, the movement of goods is beyond the scope of the present document. For people, bus systems were generally thought to be the most optimal solution. However, with the increasing number of private vehicles, bus-based systems face the problems of competition, congestion and an overall image of degradation.

The BRTS is a concept that promotes segregation of buses from other traffic. It is a bus-based, high quality and high capacity system that delivers fast, comfortable, accessible, convenient, and cost-effective urban mobility. In this arrangement, lanes provided exclusively for buses serve to prevent congestion on the road. At the same time, other motorised traffic benefits from the shifting of buses to dedicated lanes.

However, BRTS is more than just segregated bus lanes. It also includes high quality transit infrastructure, advanced ITS technology and excellent customer service of an enhanced quality. The objectives of BRTS thus include more than just a good bus service. It is evolving as one of the most popular systems across the cities of the world, particularly where congestion on the roads is high.

View of typical median BRTS bus station and lanes

System Types

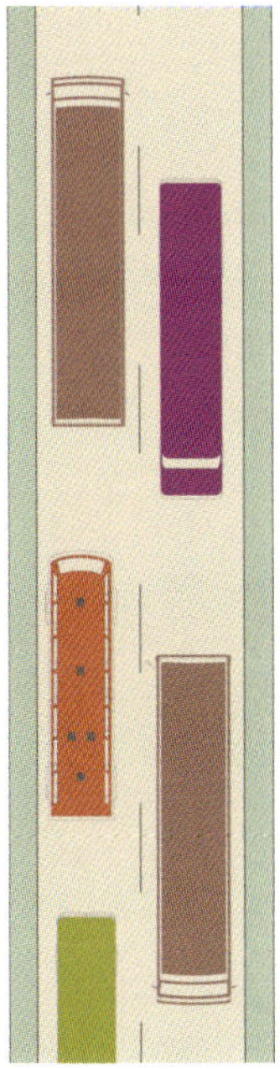

Open System

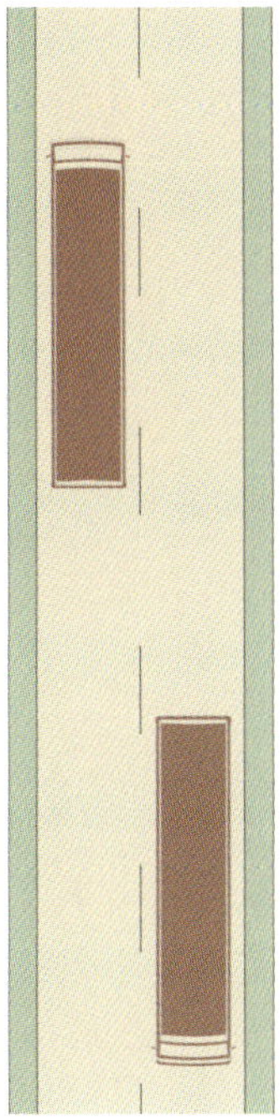

Closed System

Two kinds of BRT system are possible—open and closed. In an open system, the BRT lane is kept open for all bus operators, to whom the benefits of dedicated infrastructure become available. They largely continue to run the same routes they did previously, thereby utilising the bus-way infrastructure wherever it coincides with their previous routes, while they may also operate on parts of their existing routes, without bus-way infrastructure, outside the segregated corridor. The open system is quicker to implement as it does not include bus sector reform. The focus is on creating segregated bus lanes and allowing the existing operator/s to run the same buses on existing routes.

However, the open system has significant limitations. If the buses lack uniform configurations (length, position of doors, floor height), docking at bus stations becomes an issue. Higher dwell time at bus stations may lead to lower average speed. If buses exit the corridor at the same junction, signal phasing becomes a problem. For example, if a bus needs to turn left at a junction and the other needs to go straight or right, a separate signal phase will have to be provided, adding to the overall signal cycle time. The reliability of the system is compromised. This can affect the BRTS 'brand' and invite criticism from users. Predictability of service cannot be assured as the buses move in both controlled (bus-way) and uncontrolled (outside bus lane) environments. Hence, the reliability of features such as advance information on their arrival, departure and next stop details will be reduced.

In a closed system, the BRT lane is exclusively for BRTS buses. BRTS operators are its only beneficiaries and can be made accountable for efficiency and maintenance. In this system, the corridor is generally segregated. However, in cases where local conditions demand, short stretches may be non-segregated.

The closed structure is more conducive to efficient operations. Since the number of operators and vehicles are rationally selected and carefully controlled, such a system can be designed around the optimal conditions for user movement. A closed system brings along with it bus operators' reforms. Ticketing is generally off-board. Bus configuration is standardised, with same width and position of door and floor height. Junctions are easier to manage with fewer signal phases. Average speed in a closed system is invariably higher than in an open system. Janmarg uses the closed system.

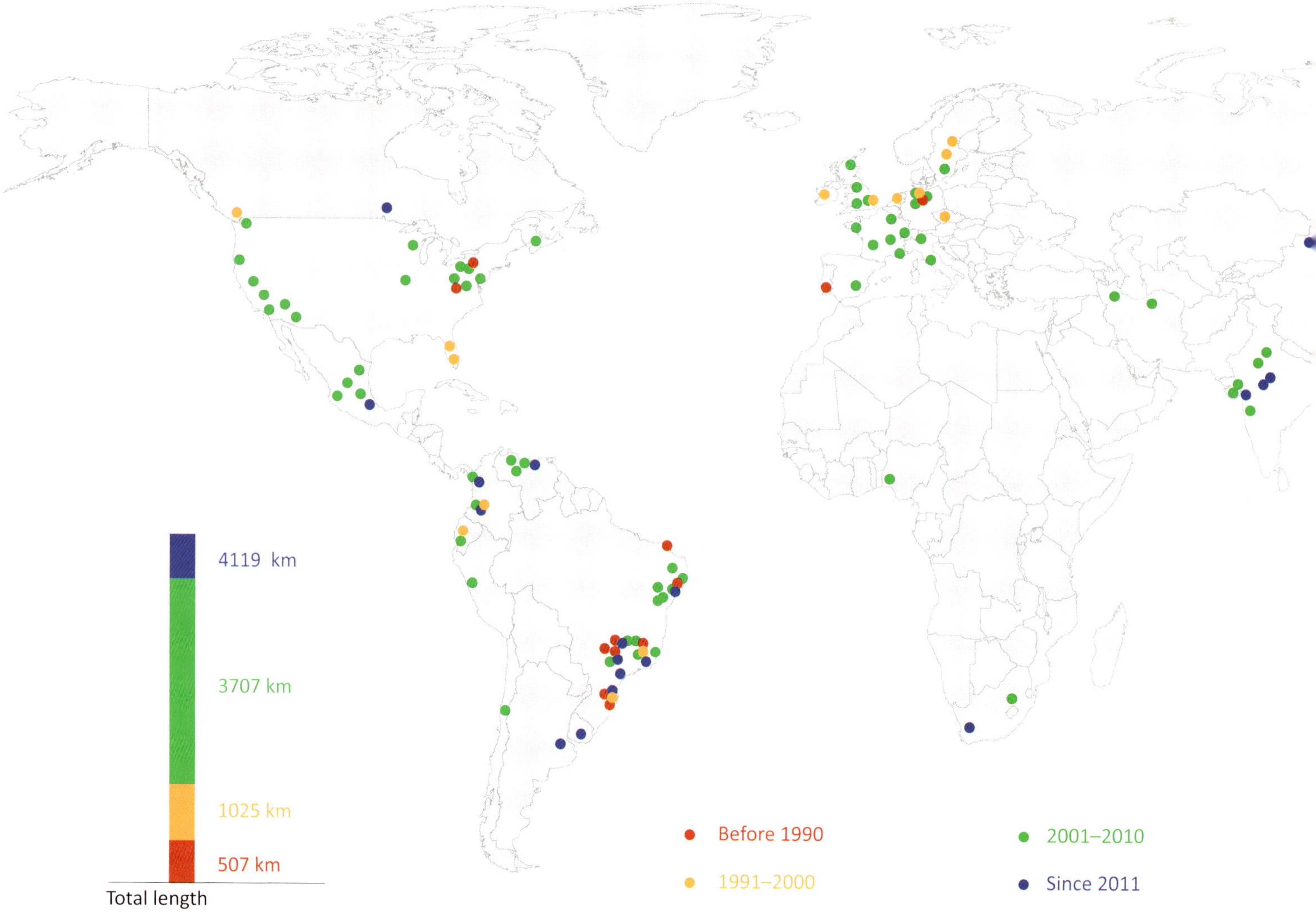

BRTS cities worldwide
(Recreated from the source: http//brtdata.org, October 2013)

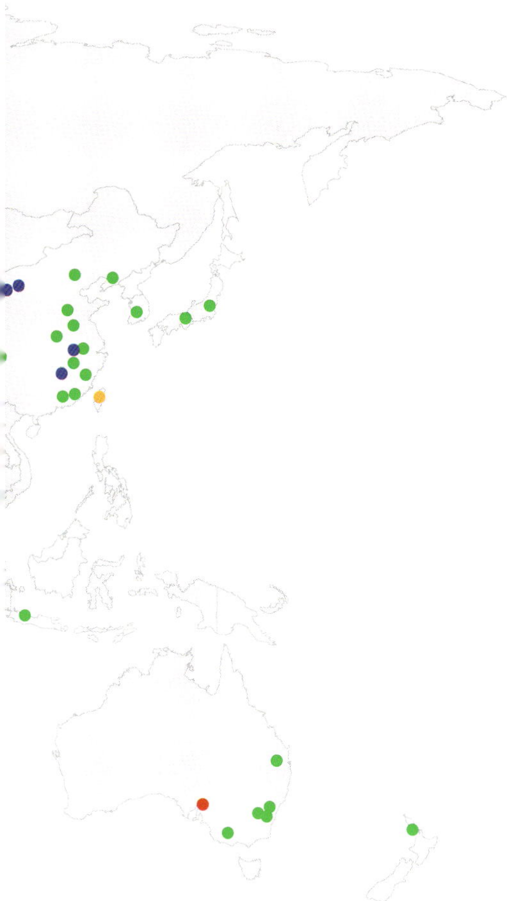

Status of BRTS in India

Janmarg at Jhansi ki Rani: A closed system with segregated lanes only for specially designed buses

About Janmarg

Janmarg was designed as a strategic intervention to ease existing traffic congestion, to attract latent transit demand, to improve air quality, and help the city remain compact. The guiding principle for the selection of the network corridors was to reach the largest possible segment of people. Also considered was the ability of the corridors to accommodate BRTS treatment, to integrate with the existing infrastructure, to contribute to significantly ease traffic problems, to create opportunities for improvement in land use, to allow for quick and inexpensive implementation, and to yield potential for cost-recovery.

The system is managed by Ahmedabad Janmarg Ltd (AJL), a special purpose vehicle (SPV) formed under the Companies Act. However, AJL does not own most of the infrastructure. For example, its buses are owned by a private operator, who operates them as per schedules set by AJL. The drivers or system operators are also provided by the private operator, who is paid as per a 'gross cost contract' model which guarantees a certain number of kilometres per day. The contract between AJL and the operator lays down the bus specifications and quality. Fare collection is also outsourced to a private operator. In effect, AJL plays the role of regulator and manager.

The system operators are trained for reliability, safety and ideal speed. Staff at the bus stations is trained for issuing tickets, smart cards and providing any other assistance that is needed. All people involved in Janmarg operations have special uniforms to assert its distinct brand identity.

The Board of Directors for AJL includes the Municipal Commissioner (Chairman), Mayor, Standing Committee Chairman, Leader of the Ruling Party in the Ahmedabad Municipal Corporation (AMC), Leader of the Opposition, Traffic Police Commissioner, a representative of the State Government, a Deputy Municipal Commissioner (Executive Director) and two subject experts.

Today, Janmarg operates over a route network of 88 km and has a daily ridership of 1.6 lakh people. One hundred and fifty buses operate every day, with headway of 2 minutes in the peak hours. Almost 20 per cent of the commuters on Janmarg today have changed over from motorised two-wheelers. By December 2014, it would be operating seven routes and carrying an estimated three lakh passengers daily. Plans have been finalised to extend the network by another 21 km, taking the corridor length to 110 km by the end of 2016.

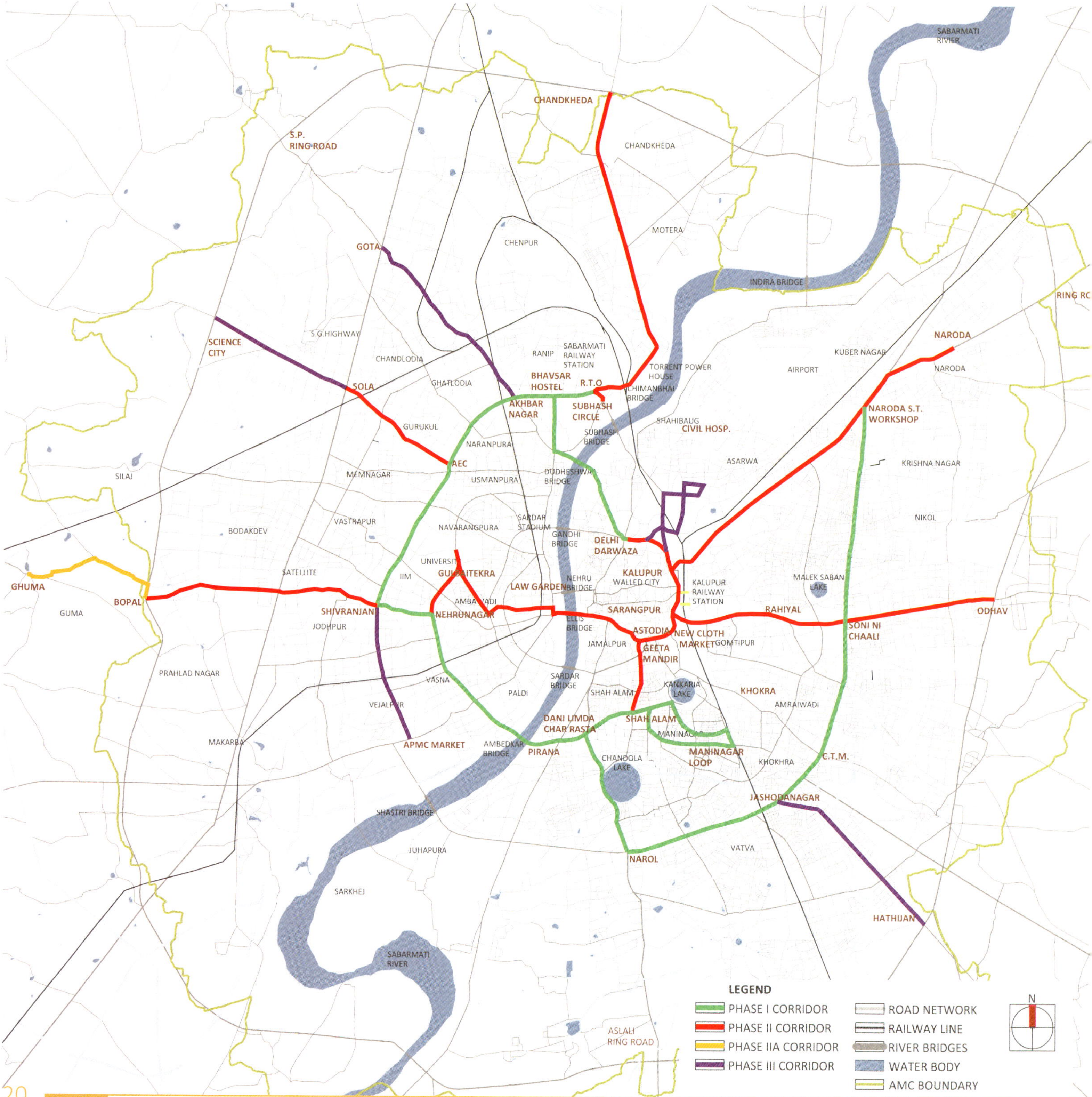
SABARMATI RIVIER
CHANDKHEDA
CHANDKHEDA
S.P. RING ROAD
MOTERA
INDIRA BRIDGE
RING RO
CHENPUR
GOTA
S.G HIGHWAY
SCIENCE CITY
CHANDLODIA
RANIP
SABARMATI RAILWAY STATION
TORRENT POWER HOUSE
AIRPORT
KUBER NAGAR
NARODA
NARODA
SOLA
GHATLODIA
BHAVSAR HOSTEL
R.T.O
CHIMANBHAI BRIDGE
AKHBAR NAGAR
SUBHASH CIRCLE
NARODA S.T. WORKSHOP
GURUKUL
SHAHIBAUG
CIVIL HOSP.
NARANPURA
SUBHASH BRIDGE
AEC
ASARWA
KRISHNA NAGAR
SILAJ
MEMNAGAR
USMANPURA
DUDHESHWAR BRIDGE
VASTRAPUR
SARDAR STADIUM
NIKOL
BODAKDEV
NAVARANGPURA
GANDHI BRIDGE
DELHI DARWAZA
UNIVERSITY
SATELLITE
GULBAITEKRA
KALUPUR WALLED CITY
MALEK SABAN LAKE
IIM
NEHRU BRIDGE
KALUPUR RAILWAY STATION
GHUMA
LAW GARDEN
BOPAL
AMBAWADI
GUMA
SHIVRANJANI
NEHRUNAGAR
SARANGPUR
RAHIYAL
ODHAV
ELLIS BRIDGE
JODHPUR
ASTODIA
NEW CLOTH MARKET
SONI NI CHAALI
GOMTIPUR
JAMALPUR
GEETA MANDIR
PRAHLAD NAGAR
VASNA
SARDAR BRIDGE
KANKARIA LAKE
KHOKRA
PALDI
SHAH ALAM
AMRAIWADI
VEJALPUR
DANI LIMDA CHAR RASTA
SHAH ALAM
MANINAGAR
MAKARBA
APMC MARKET
AMBEDKAR BRIDGE
PIRANA
MANINAGAR LOOP
C.T.M.
CHANDOLA LAKE
KHOKHRA
JASHODANAGAR
SHASTRI BRIDGE
JUHAPURA
VATVA
NAROL
SARKHEJ
HATHIJAN
SABARMATI RIVER
ASLALI RING ROAD
LEGEND
PHASE I CORRIDOR
PHASE II CORRIDOR
PHASE IIA CORRIDOR
PHASE III CORRIDOR
ROAD NETWORK
RAILWAY LINE
RIVER BRIDGES
WATER BODY
AMC BOUNDARY
N

Planning for Janmarg

Until the year 2008, the only options for public transport in Ahmedabad were AMTS buses or auto rickshaws. These options were very few for a mega-city. It required an affordable public transport network that would enable people to reach their destinations in the shortest possible time, in the easiest possible manner. The system also had to be affordable. The city therefore chose to move towards an integrated transit system with judiciously planned interchanges between metro, regional rail, BRTS and regular bus services, all planned to be progressively improved. The aim is to increase the public transport system's share of passenger trips from 7 per cent in 2000 to 40 per cent by 2020. The BRTS component is the first major step in this strategy, in keeping with which the trans-vision of Ahmedabad is captioned as 'Accessible Ahmedabad'.

Janmarg is based on several considerations. The most crucial of these is its focus on equitable sharing of road space and an inclusiveness that encourages people from all socio-economic segments and groups to board the bus. In 2004, more than half the city's population did not own any personalised motor vehicle and was captive to public transport. Data revealed that almost 37 per cent of the people walked while 17 per cent used bicycles. Hence, the Janmarg design includes giving priority to cycle tracks and adequate footpaths.

In today's world of advanced technologies, Janmarg employs an Intelligent Transport System (ITS) to improve customer convenience, speed, reliability and safety. This system continuously monitors buses from the control centre through GPS devices fitted in all the buses. It gives passengers real-time information on bus arrivals at the stations. On-board announcements identify the station being approached or reached. Regular reports are prepared to enable study of mobility patterns and to structure future scheduling.

Phase I Corridors (58.3 km)	**Length (km)**
RTO–Pirana	12.50
Narol–Naroda	13.50
Kalupur darwaza–Naroda gaam	8.50
Pirana–Dani Limda–Narol and Maninagar	12.20
Bhavsar Hostel–Wadaj–Dudheshwar–Prem Darwaza	5.0
Shah Alam–Geeta Mandir–Sarangpur–Soni ni Chali	6.60

Phase II Corridors (30.5 km)	**Length (km)**
RTO–Chandkheda	6.60
AEC–Sola	3.10
Soni ni Chali–Odhav	3.60
Nehrunagar–Astodia	6.20
Shivranjani–Bopal	6.50
Kalupur Elevated Corridor	4.50
Phase II A Corridor (3.5 Km)	**Length (km)**
Bopal–Ghuma	3.50

Phase III Corridors (20 .90 km)	**Length (km)**
Shivranjini–APMC	3.25
Jashodanagar–Hathijan	4.50
Sola–Science City	3.50
Akhbarnagar–Gota Chowkdi (S.G. Highway)	4.80
Civil Hospital Loop	4.85

BRTS network showing Phase I, Phase II and Phase III corridors

BRTS bus station near Gujarat University campus

BRTS Design

Basic Layout

BRT Lanes: Side or Median?

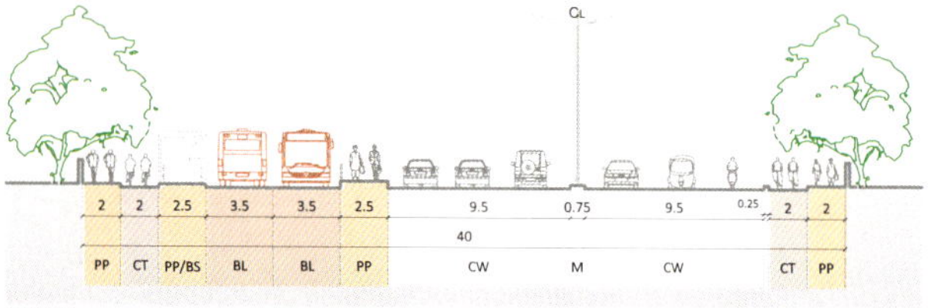

BRT lanes on one side

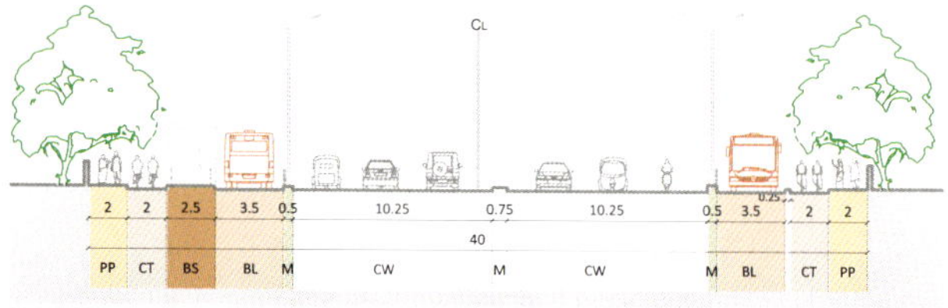

BRT lanes on either side

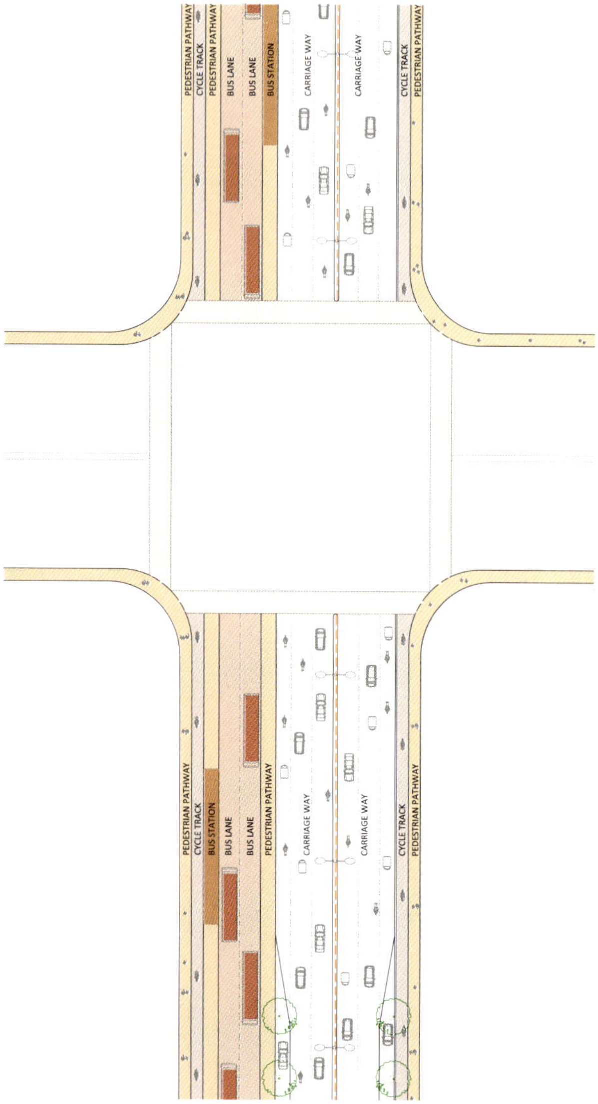

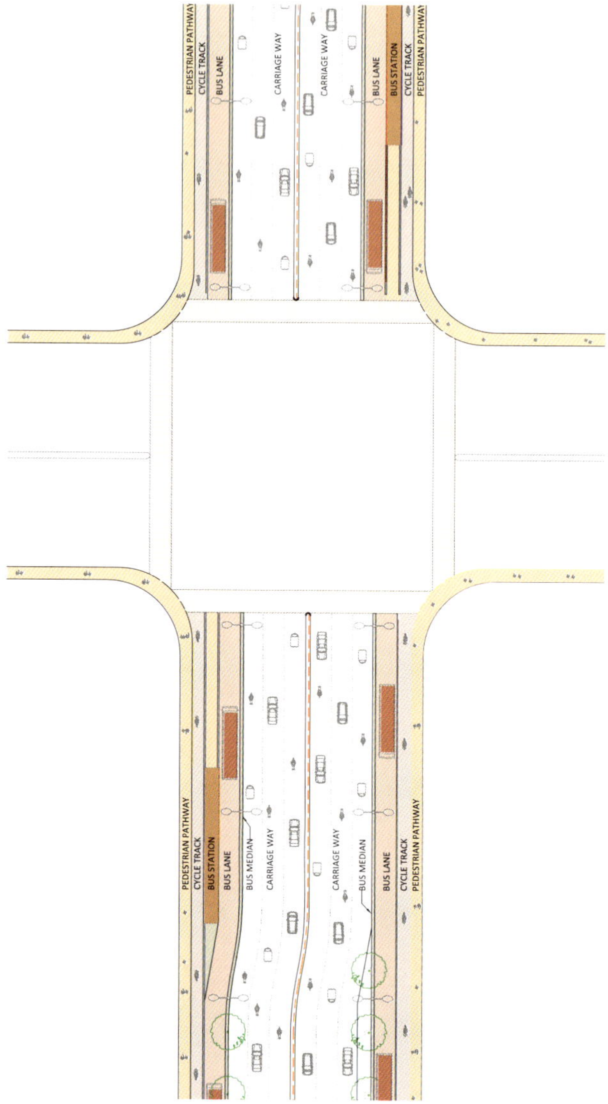

The location of the bus lanes is the first step towards finalising the design. Conventional wisdom would suggest locating them on the side, since that is where buses traditionally operate. The stations can be accommodated on the footpath. In Ahmedabad, the planners considered both options. A median bus lane was a major departure from the norm. There were apprehensions about user acceptance.

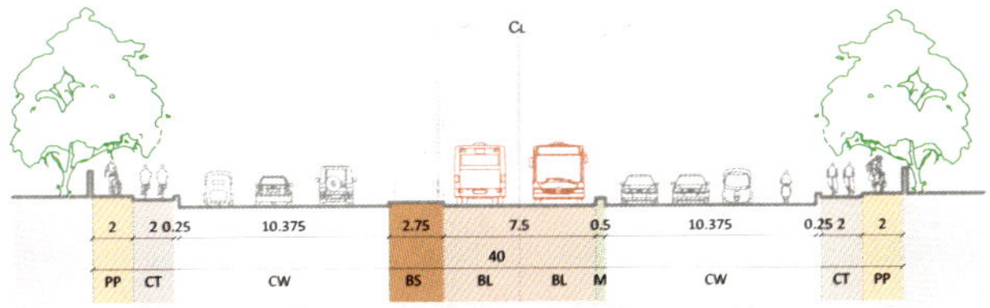

Median BRT lanes with kerb-side bus stops

The advantages and disadvantages of both designs were debated.

Comparison between side and median BRT lanes:

Side lane	Median lane
Junction management is an issue. Buses interfere with left turning traffic.	Junction management is easier. Bus flows can be integrated with other flows.
Bus stations are perceived to provide easier access from the pedestrian way.	It appears that commuters would have to cross the road to access bus stations.
Abutting property access will be affected in case of side lanes.	There is no issue with access to abutting properties.
Overall system speed is lower owing to frequent slowdown for left-turning or parked vehicles and pedestrians accessing properties.	Overall system speed is higher, since the bus lanes are not subject to interruptions from other traffic.

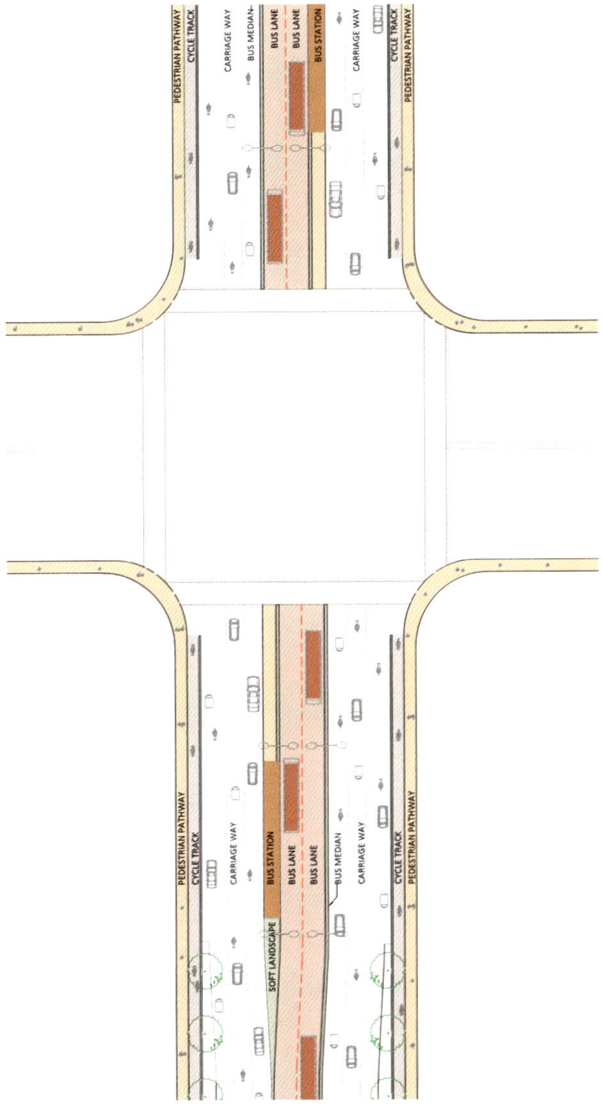

Experience from around the world showed that median lanes were widely used and appeared to be successful. Other than the perceived issue of tradition and accessing stations in the centre, the overall traffic movement appeared to be much better organised with median bus lanes. The station access too could be resolved with appropriate design. Janmarg chose to go with the median bus lane option, with a focussed campaign to build consensus on this among stakeholders.

Bus Station: Kerb or Median?

Location of bus stations on bus lanes is a much-debated issue. Two options exist. In the first, bus stations may be located on the left hand side (LHS) of the lane with access to buses through conventional LHS doors. This design demands two station structures—one for each direction of travel. The second option is a single median bus station, with access to buses through doors specially provided on the right hand side. In this option, a single station structure serves traffic in both directions. Both options have their advantages and disadvantages.

Kerb-side Bus Station

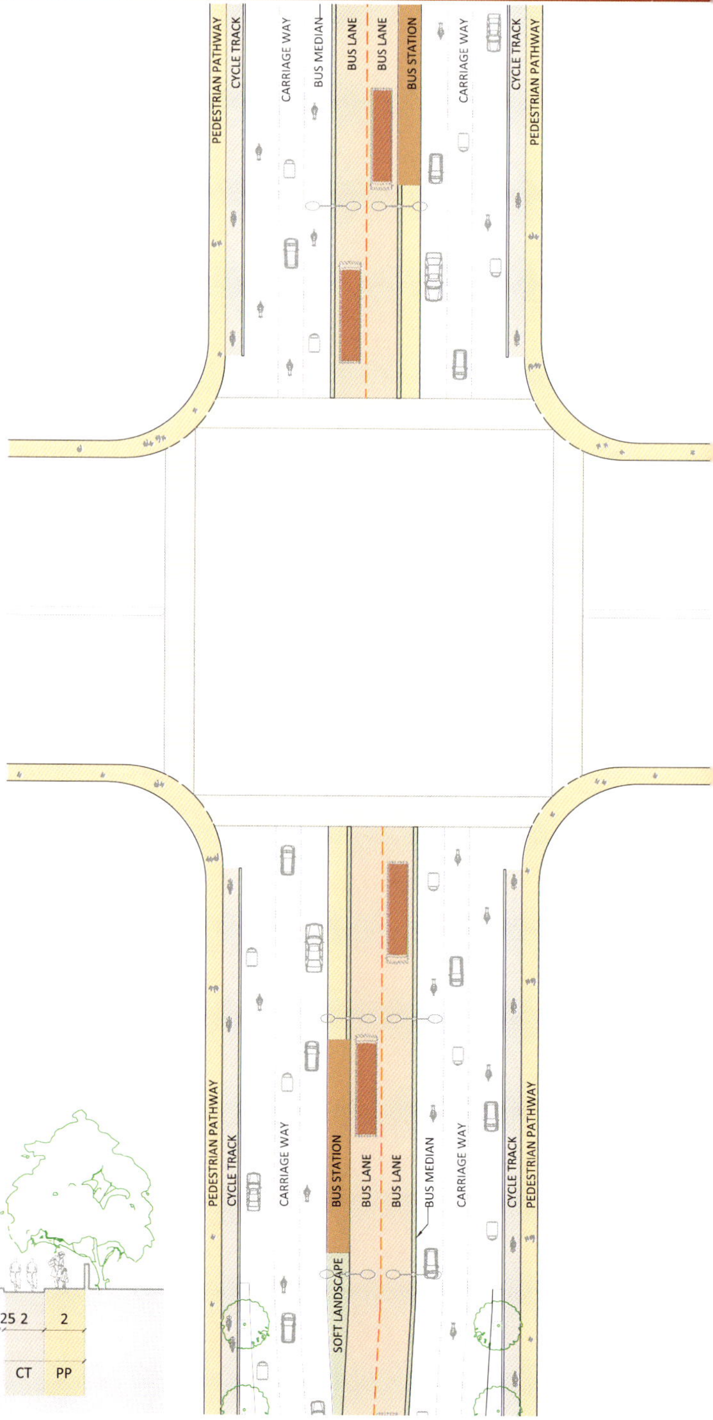

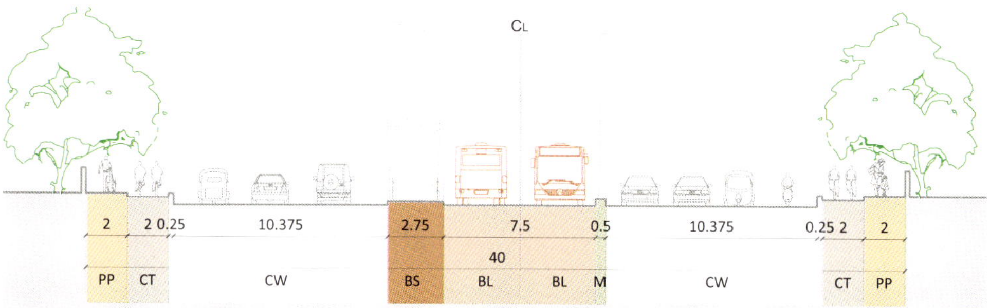

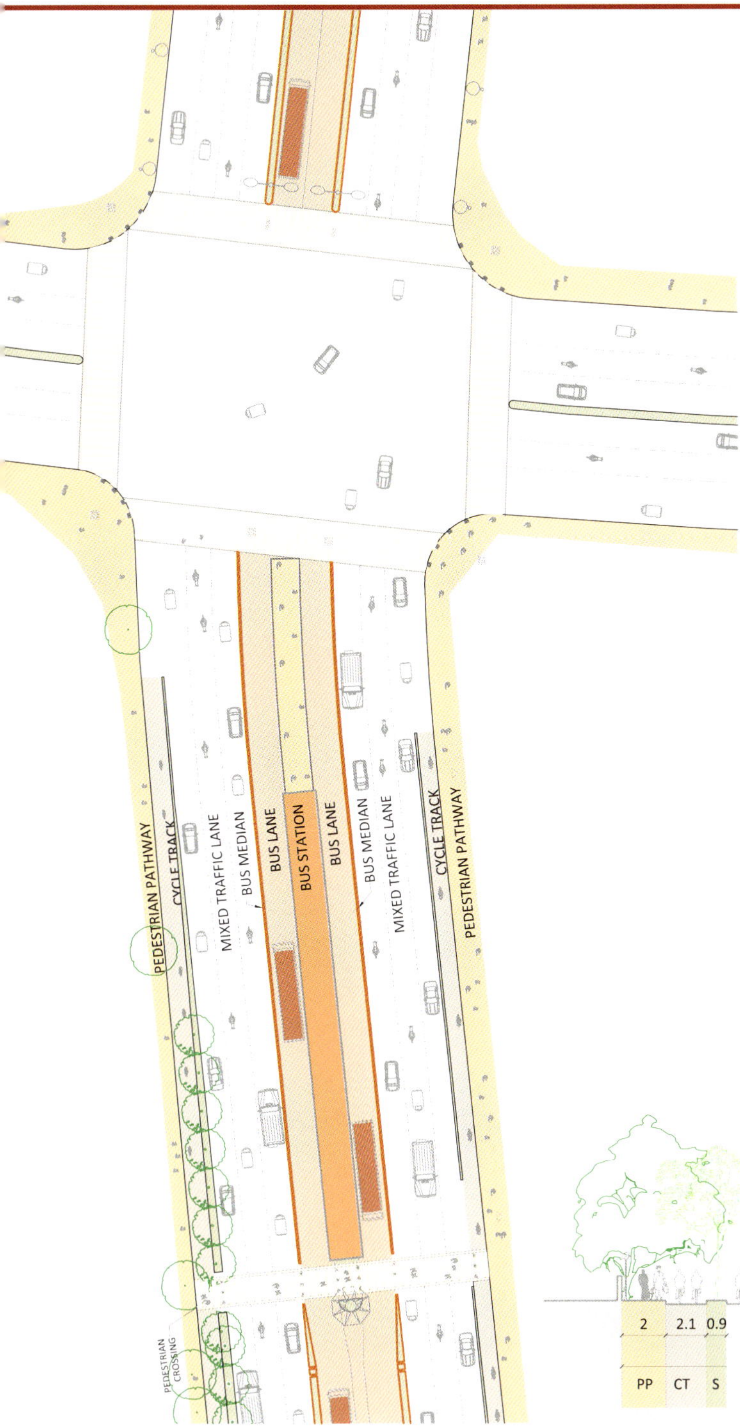

Comparison between kerb-side and median bus stations:

Kerb-side Bus station	**Median Bus station**
Two station structures at each location	Single structure at each location
Higher construction costs	Lower construction costs
Higher operation and maintenance cost	Lower operation and maintenance cost
Commuters must exit one station and cross the carriageway to transfer to another route	Transfers are easy within the station
Normal buses with LHS doors can be used	Special buses with RHS doors have to be used

Janmarg decided on median stations, primarily for passenger convenience, enabling easy transfers, and to reduce construction and operation costs.

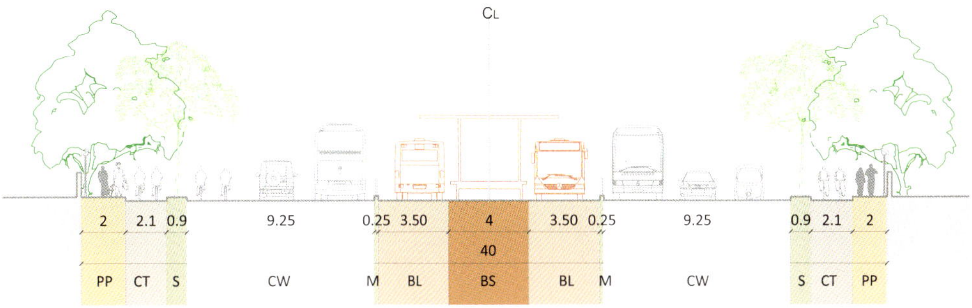

Bus Station: Location

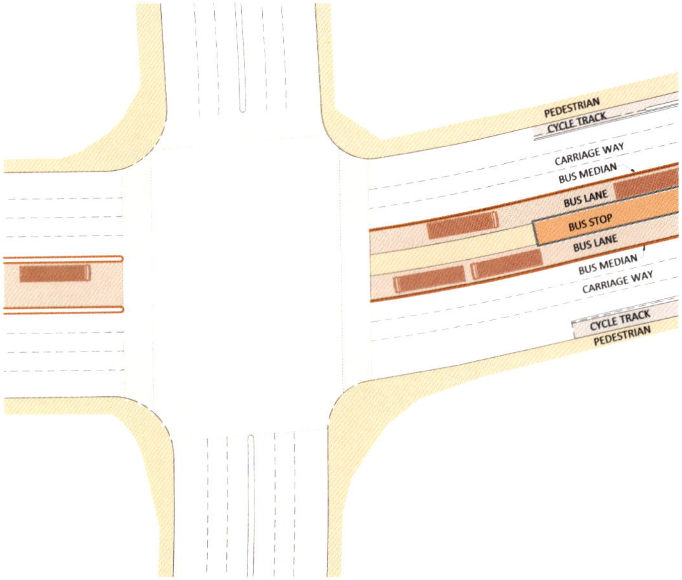

Locating bus stations near junctions

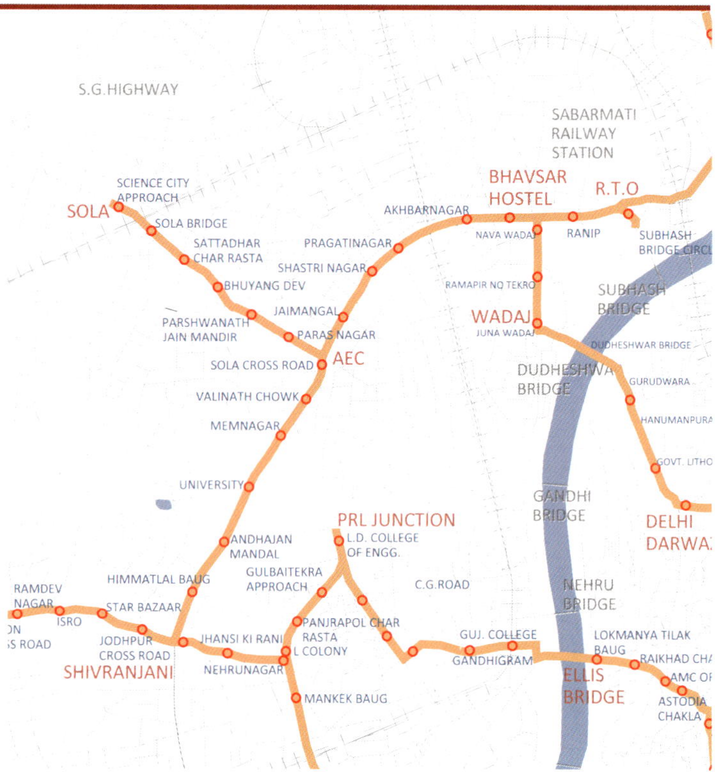

Spacing between bus stations

Near junctions

Bus stations located near road junctions offer easy access to commuters approaching them from crossroads. However, they should not be too close to the junctions, which would create queuing of buses when, after off-loading and taking on new passengers, they are held up by a red signal at the junction, blocking access to the station for buses that are immediately following. Some distance between the station and the junction will allow buses that have completed their halt to move ahead and wait at the junction.

Janmarg keeps a distance of 24-36 m (two standard buses or one articulated bus) between the station and the stop line. If a bus station cannot be provided near a junction, it is located at mid-block.

Spacing

The spacing between two bus stations is critical. It determines how much commuters would have to travel/ walk to reach the nearest station. A 500 m distance between two bus stations is considered ideal in an urban area. It may be 300-350 m in the Central Business District (CBD) and 600-800 m in suburban areas. This is considered the optimal distance in which a bus may reach cruising speed before decelerating for the next halt. For a commuter, walking time to the station is a major part of the total trip time. With increase in distance between stations, walking time and overall journey time also increase. Therefore, an optimum distance of 500 m is recommended.

Janmarg has adopted an average spacing of 500 m between bus stations.

BRTS Design

Cross Sections

In urban areas, it is difficult to increase the Right of Way (RoW) of roads. The BRT corridor has been designed as a strategic intervention keeping in mind constraints with respect to available road widths, encroachments and traffic.

The design team explored various possibilities to arrive at a functional and appropriate design for varying road widths and local situations. The cross section includes street elements such as dedicated BRT lane, carriageway, service lane, parking spaces, bicycle track, pedestrian pathway, street furniture and landscaping.

The overall infrastructure design is a process of development of different stages. The planning and design team explored design elements on the basis of emerging operations plan and made conceptual designs for each element.

The closed system adopted by Janmarg reserves the bus lane exclusively for the BRT operator and buses. The segregated corridor acts as the trunk route of BRTS network. Other buses feed this corridor.

Various alternative cross-sections were initially analysed—with and without cycle track and varying widths of mixed lane and footpaths for each RoW category. The recommended cross sections not only consider the requirements of BRT buses but also accommodate the needs of other users of the corridor, such as non-BRT motorised traffic, bicycles and pedestrians. Emphasis is given to the proposed improvement over full roadway width that ensures better mobility level on the corridor as a whole.

This section elaborates on the physical design of street cross section for all categories of available RoWs. It also discusses the special designs evolved in response to local constraints.

Right of Ways (RoWs) along the BRTS network (Phase I & II)

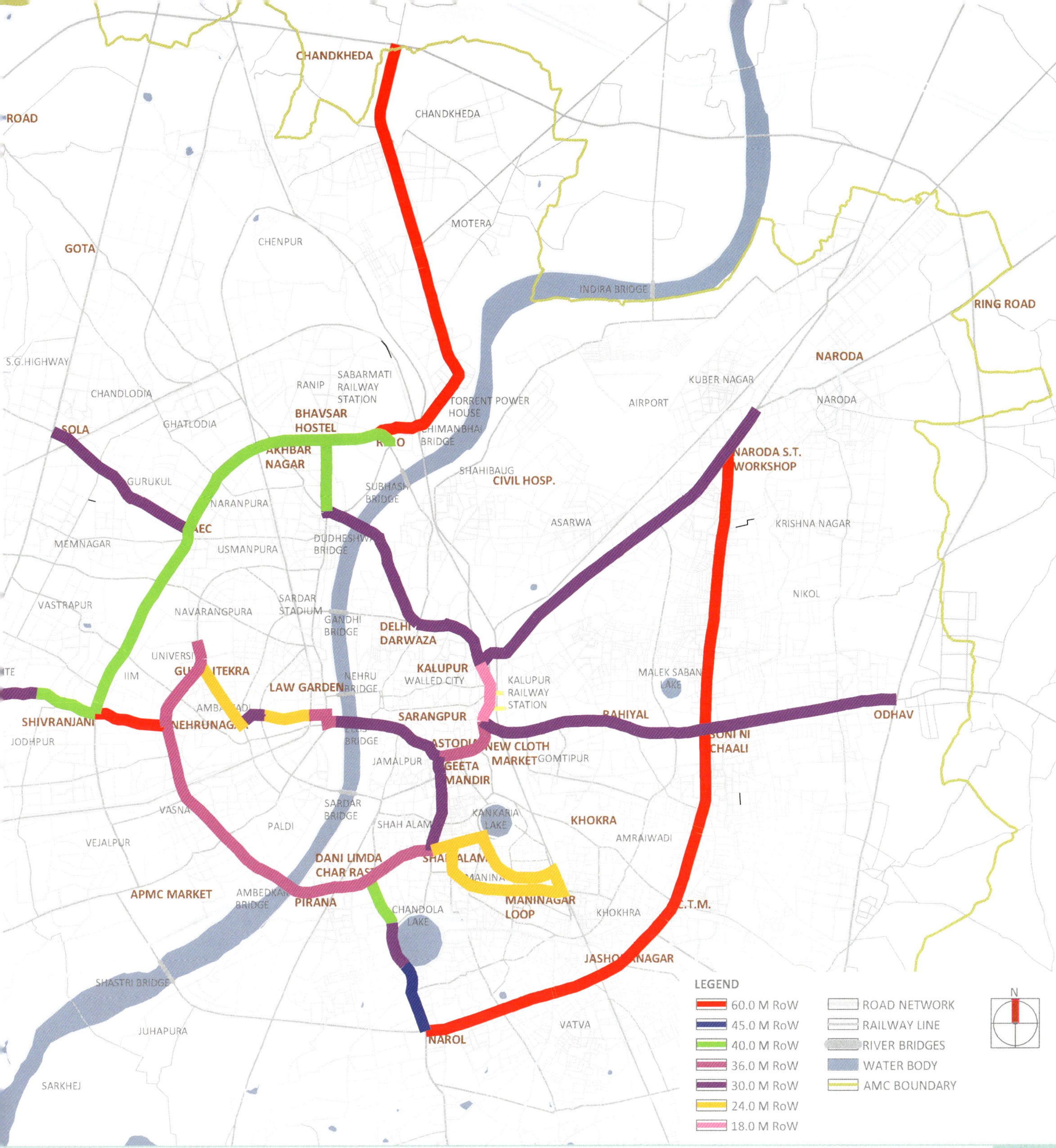
CHANDKHEDA
ROAD
CHANDKHEDA
MOTERA
GOTA
CHENPUR
INDIRA BRIDGE
RING ROAD
NARODA
S.G.HIGHWAY
CHANDLODIA
RANIP
SABARMATI RAILWAY STATION
TORRENT POWER HOUSE
KUBER NAGAR
AIRPORT
NARODA
BHAVSAR HOSTEL
GHATLODIA
SOLA
AKHBAR NAGAR
HIMANBHAI BRIDGE
SHAHIBAUG
CIVIL HOSP.
NARODA S.T. WORKSHOP
GURUKUL
NARANPURA
SUBHASH BRIDGE
ASARWA
KRISHNA NAGAR
MEMNAGAR
USMANPURA
DUDHESHWAR BRIDGE
VASTRAPUR
NAVARANGPURA
SARDAR STADIUM
GANDHI BRIDGE
DELHI DARWAZA
NIKOL
IIM
ITEKRA
LAW GARDEN
NEHRU BRIDGE
KALUPUR
WALLED CITY
KALUPUR RAILWAY STATION
MALEK SABAN LAKE
ODHAV
SHIVRANJANI
NEHRUNAGAR
SARANGPUR
RAHIYAL
JODHPUR
BRIDGE
NEW CLOTH MARKET
GOMTIPUR
SONI NI CHAALI
JAMALPUR
GEETA MANDIR
VASNA
SARDAR BRIDGE
PALDI
SHAH ALAM
KANKARIA LAKE
KHOKRA
AMRAIWADI
VEJALPUR
DANI LIMDA
APMC MARKET
AMBEDKAR BRIDGE
PIRANA
CHANDOLA LAKE
MANINAGAR LOOP
KHOKHRA
C.T.M.
SHASTRI BRIDGE
JUHAPURA
NAROL
VATVA
SARKHEJ
LEGEND
60.0 M RoW
45.0 M RoW
40.0 M RoW
36.0 M RoW
30.0 M RoW
24.0 M RoW
18.0 M RoW
ROAD NETWORK
RAILWAY LINE
RIVER BRIDGES
WATER BODY
AMC BOUNDARY
N

Phase I: Right of Way

60m

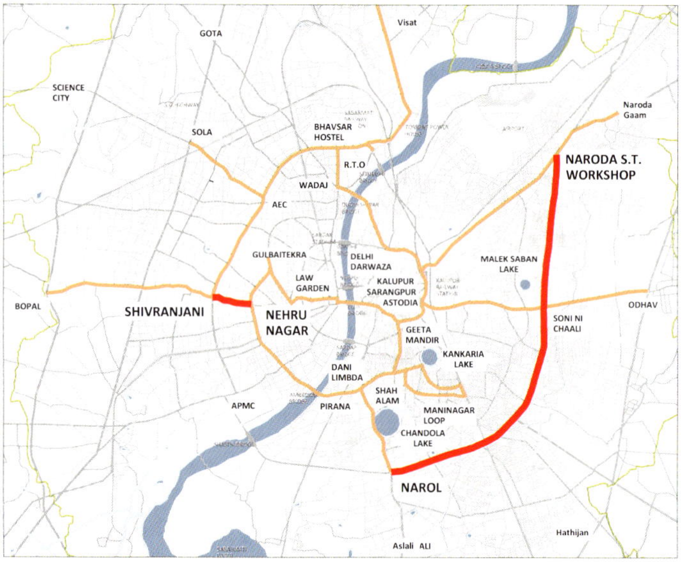

Key Map showing 60 m RoW corridors
Narol to Naroda—13.5 km (Phase I Eastern Corridor)
Shivranjini to Nehrunagar—1.4 km (Phase I Western Corridor)

The Narol–Naroda corridor was under the jurisdiction of the National Highways Authority of India (NHAI) during the period of implementation of BRTS. Although it is a National Highway, it has become an urban arterial over the years as the city expanded around it. Along or just off the corridor are three major industrial estates (Narol, Vatva and Naroda). It is also surrounded by dense residential settlements. The traffic mainly consists of trucks and heavy vehicles, and shared auto-rickshaws. Parking of heavy vehicles is a major issue on this corridor, considered the most accident-prone in Ahmedabad before BRTS implementation.

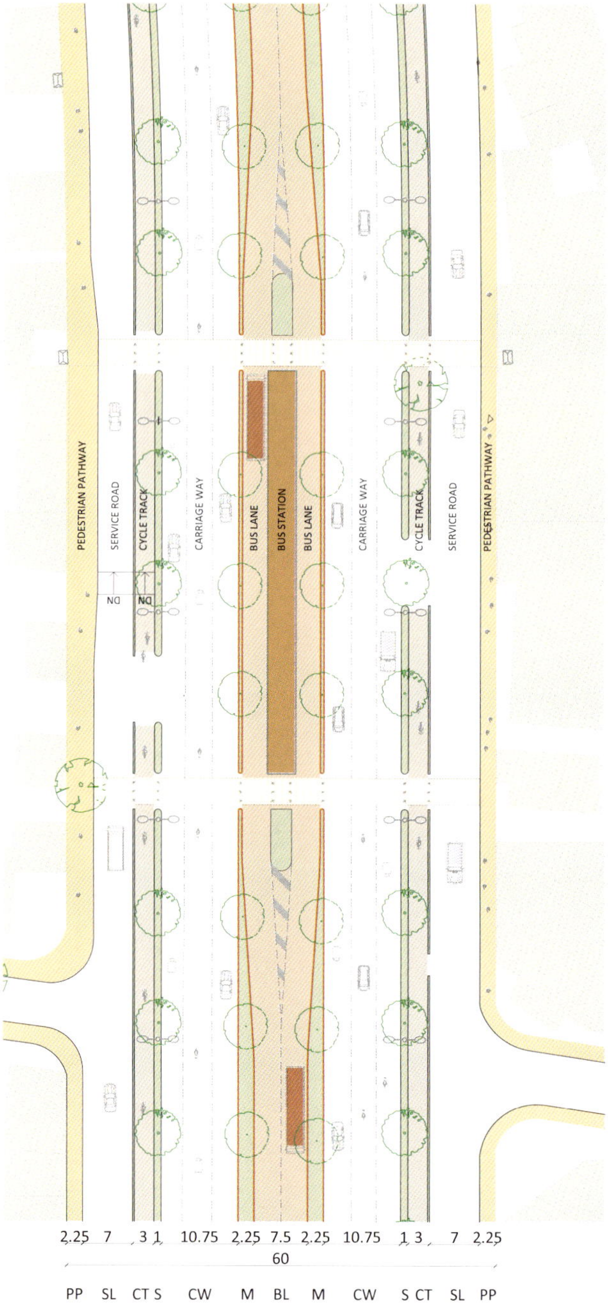

Plan for 60 m RoW corridor

The initial designs considered options to develop activity areas along the road, which would offer opportunities for landscaping, street shopping and rest areas. Separate service roads would cater to local traffic, while a two-lane carriageway in each direction would carry through traffic. Segregated cycle tracks were also proposed.

To meet NHAI standards, the final design was modified to include an extra lane for through traffic at the cost of the activity area. The service road and cycle track were retained. However, this meant that many activities envisaged in the activity area could not be accommodated.

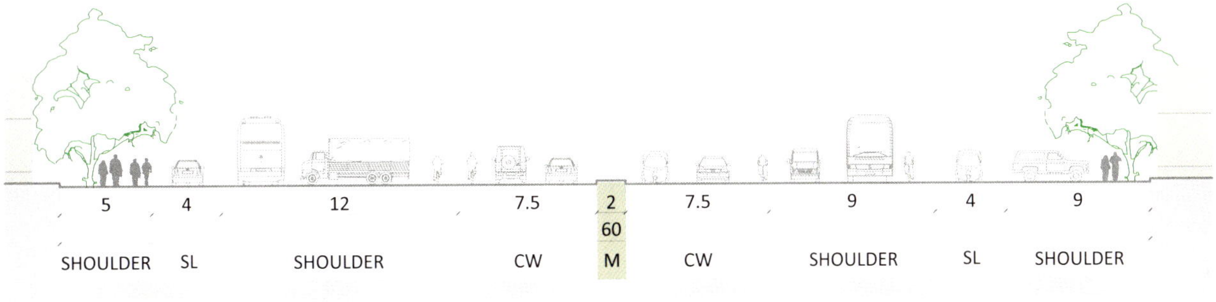

Earlier situation near Ramrajyanagar on Narol–Naroda stretch

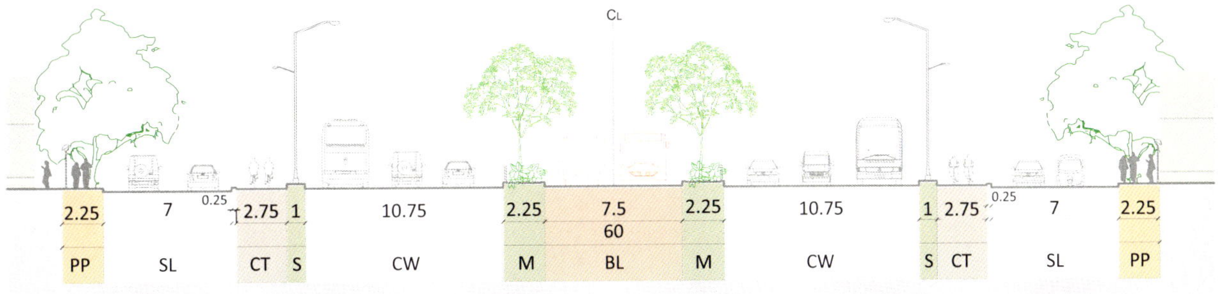

Existing typical cross section on Narol–Naroda stretch

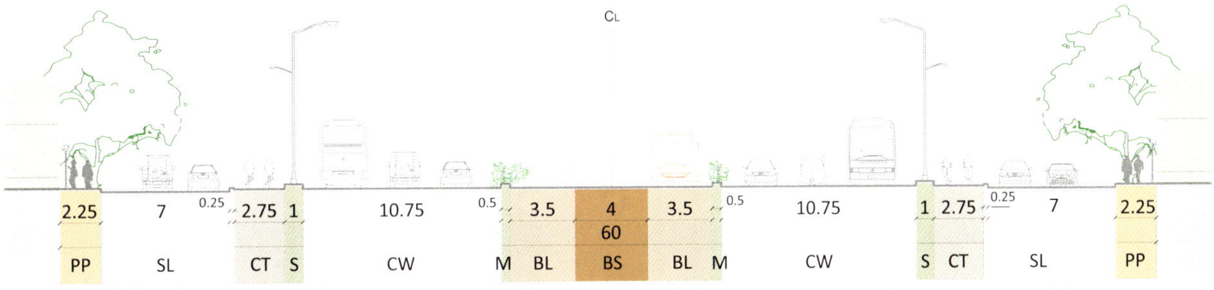

Existing cross section at bus station location

Traffic situation near the Expressway junction before BRTS

The BRTS track near Expressway junction. The Right of Way is redesigned, traffic flow is streamlined and buses get priority.

45m

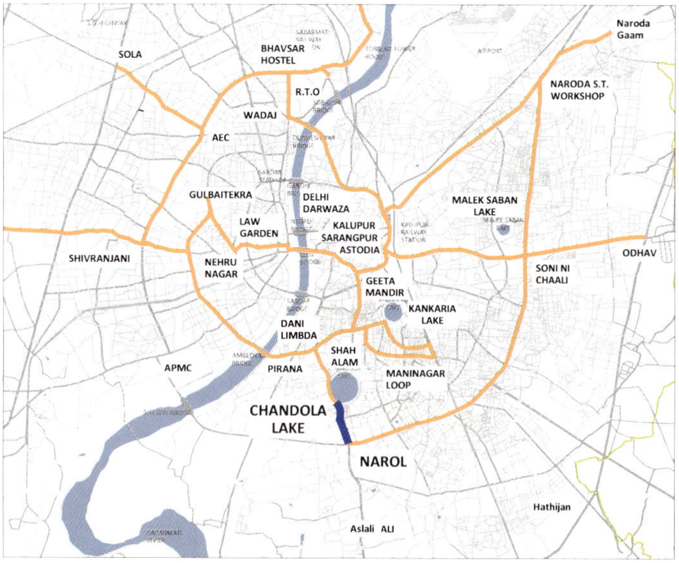

Key map showing 45 m RoW corridor
Chandola lake to Narol—0.6 km (Phase I Eastern Corridor)

This Right of Way is over a very short stretch in the entire network. However, the distinct nature of land use abutting it is important to understand. The corridor passes through an area of predominantly mixed use, with small-scale industries and workshops along the road's edge, where heavy vehicles tend to park, and loading and unloading activities happen.

On both sides of the corridor, alongside the mixed traffic lanes conveying traffic in either direction, and separated from them by 1 m wide medians, run 6.25 m wide service lanes. These cater to truck movement to industries along the corridor. Some parking is also permitted on the service lanes to keep the main carriageway free of stopping or standing vehicles.

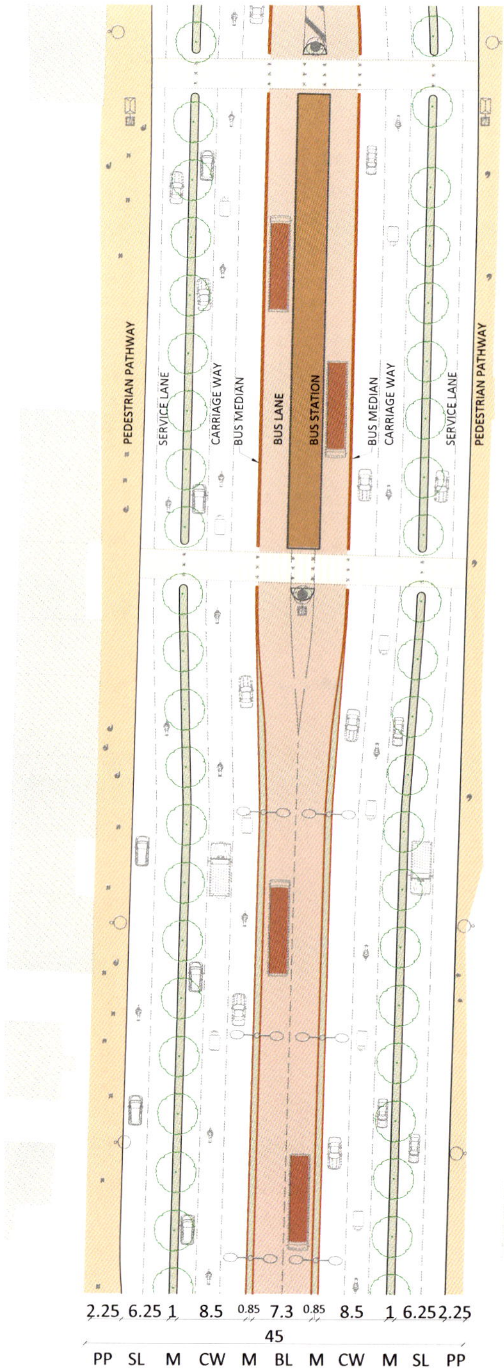

Plan for 45 m RoW corridor

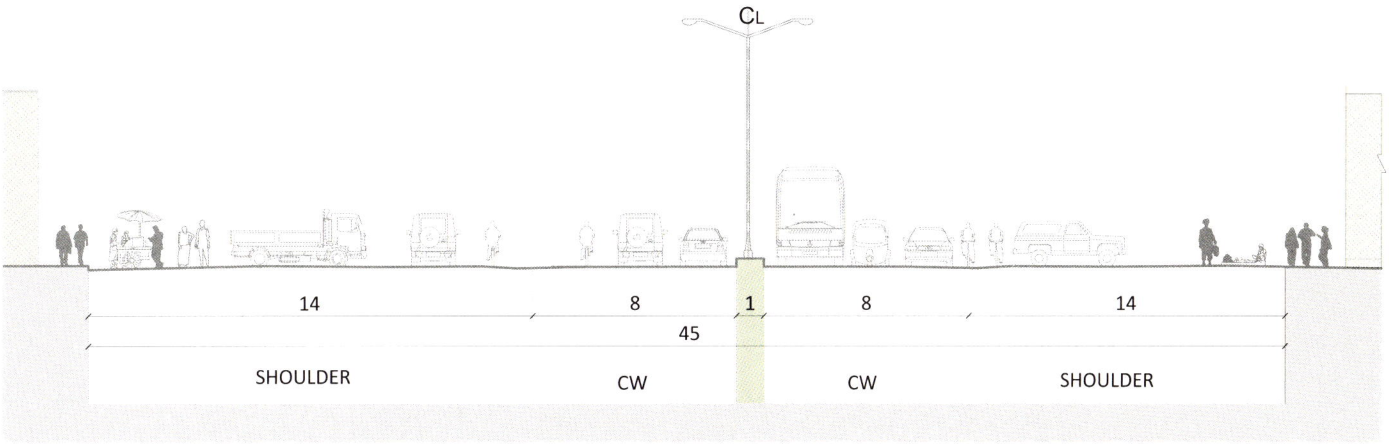

Earlier cross section showing 45 m corridor

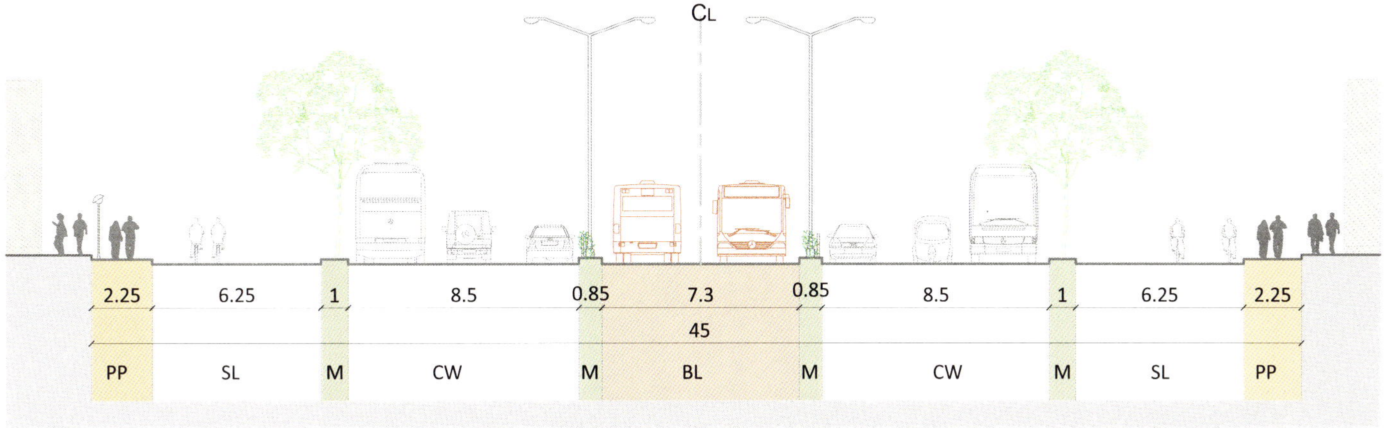

Existing typical cross section design at Dani Limda–Narol stretch

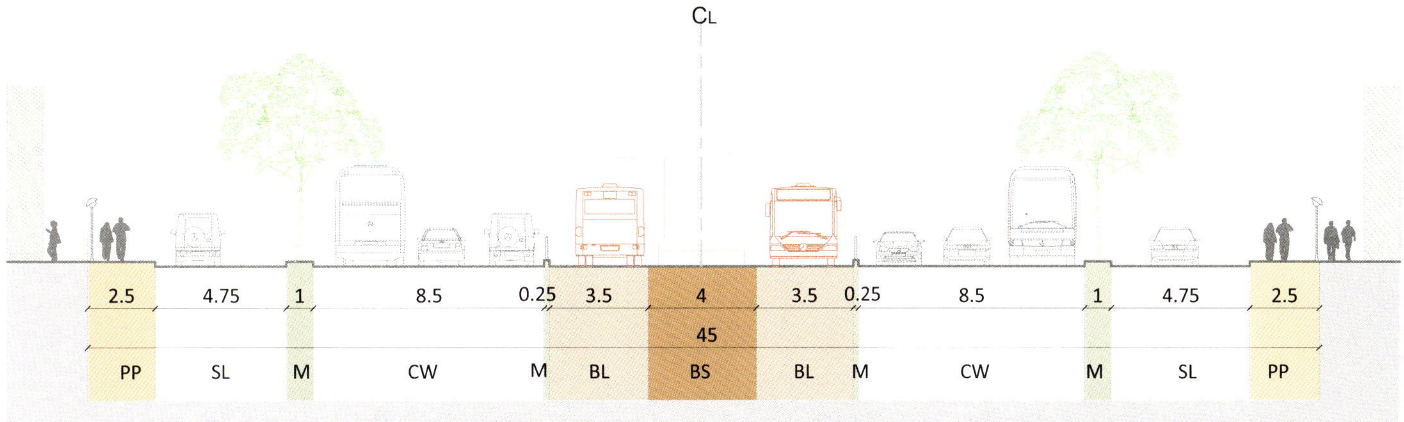

Existing typical cross section design at bus station location

BRTS track near Narol junction. The road now has enhanced lighting and a well-defined Right of Way.

Bus station near Dani Limda. The area is now witnessing redevelopment with BRTS as the catalyst.

40m

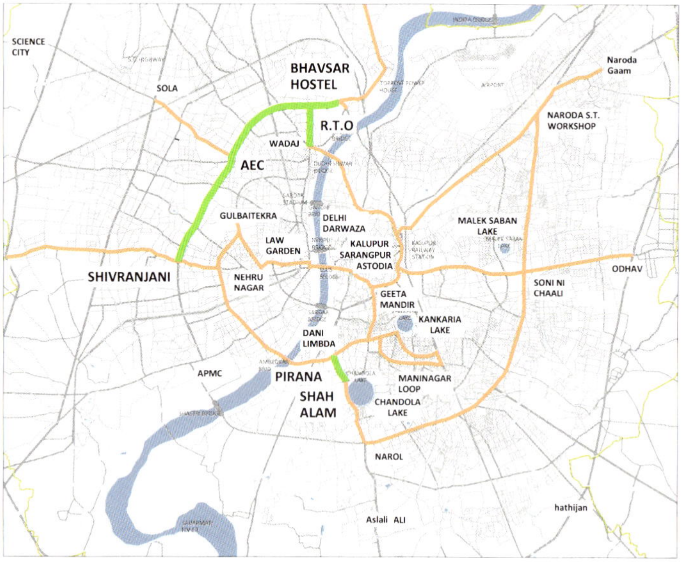

Key map showing 40 m RoW corridors
RTO to Shivranjini–7.6 km (Phase I Western Corridor)
Bhavsar Hostel to Wadaj–1.25 km (Phase I Western Corridor)

This was the first corridor to be implemented and, therefore, saw the most iterations. The footpath width, position and width of cycle track, the bus lanes width were debated extensively. Since it was among the first BRT corridors to be built in India, experiments were conducted with AMTS buses to determine appropriate width for the bus lanes. The bus lane width was changed from 7 m to 7.3 m during implementation.

In the final design, two-way central bus lanes, 7.3 m wide, replaced the existing median. This was abutted by a 0.85-m wide separator on each side for installing light poles and landscaping. Lanes for mixed traffic were kept at 9.25 m for each direction of travel. A 2-m wide parking is proposed along the roadside. A 2-m wide cycle track runs adjacent to the parking with a separator of 0.25 m between them. A 2.25-m wide pedestrian pathway runs along the street edge. This caters to pedestrian movement and access to the adjacent plots and activities on the street edge. Tree pits are located within the parking bay at every 12–18 m.

Over time, the cycle track has not been utilised for its original purpose. Motorised two-wheelers use it if the main carriageway is congested. Some of them also use it to drive in the wrong direction.

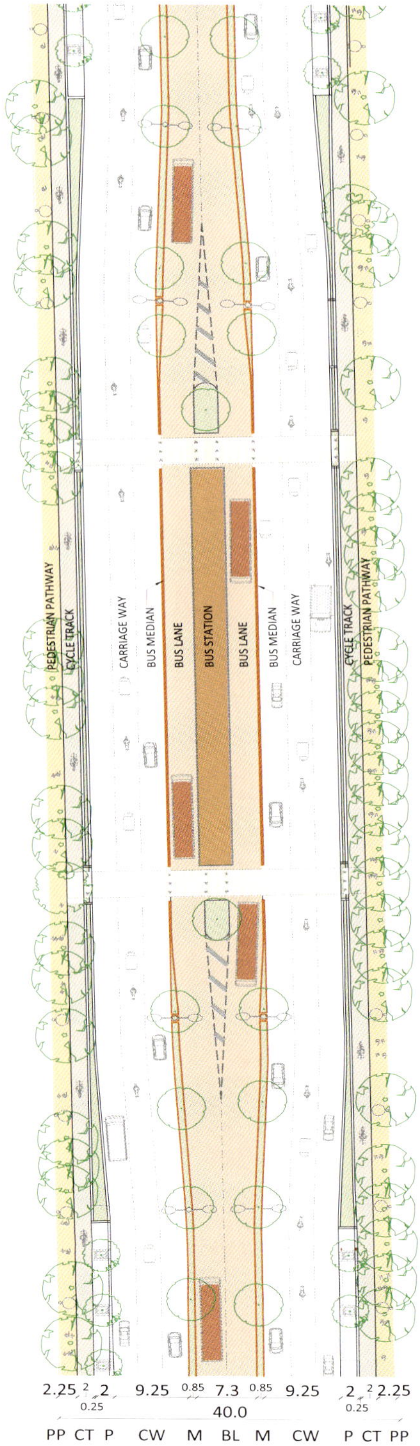

Plan for 40 m RoW corridor

The location of the cycle track has become a problem. It is aligned between the main carriageway and private properties abutting the edge. It works fairly well in stretches where entrances to such properties are few, but creates difficulties where there are many such entrances in a short stretch.

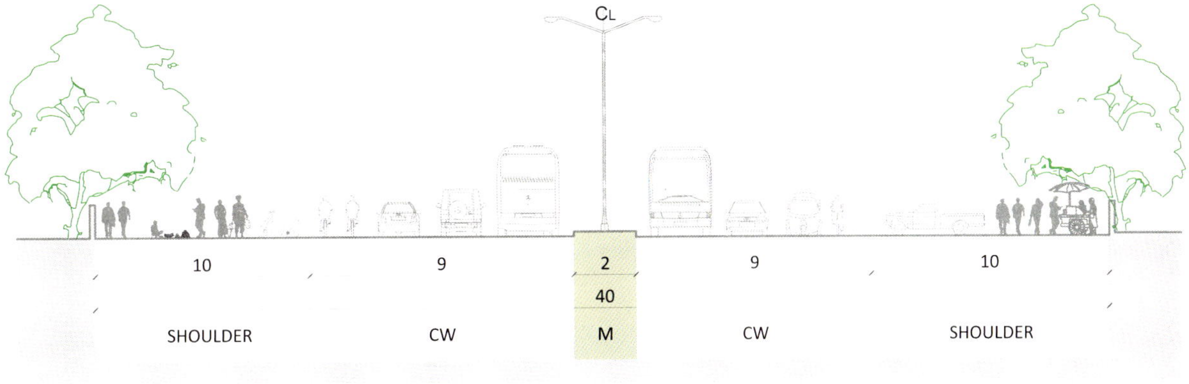

Earlier cross section showing 40 m corridor: Phase I

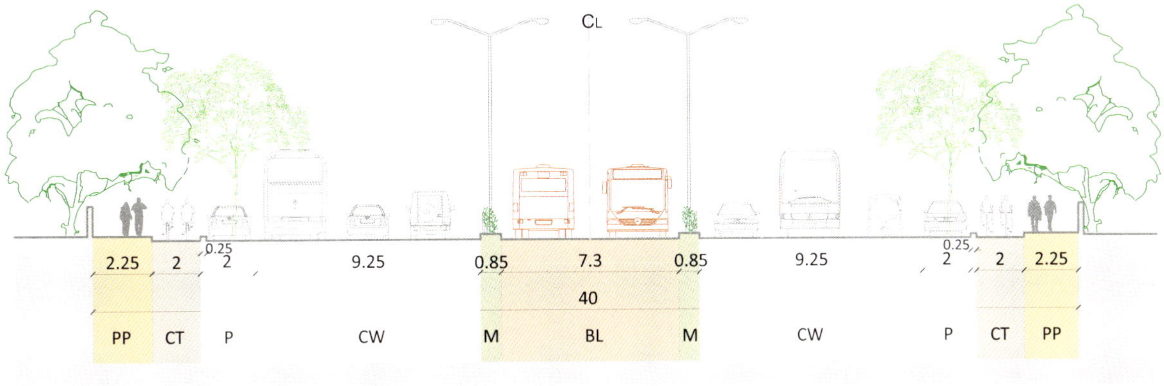

Existing typical cross section design at RTO–Pirana stretch

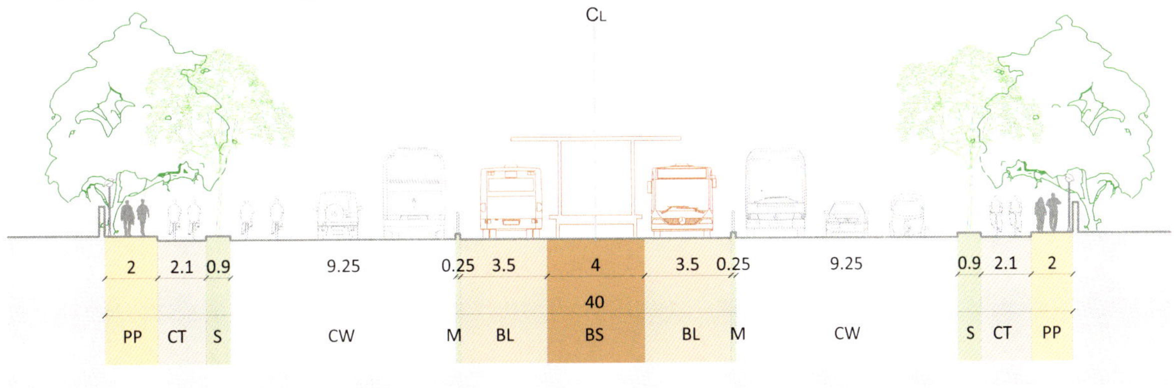

Existing typical cross section design at bus station location

Cross Sections

RTO–Pirana: Near Gujarat University area.
Cycle track works efficiently because it adjoins large institutional campuses with very few entry points.

RTO–Pirana: Near Pragatinagar.
Cycle track gets interrupted because of several entry points to adjoining residential properties.

Typical scene at the BRTS bus station near Blind People's Association during peak traffic hours in the morning

TAXI
TATA
PRESS
CNG

36m

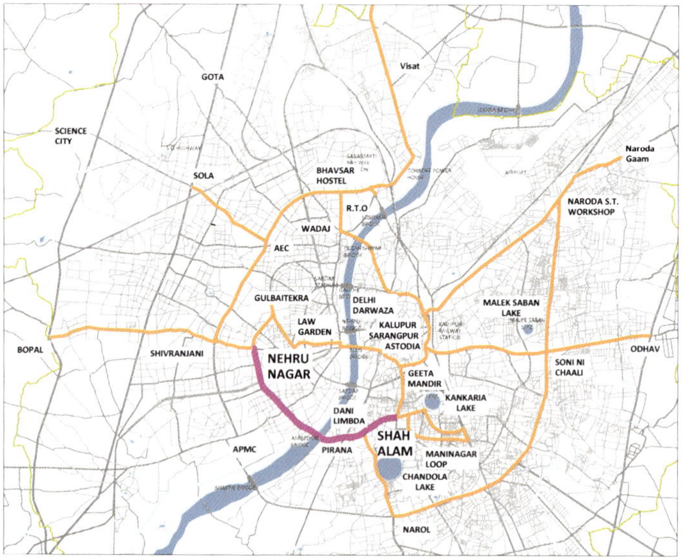

Key map showing 36 m RoW corridors
Nehrunagar to Pirana—3.5 km (Phase I Western Corridor)
Pirana to Shah Alam—2.6 km (Phase I Eastern Corridor)

The 36 m RoW corridors traverse mainly middle class residential neighbourhoods in the west and industrial areas east of the river. However, this road is also part of one of the five rings of Ahmedabad and plays a major role in moving people in the city.

The cycle track here is segregated with a painted line, while the rest of the configuration remains similar to the 40 m RoW. Parking is provided only where space is available. However, after implementation the cycle track has become the de facto parking lane.

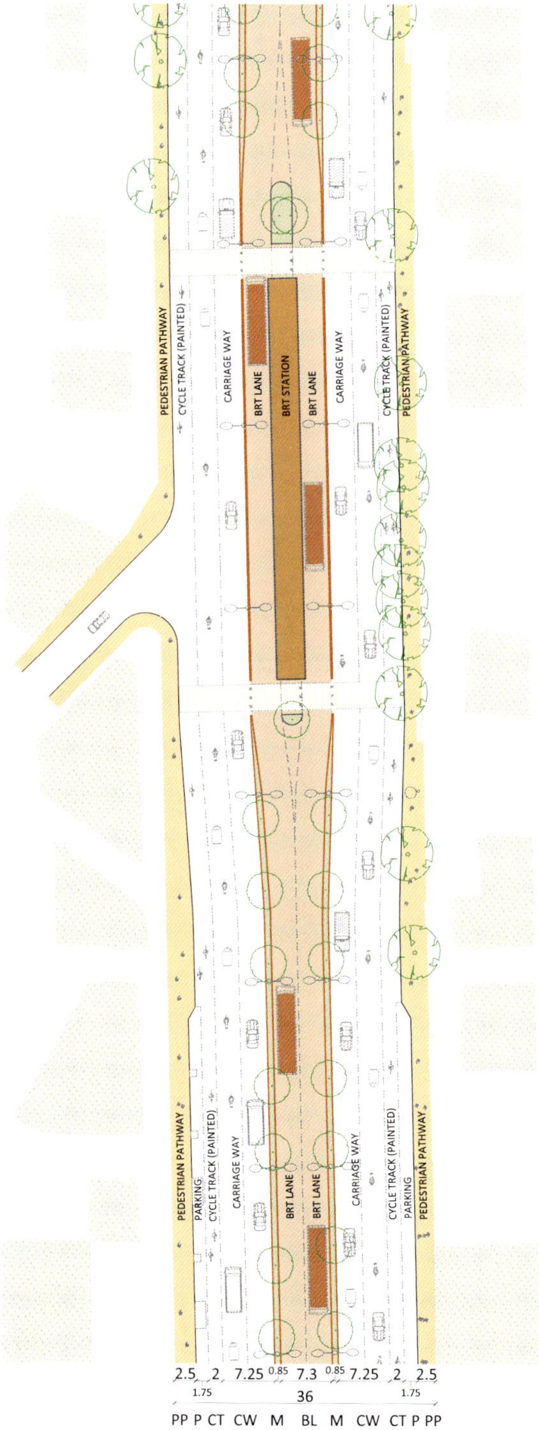

Plan for 36 m RoW corridor

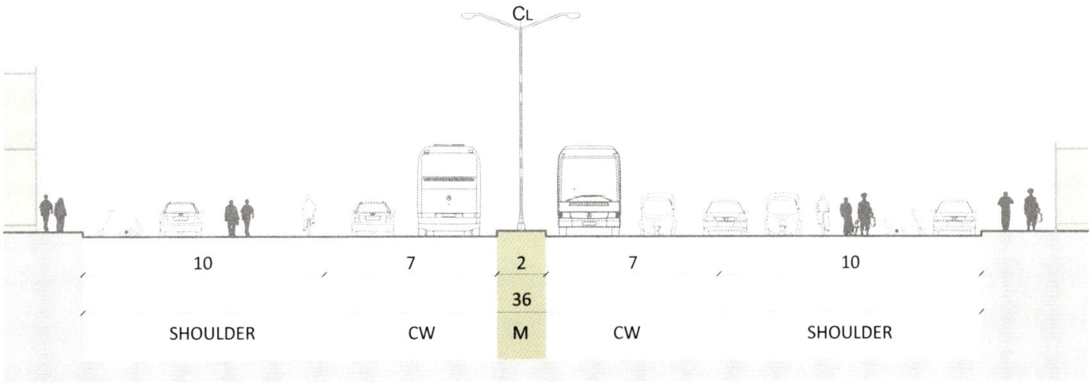

Earlier cross section of 36 m RoW

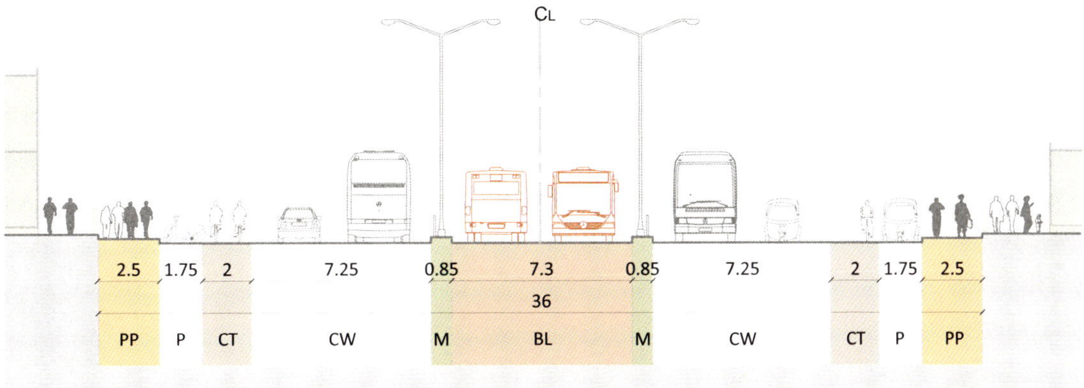

Existing typical cross section design for 36 m RoW

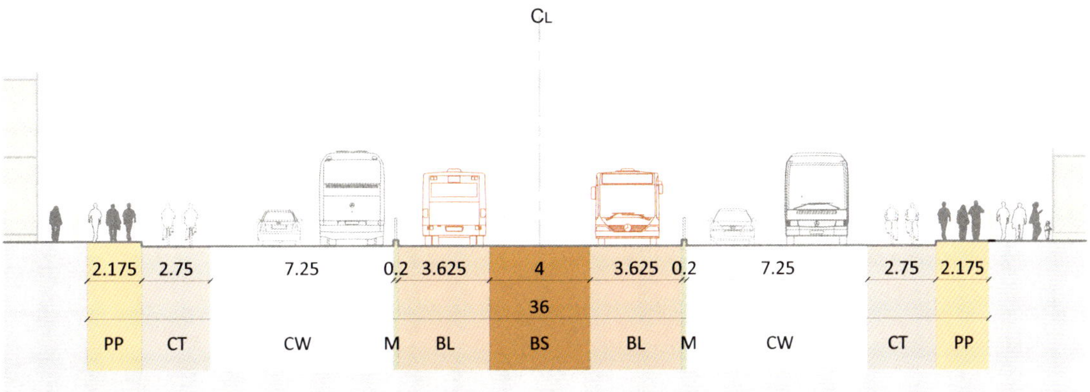

Existing typical cross section design at bus station location

Manekbaug to Nehrunagar: Typical cross section *Before*

Manekbaug to Nehrunagar: Typical cross section *After*

30m

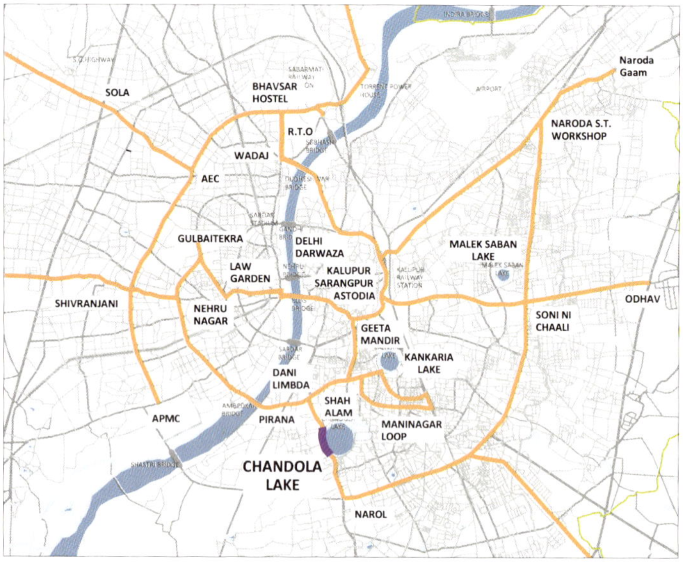

Key map showing 30 m RoW corridor
Chandola Lake Stretch—2.4 km (Phase I Eastern Corridor)

The 30 m RoW corridor passes through the industrial areas near Chandola Lake. Owing to the constricted RoW, cycle tracks are not provided. Parking is provided where possible.

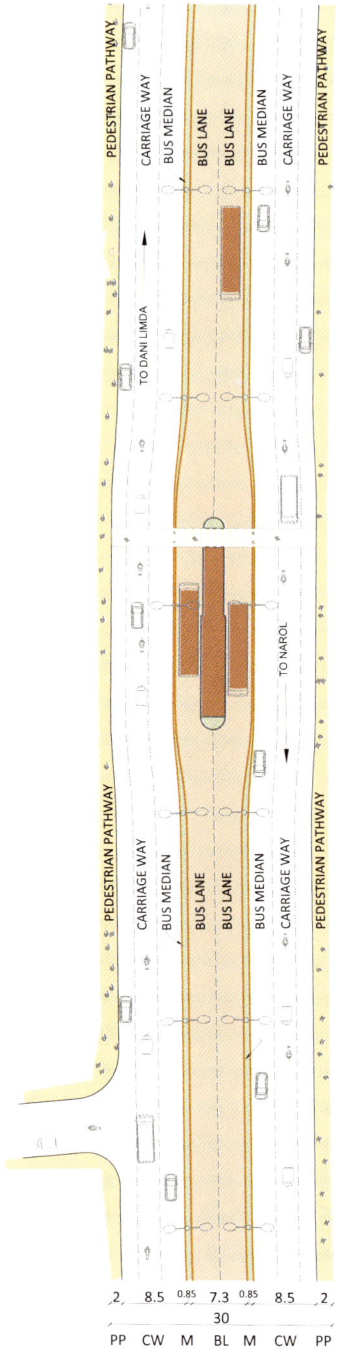

Plan for 30 m RoW corridor

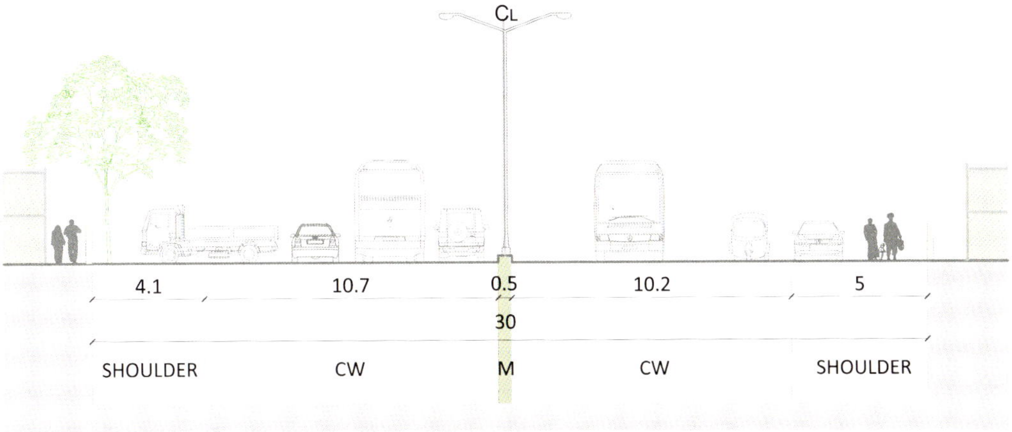

Earlier cross section of 30 m RoW

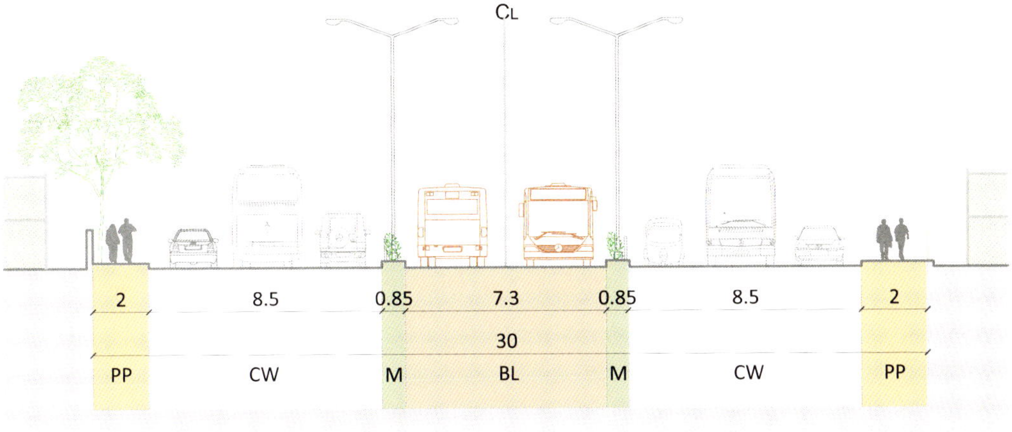

Existing typical cross section design of 30 m RoW

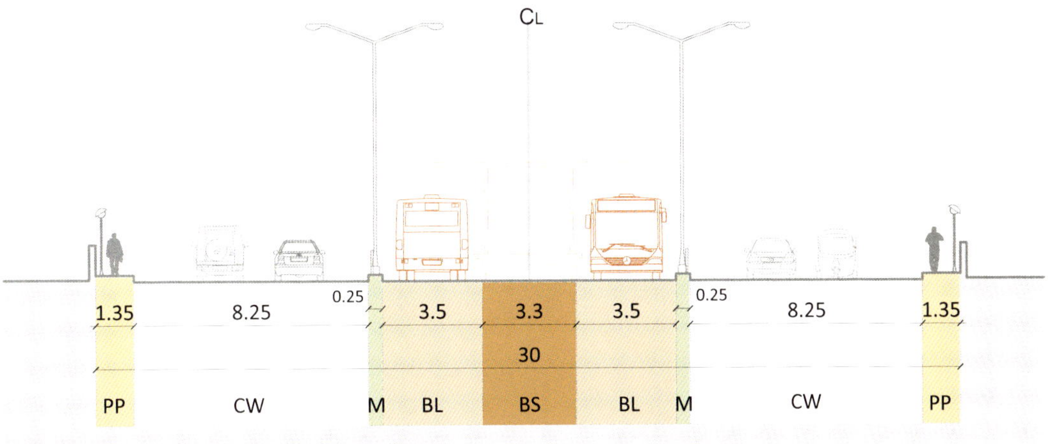

Existing typical cross section design at bus station location

24m

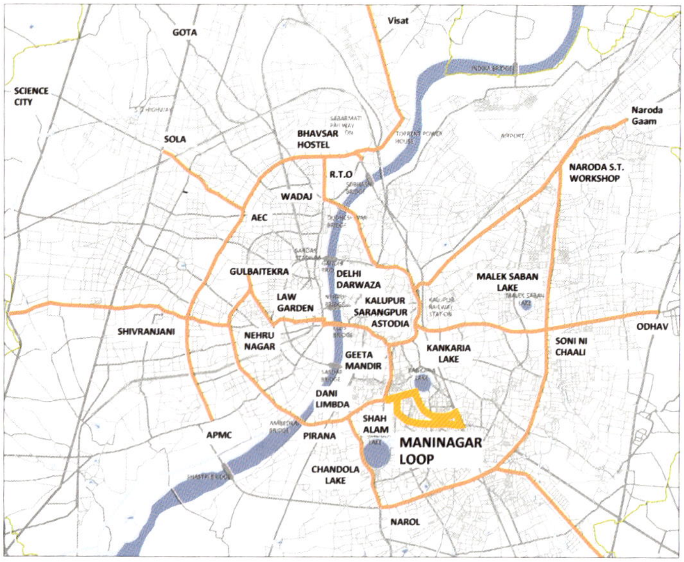

Key map showing 24 m RoW corridor
Shah Alam to Maninagar—5.65 km (Phase I Eastern Corridor) One-way BRTS

One of the design challenges faced was in treating corridors with RoW less than 30 m. For a two-way BRTS with two-way mixed traffic, anything less than 30 m is difficult to manage. The options are to make either the mixed traffic or the BRTS lane one-way. Both have advantages and disadvantages. For BRTS, the network has to be such that the one-way is for a short distance only. Even for mixed traffic, a one-way system with the BRTS presents problems since a service lane would have to be provided anyway for access to private properties.

After weighing both options, one-way BRT lane with normal mixed traffic movement was chosen. The BRT lane here forms a 5-km unidirectional loop before joining the main network again. The bus stations are modified to suit this arrangement.

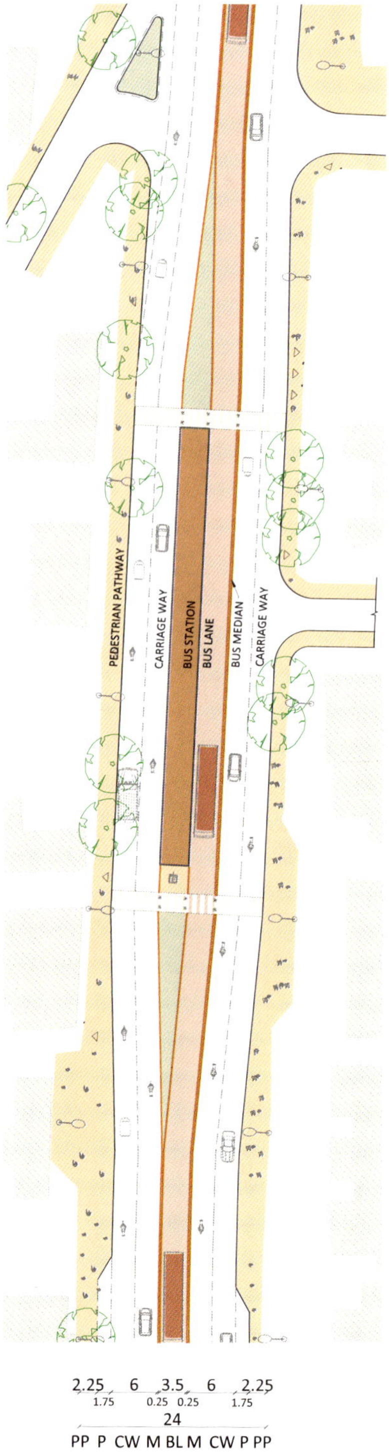

Plan for 24 m RoW corridor

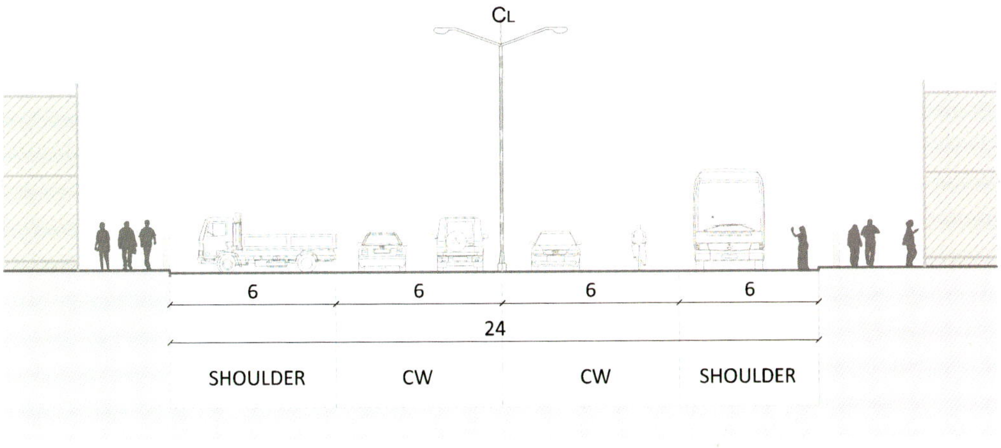

Earlier cross section of 24 m RoW: Phase I

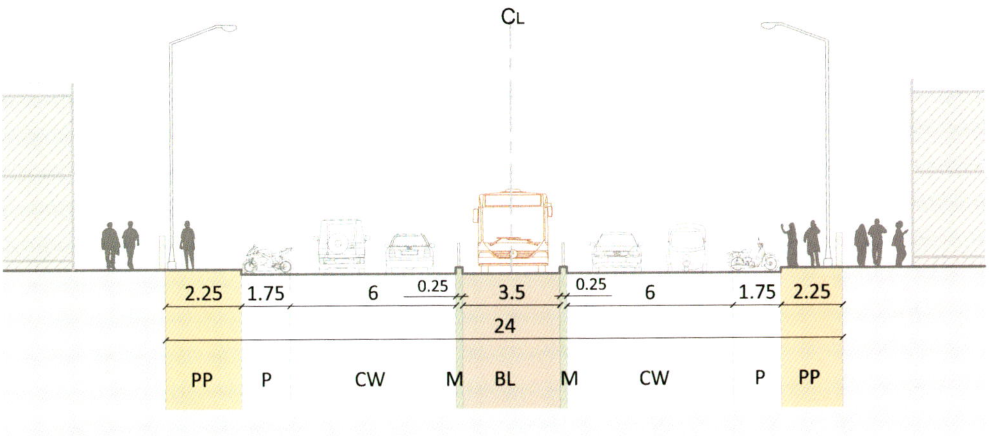

Existing typical cross section design of 24 m RoW: Phase I

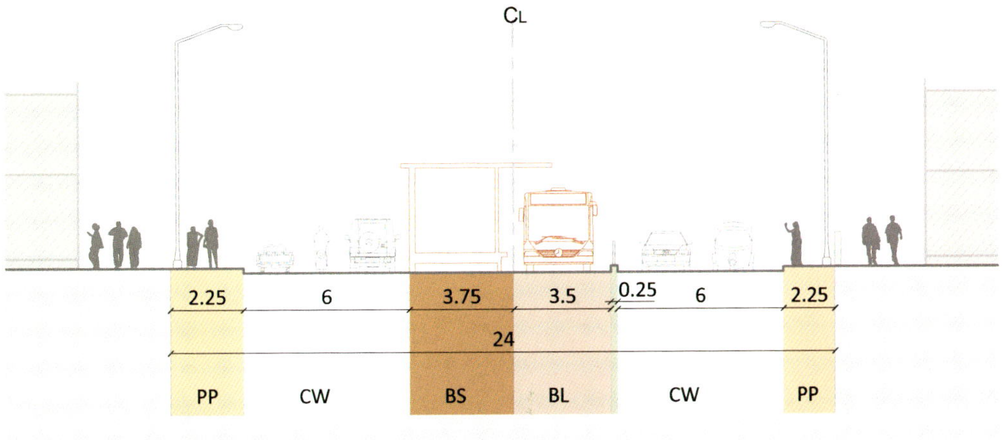

Existing typical cross section design at bus station location

Before

After

Maninagar one-way loop: Typical cross section

Before

After

Bus station on Maninagar one-way loop: Typical cross section

Overtaking Lanes

The decision to add overtaking/ passing lanes was taken later in the project to allow for express services. An additional lane of 3.5 m is provided on either side of the station making the bus lane 7 m. Thus, the cross section here gets widened to 18 m for BRTS. However, these passing lanes, proposed at four locations in the corridor, are not utilised at present as express services have not been scheduled.

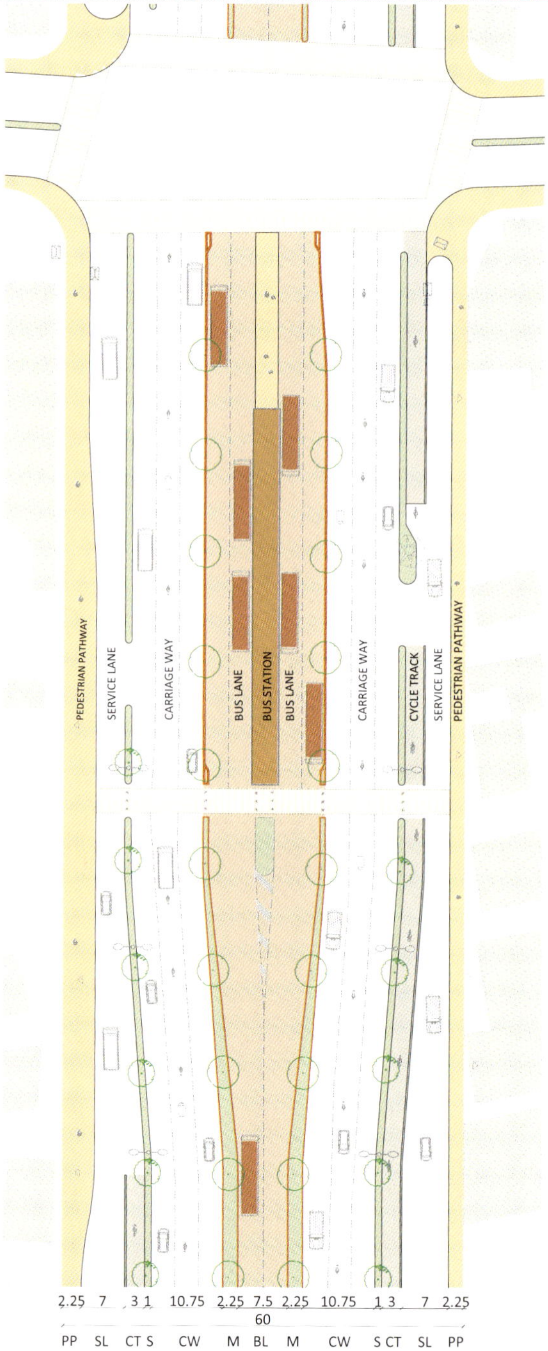

Plan for 60 m RoW corridor showing overtaking lanes

Overtaking lanes at Rabari Colony: This will enable express services to operate in future.

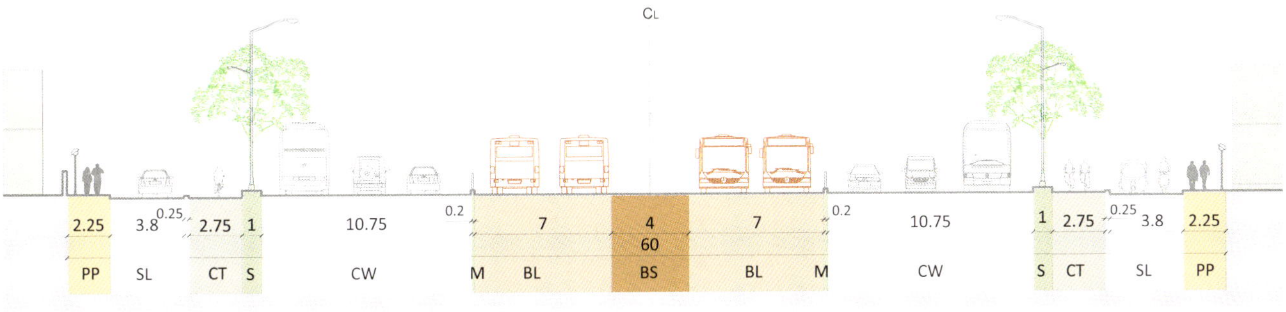

Proposed cross section showing overtaking lanes with bus station location

Adapting Design for Special Situations

While Ahmedabad roads generally have a uniform RoW with few encroachments, some situations require the design to be modified to accommodate specific site contexts. One such case is Krishnanagar on the Narol–Naroda corridor.

The temple here is a vibrant place throughout the day, where people from surrounding areas visit and spend time with friends and families. A small fruit and vegetable market has also sprung up to cater to local demand. In order to retain this vibrancy and respect the local context, special attention has been given to this zone by creating a public plaza with paved surfaces, merging the cycle track and creating a wider pedestrian walkway.

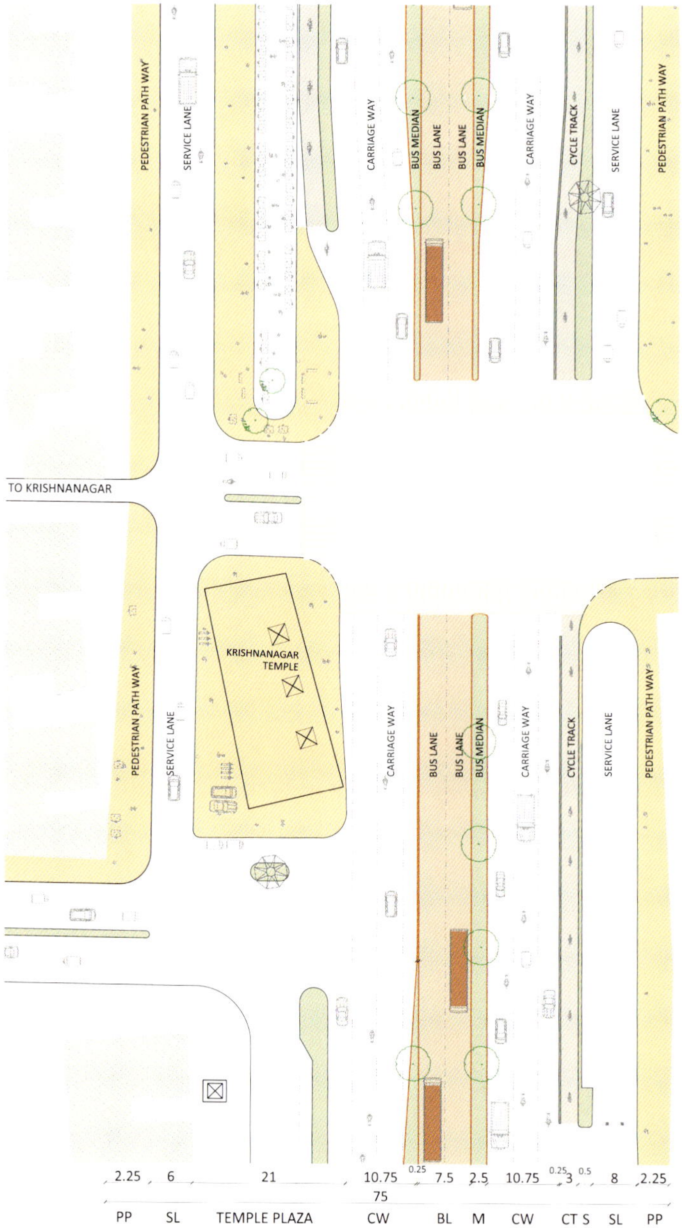

Plan for 60 m RoW showing integration of Krishnanagar temple in the design

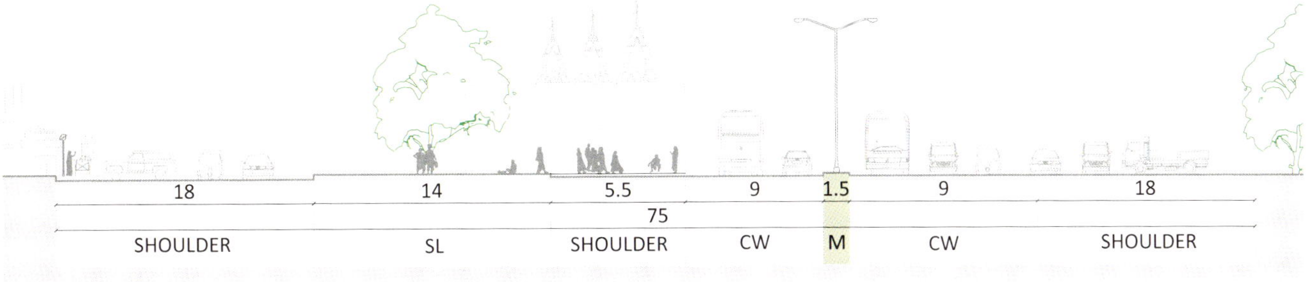

Earlier cross section at Krishnanagar temple

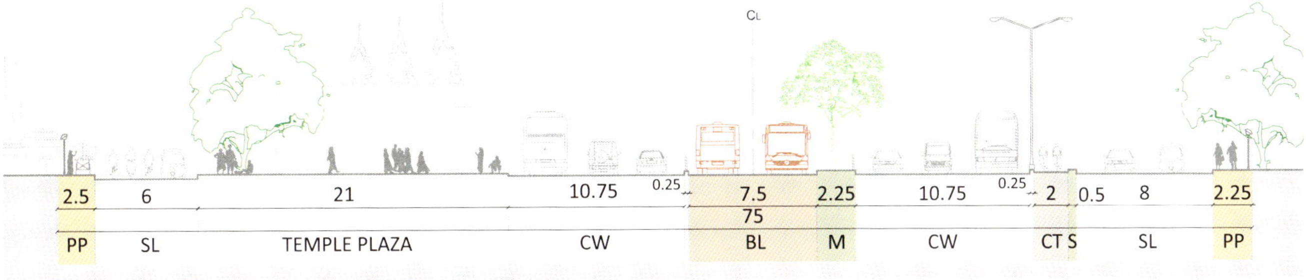

Existing cross section at Krishnanagar temple

Narol–Naroda: Krishnanagar temple

Grade Separating for Pedestrians

Facilities to enable commuters to cross the road to access bus stations are a widely debated topic. It does appear to make sense to grade separate pedestrians from the mixed traffic. Images from the famous Transmilenio BRTS in Bogotá, Colombia, also depict pedestrian overbridges. Subways are also an option. AMC prepared design options for these crossings and discussed them in detail with various stakeholders. One opinion to emerge was that some kinds of activities need to be planned on these crossings to attract pedestrians and ensure safety and maintenance.

However, the experience in India, wherever grade separated crossings have been introduced, suggests that they are rarely successful. Pedestrians are willing to risk crossing at grade. The physically challenged also find it difficult to use bridges. In subways, drainage and security are major concerns. Further investigations

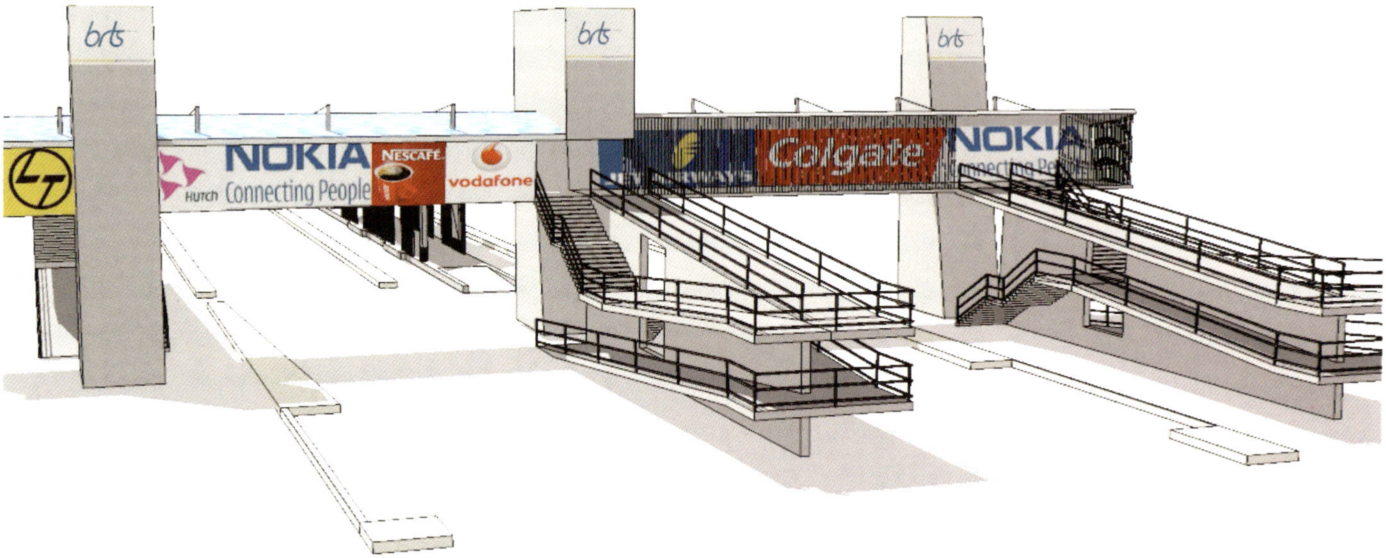

Conceptual drawings of foot overbridge for BRT station

into best practices reveal that even the Transmilenio has pedestrian bridges only across very wide roads with five to six lanes of mixed traffic in each direction. Most other BRT corridors have zebra crossings.

Janmarg generally uses zebra crossings at junctions or mid-block to access bus stations. However, a few experiments were done on the Narol–Naroda corridor. The final design consisted in elevating the mixed traffic lanes at the bus station access points and allowing pedestrians to cross at grade, without using steps, amps or elevators. This design was implemented at two locations. The experience after two years suggests that these underpasses are not well maintained. The bus stations tend to be in a canyon and are not visible from the road, creating safety issues.

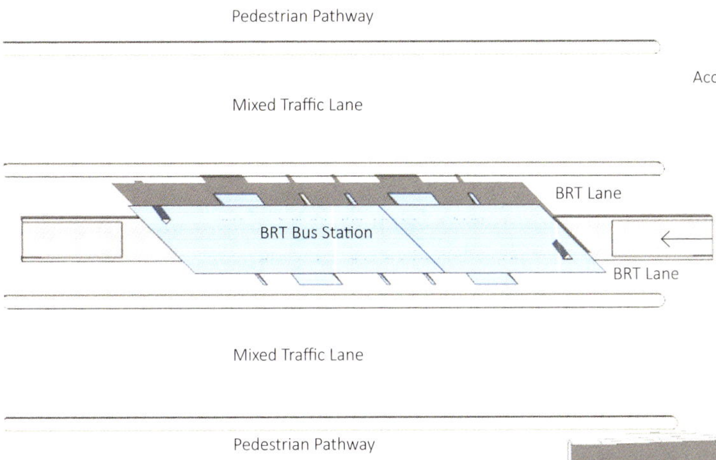

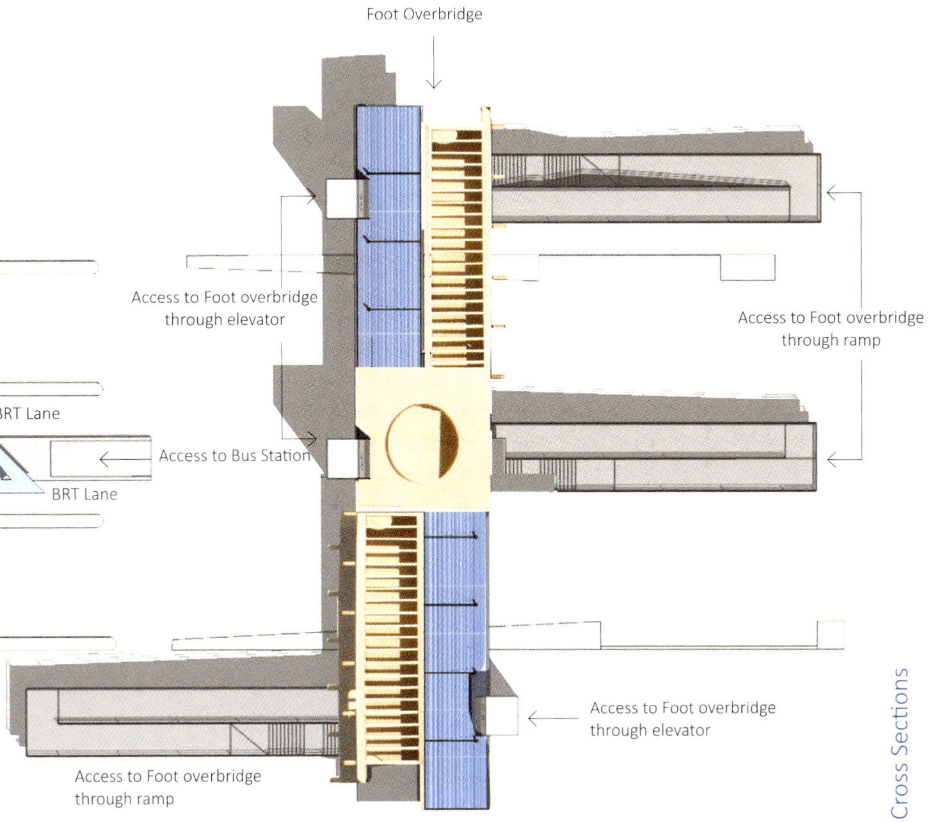

Plan showing BRT station and pedestrian overbridge

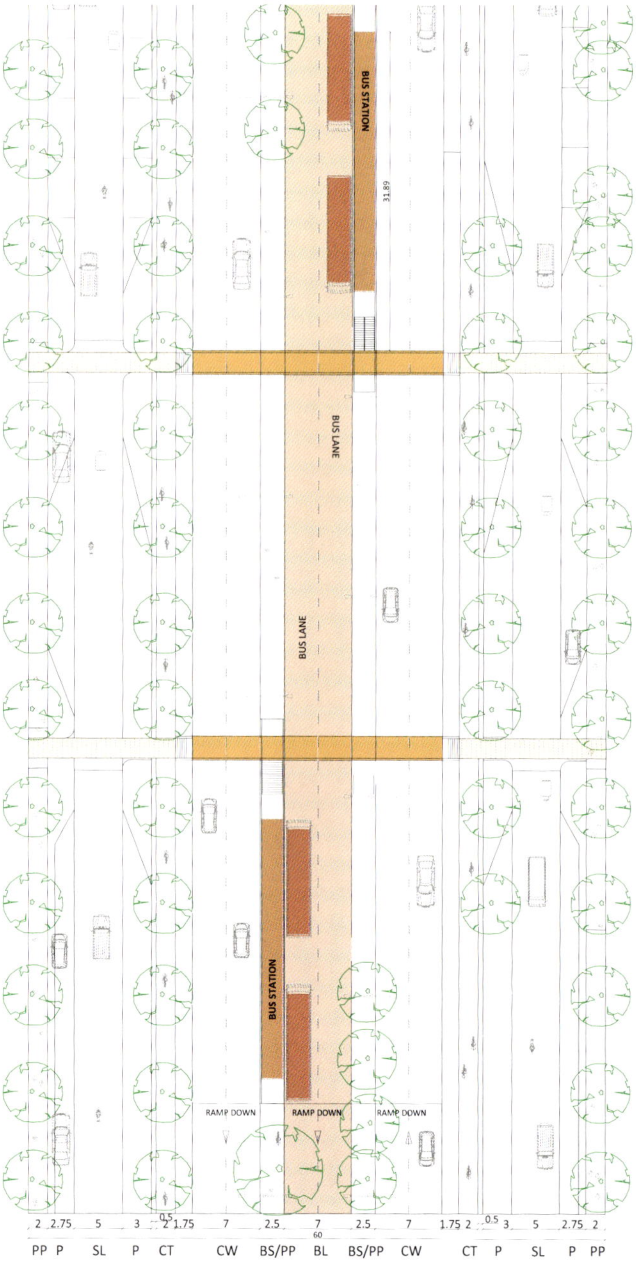

Subway design near Soni ni Chali: Earlier option

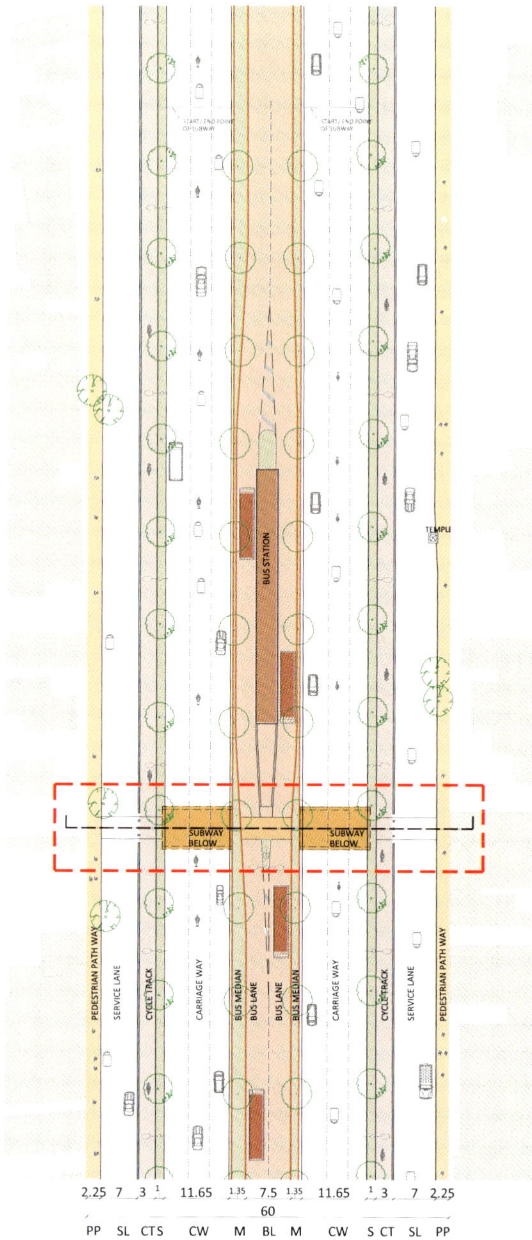

Existing subway near Soni ni Chali

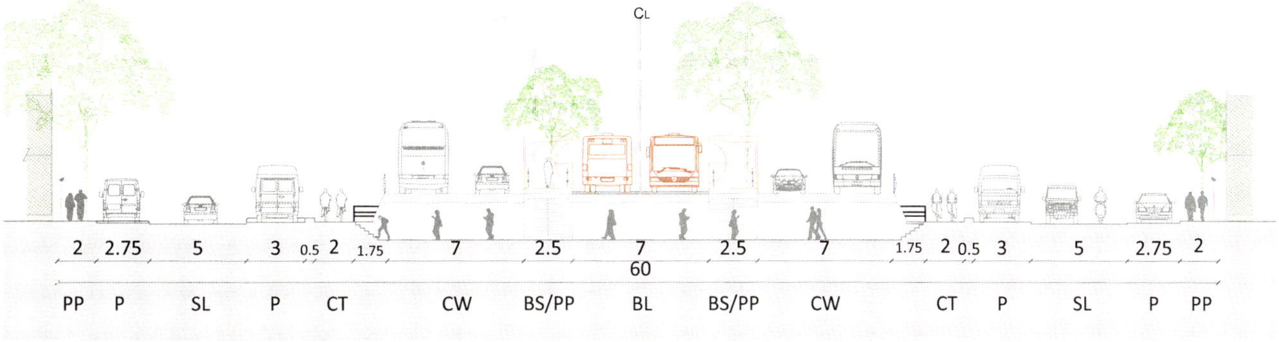

Cross section of subway: Earlier option

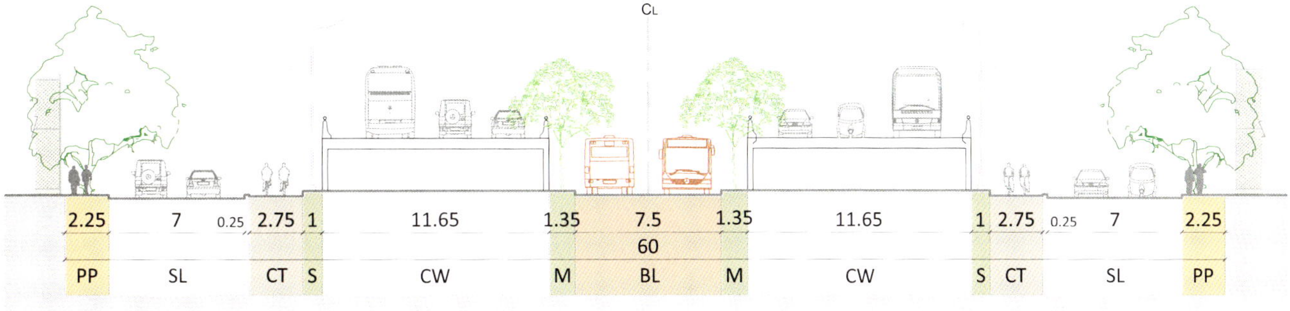

Existing cross section near Soni ni Chali

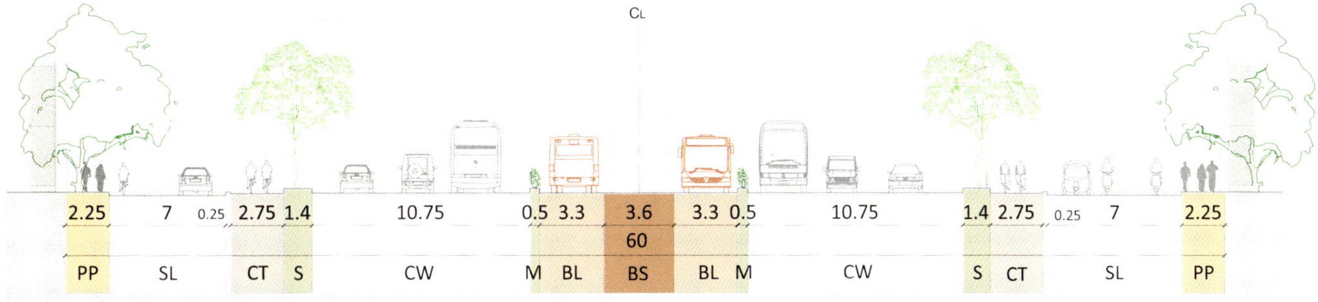

Existing cross section near Soni ni Chali at bus station location

NEMA BRT

The elevated mixed carriageway at Geeta-Gauri Cinema.
The BRTS is at-grade and passengers cross through a subway.

Splitting the Flyovers

As part of proposals to relieve congestion at critical junctions, the Ahmedabad Urban Development Authority planned flyovers. As junctions would attract more passengers from crossroads, it was not advisable for buses to use the flyovers. The bus stations had to be at grade level and close to the junction. This was a cause for major concern. If buses remained at grade, they would have to move from median lanes to the service lane next to the flyover, which would mean weaving and merging with other traffic before and after the flyover.

After discussing various options (including a flyover across the BRT corridor rather than along it), a 'split' flyover was proposed. This meant two separate arms for up and down movement of other bidirectional traffic. The bus lanes would continue in the centre at grade, with the station between the two arms of the flyover. Such split flyovers are now operational at three locations.

In later designs, the first option was always to align the flyover across the BRT corridor. Six such flyovers were constructed.

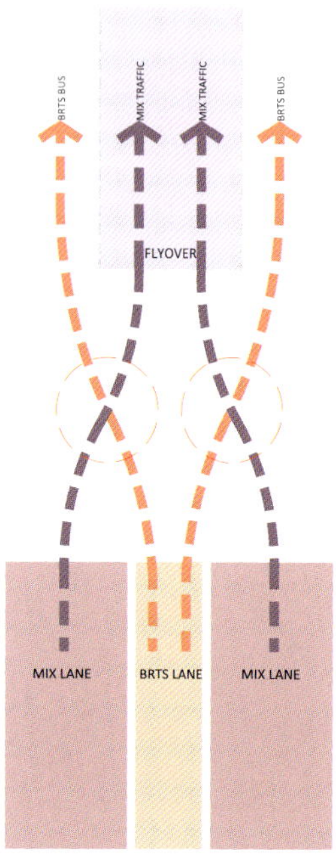

A drawing depicts the issues of merging and weaving of BRTS buses with a central flyover

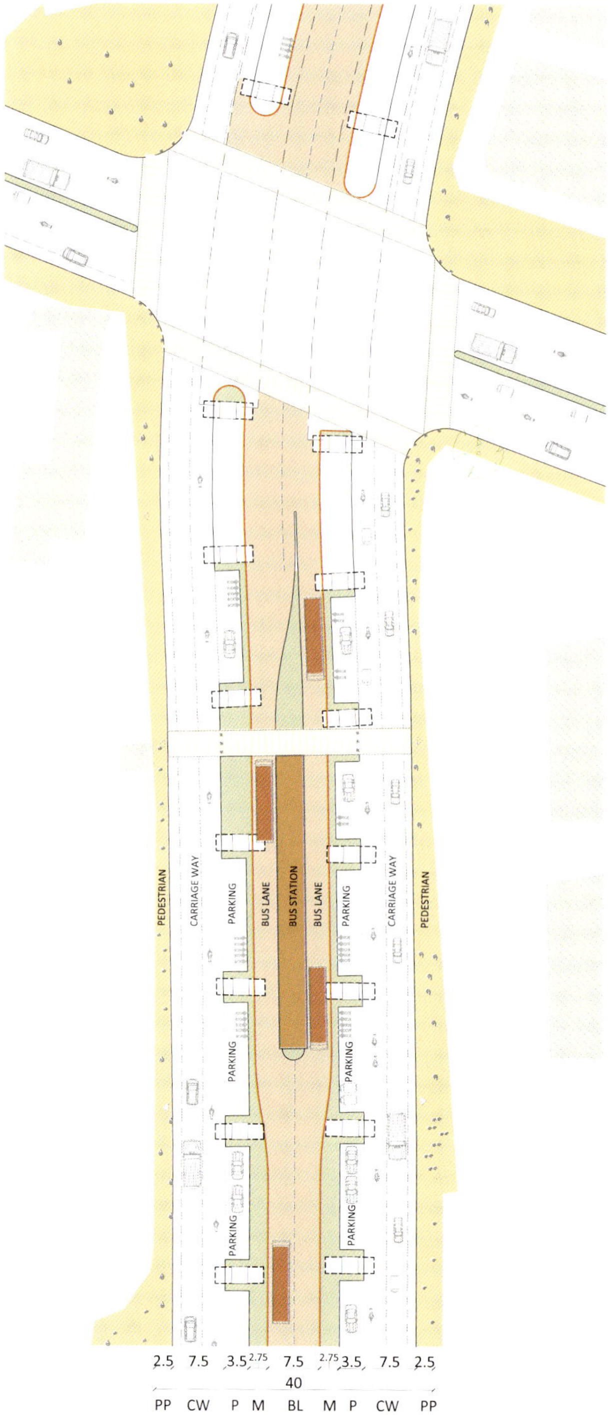

Final design for split flyover and bus station at AEC

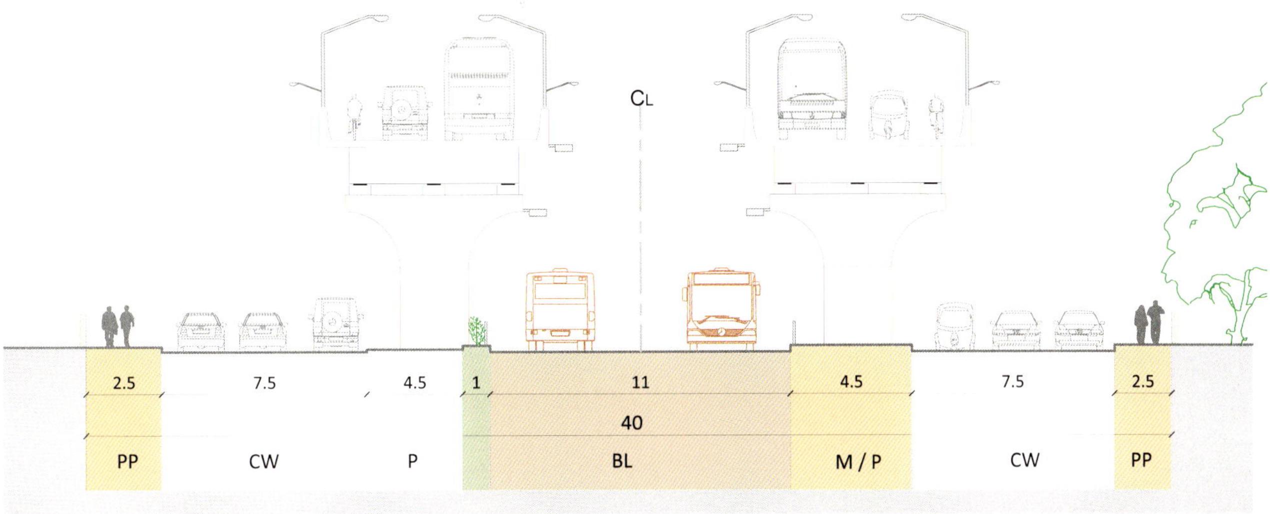

Existing cross section design at AEC flyover

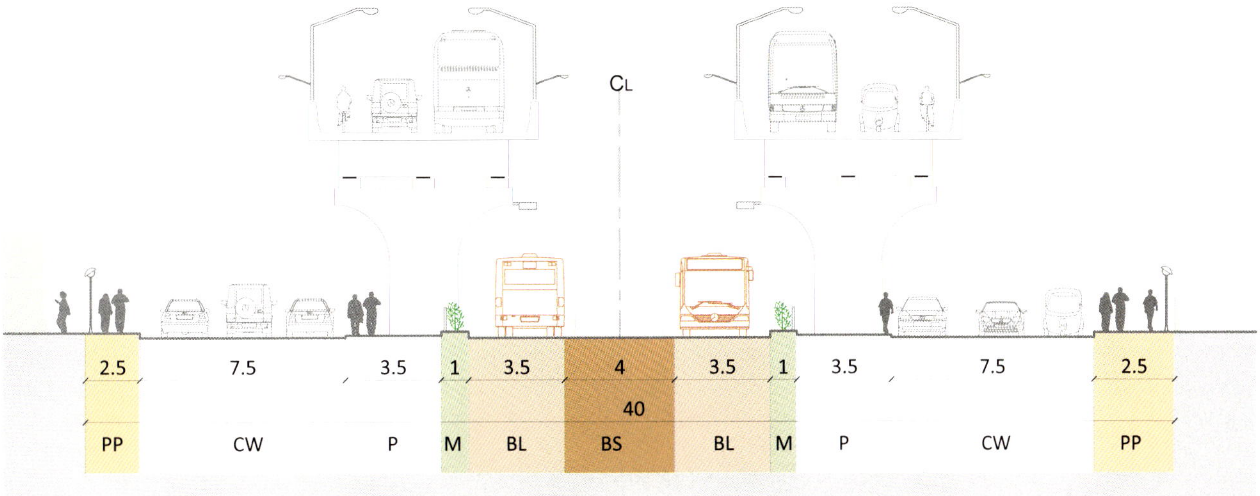

Existing cross section design at AEC flyover with BRTS bus station

Memnagar BRT station below flyover

91

Before

After

Split flyover along RTO—Pirana corridor

Accommodating High-Tension Lines

Some stretches had high-tension (HT) lines with pylons on the road edge. Realigning these is expensive and AMC chose to modify the design to accommodate them. The cycle track is opened up near HT pylons and movement of cyclists is merged with the mixed traffic. This carriageway now functions as a service lane and controls the speed of vehicles.

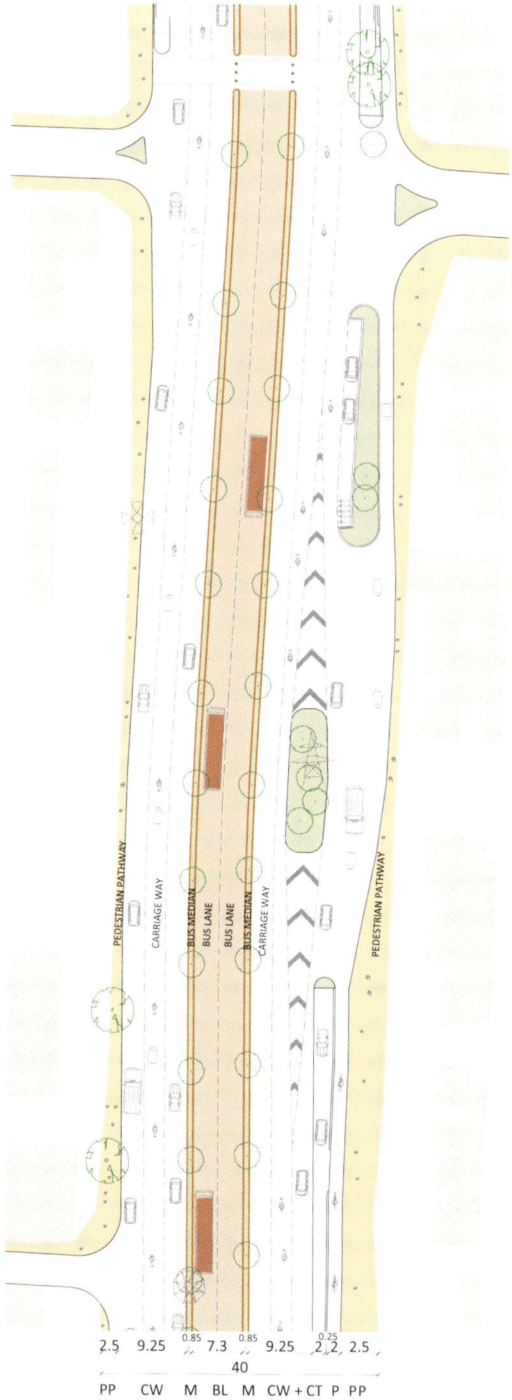

Plan showing realignment to accommodate HT lines

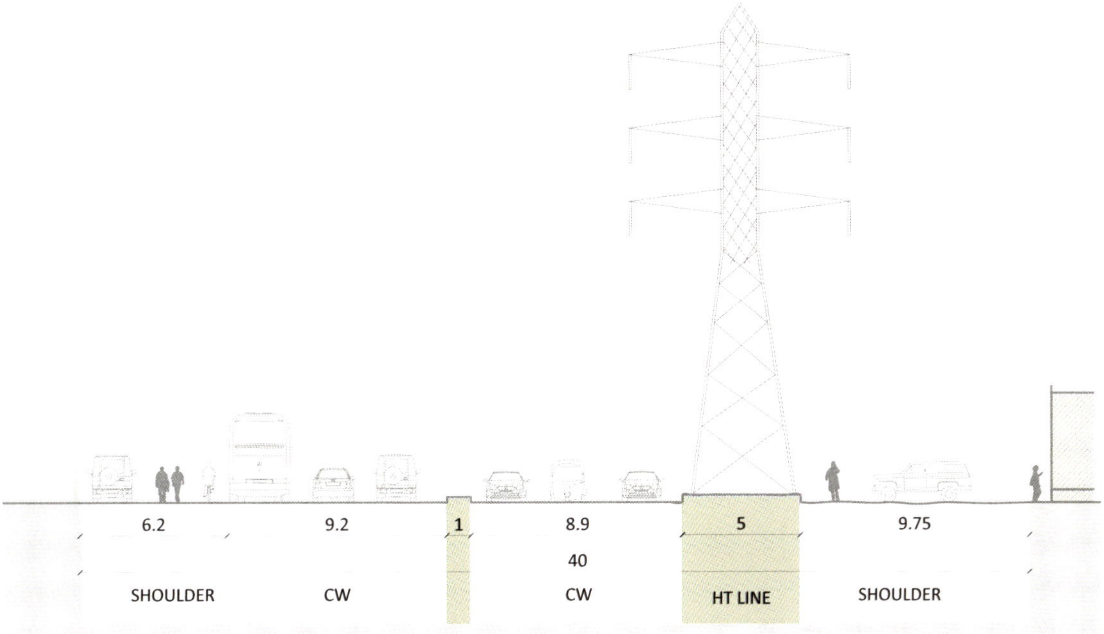

Earlier cross section along HT line

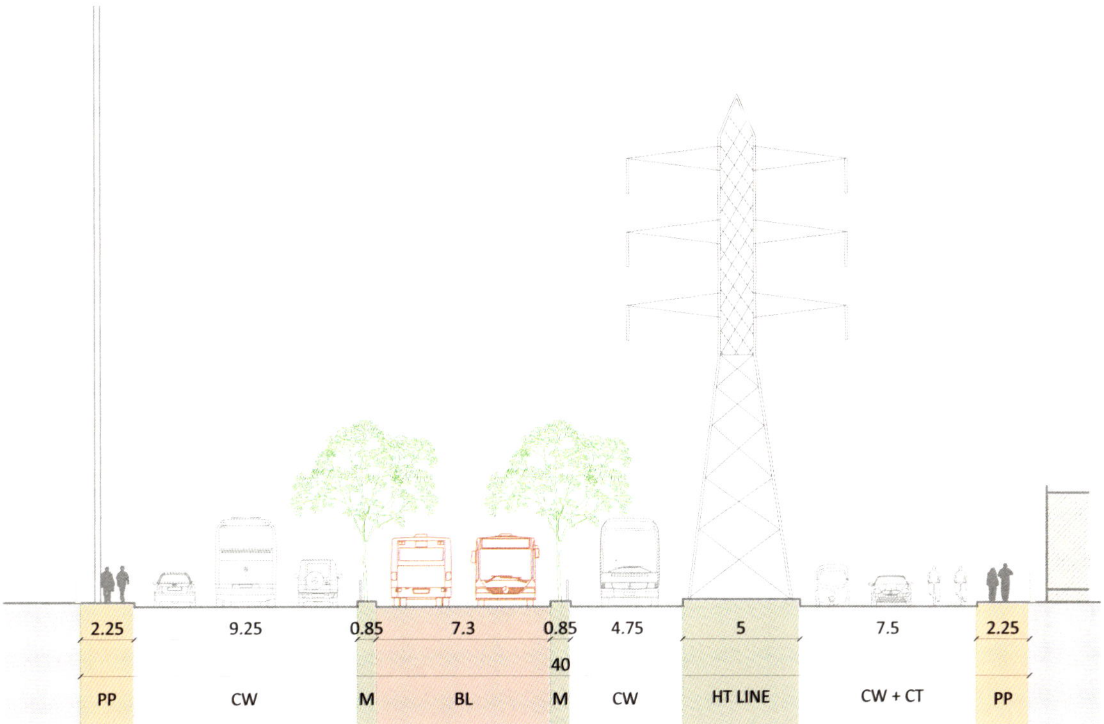

Existing cross section design along HT line with BRTS

A high-tension pylon near AEC before BRTS implementation

The same high-tension pylon accommodated in the BRTS design

Cross Sections

60m

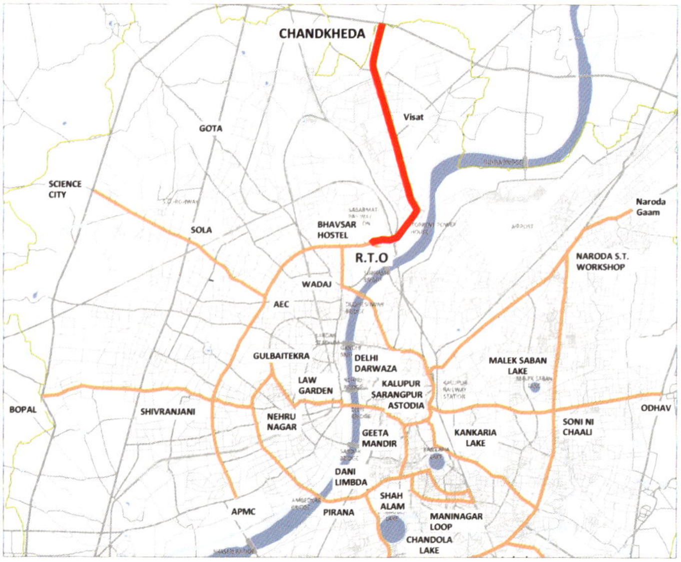

Key map showing 60 m RoW corridor
RTO to Chandkheda—6.6 km (Phase II Western Corridor)

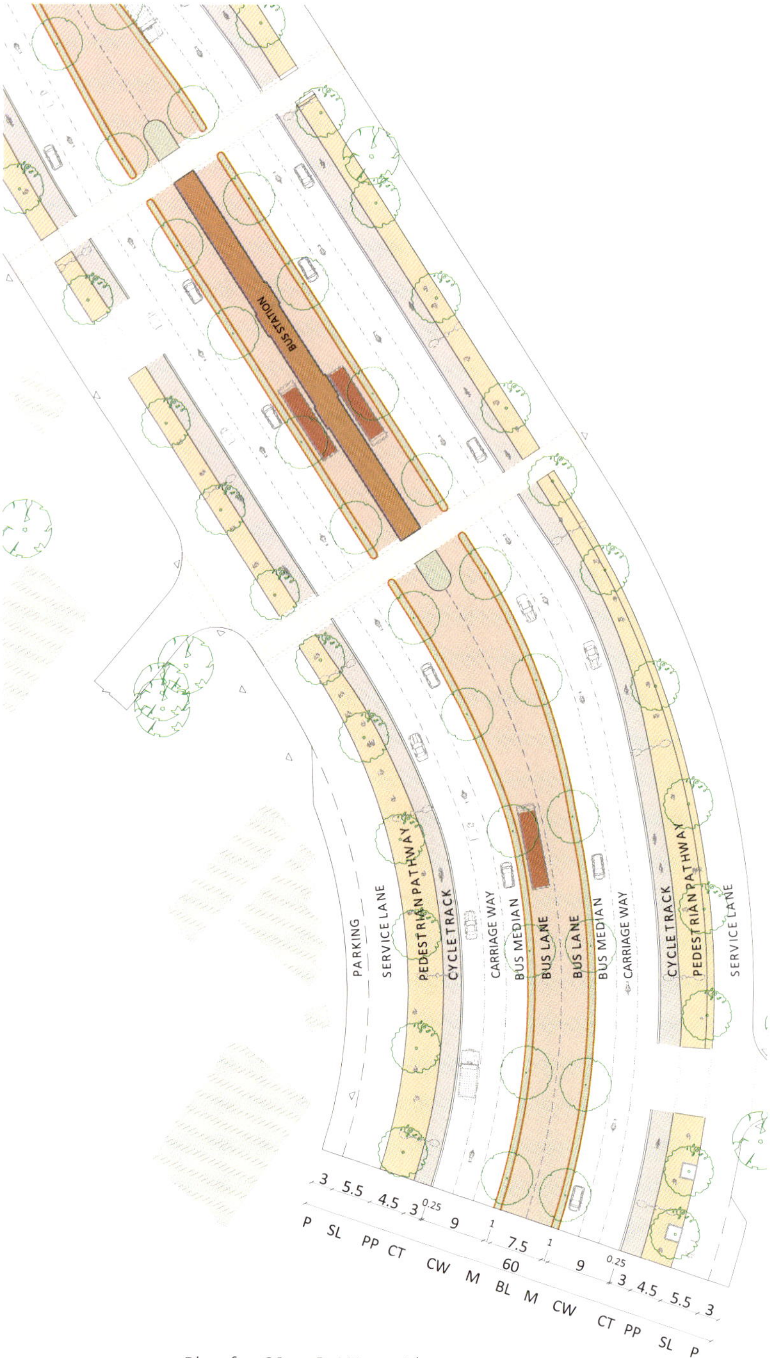

Plan for 60 m RoW corridor

After the experience of Phase I, where activity areas were completely discarded, they are included in Phase II. A 60 m wide corridor links Ahmedabad with the upcoming suburb of Chandkheda, Sabarmati railway station and Motera. The road edge is characterised by a mix of unorganised activities such as truck parking, small shops, workshops, residences, shared auto-rickshaws/local commuter stands etc. It carries major through traffic to Gandhinagar and Mehesana as well as the local traffic.

The cross section includes parking spaces, service lanes, cycle tracks, activity areas, wide pedestrian pathways and provision for future metro alignment. Passing lanes are not provided.

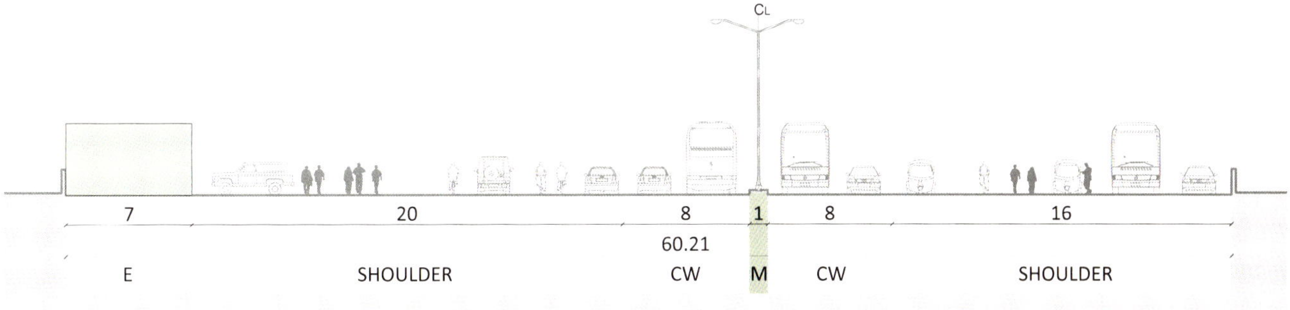

Earlier situation at RTO–Chandkheda stretch

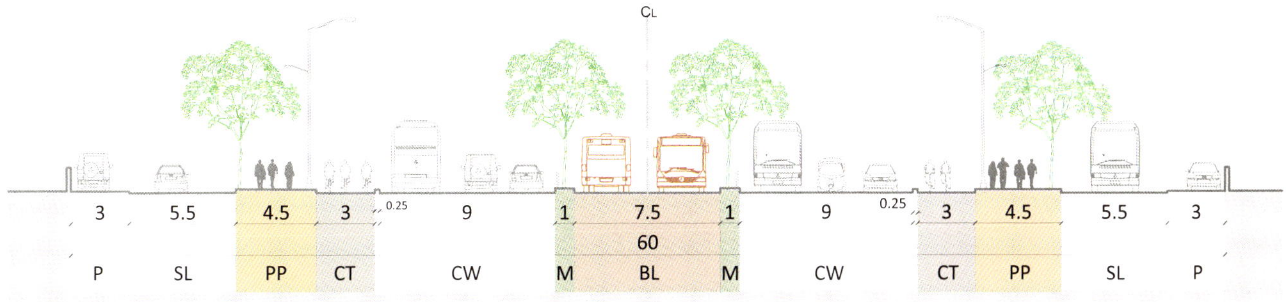

Existing typical cross section for 60 m RoW for Phase II corridor

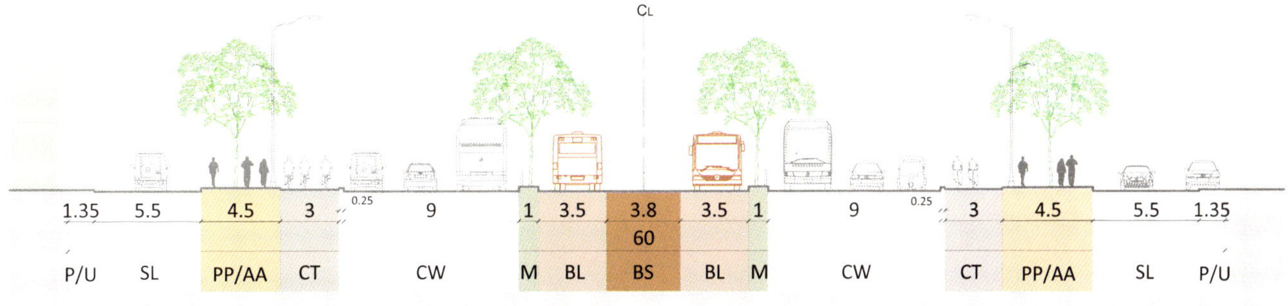

Existing typical cross section at bus station location

Typical view of BRTS section near Sabarmati. The stretch has trees planted along the medians.

Access to Sabarmati police station BRT station from junction

40m

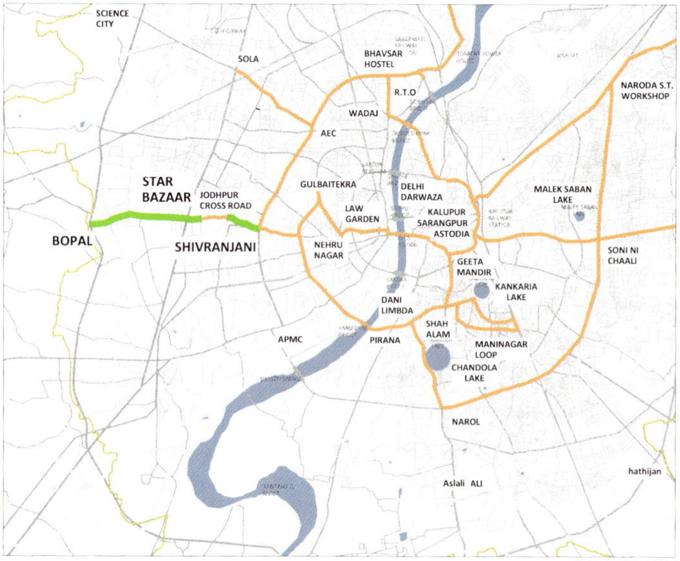

Key map showing 40 m RoW corridor
Shivranjini to Bopal—5.5 km (Phase II Western Corridor)

Based on experience from Phase I, certain changes were made in the design for Phase II. Here, the corridor passes through an upcoming commercial area. The edge of the road has many openings that serve private entrances. Therefore, the cycle track has been removed and a wider footpath built.

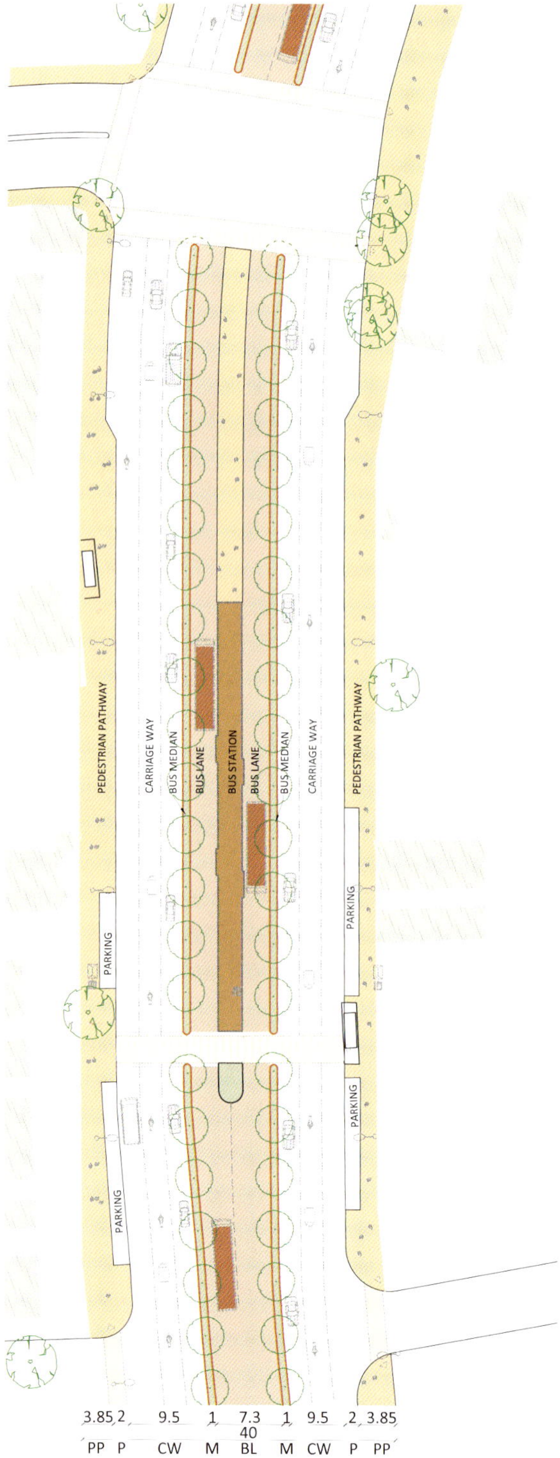

Plan for 40 m RoW corridor

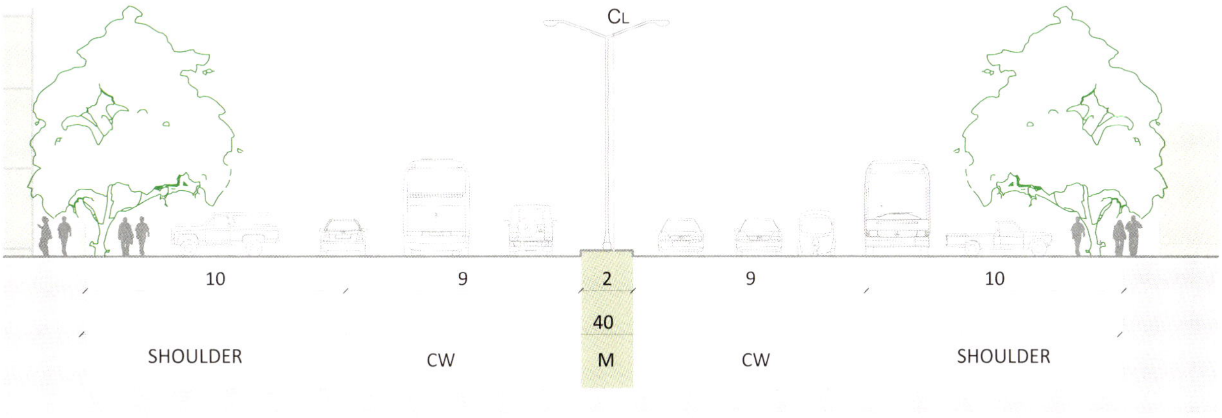

Earlier cross section of 40 m RoW—Phase II

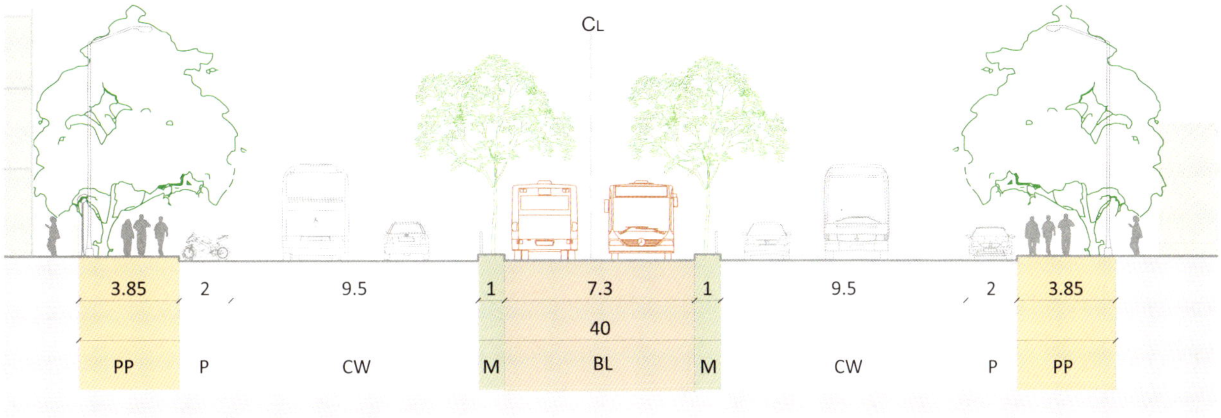

Existing typical cross section design of 40 m RoW—Phase II

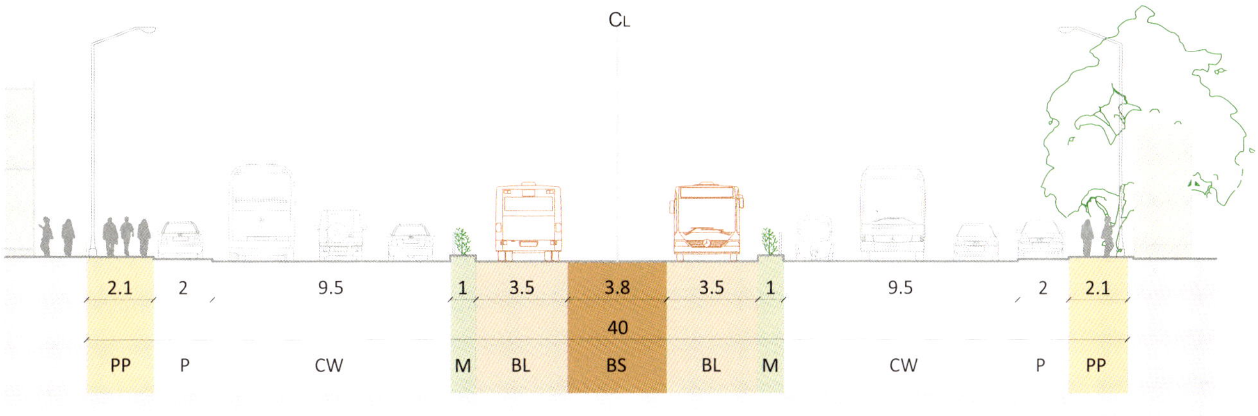

Existing typical cross section design at bus station location

Star Bazaar junction *Before*

After

36m

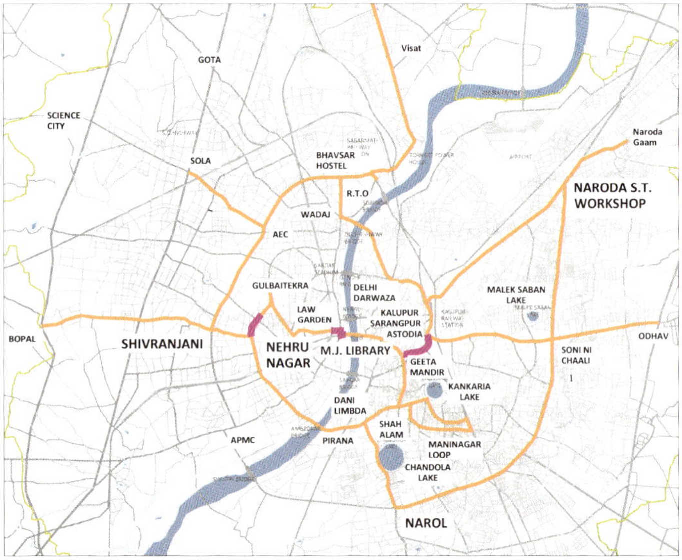

Key map showing 36 m RoW corridors

Nehrunagar to Gulbai Tekra—0.85 km (Phase II: Western Corridor)
Ashram road to Ellis bridge—0.125 km (Phase II: Eastern Corridor)
M.J. Library stretch

The painted cycle track has been removed and the footpath has been made wider. Three lanes have been provided for other traffic.

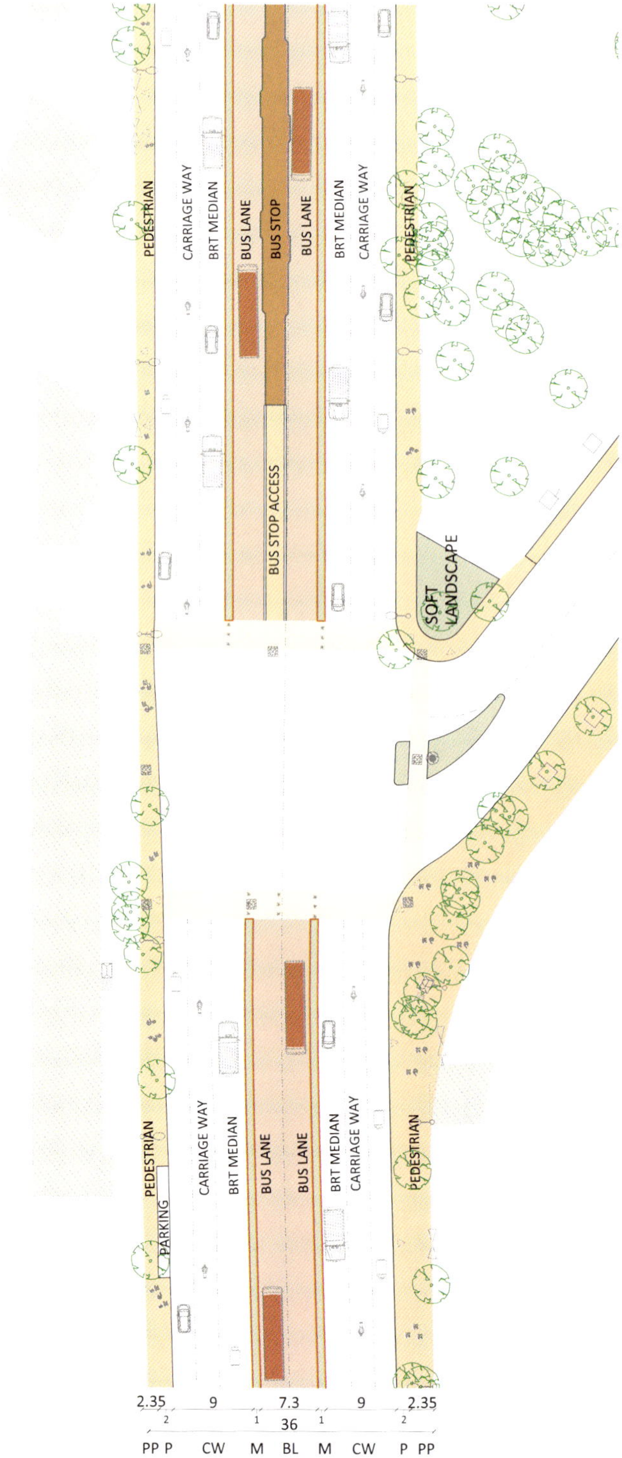

Plan for 36 m RoW corridor

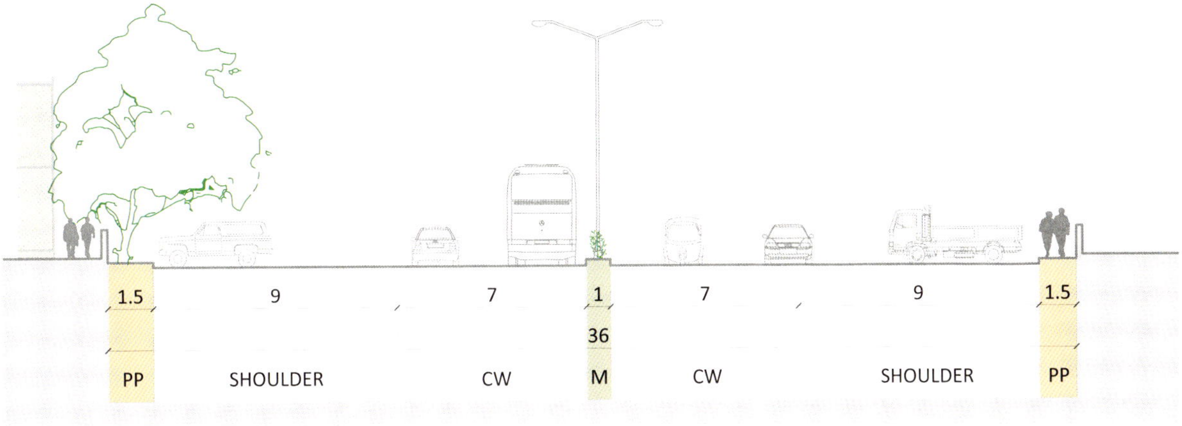

Earlier cross section of 36 m RoW—Phase II

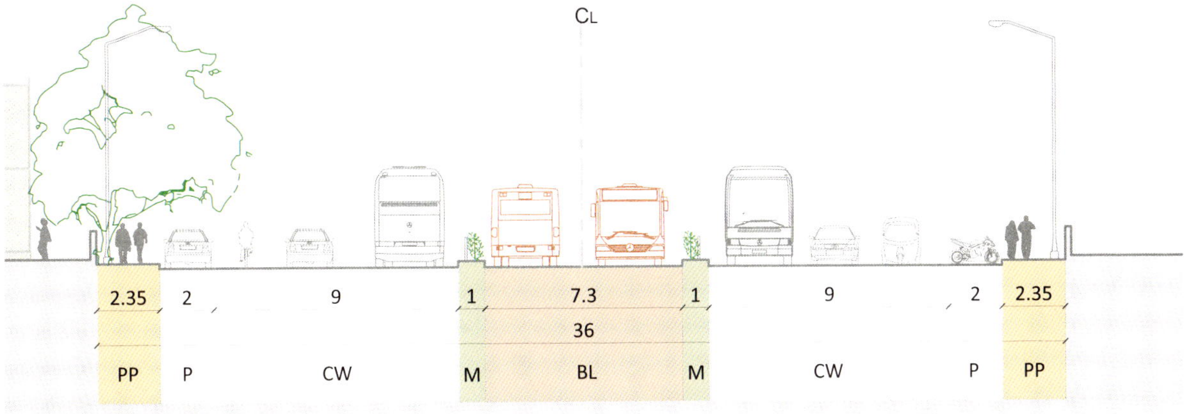

Existing typical cross section design of 36 m RoW—Phase II

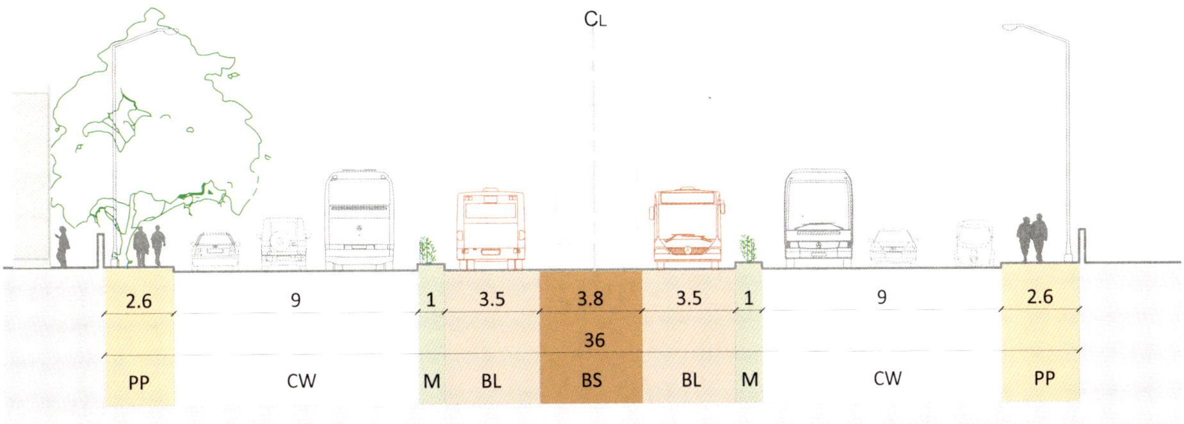

Existing typical cross section design at bus station location

30m

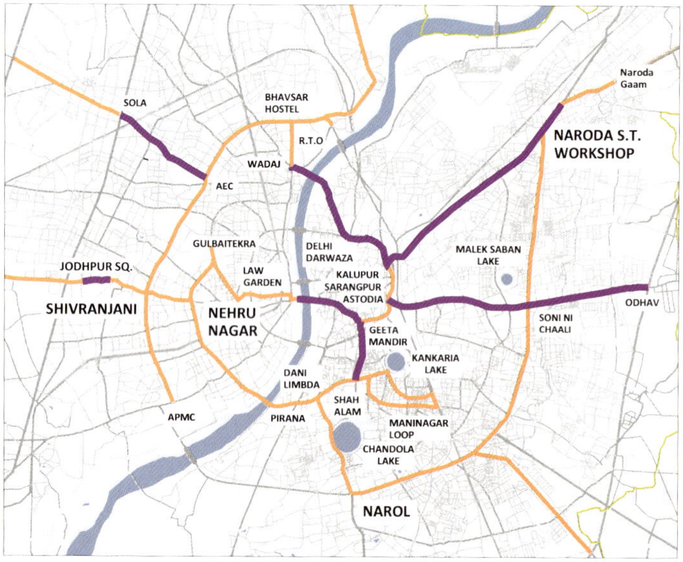

Key map showing 30 m RoW corridors

AEC to Sola—3.1 km (Phase II: Western Corridor)
Soni ni Chali to Odhav—3.6 km
Kalupur bridge to Naroda gaam—8.5 km
ISRO to Ramdevnagar—1 km

Many roads in Phase II have 30 m RoW. These are some of the most important roads in the city, connecting important transport nodes like the intercity bus terminal and railway station, industrial areas in the east and dense residential areas. Two lanes are provided in each direction for mixed traffic, with wide footpaths along the edge. Parking is provided only where space is available.

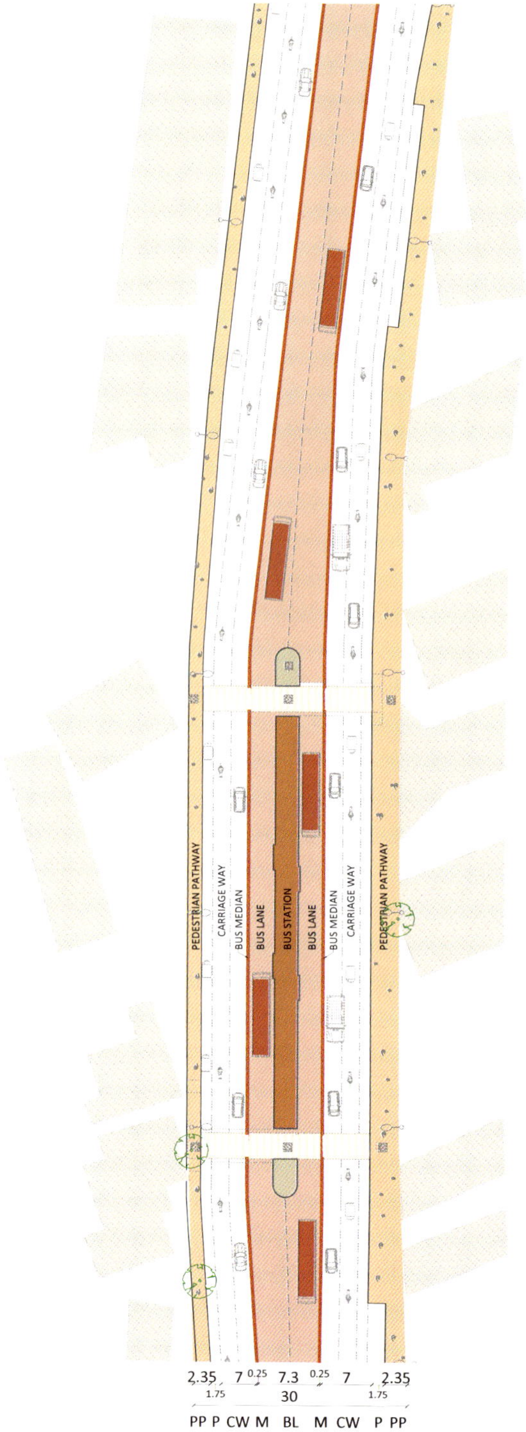

Plan for 30 m RoW corridor

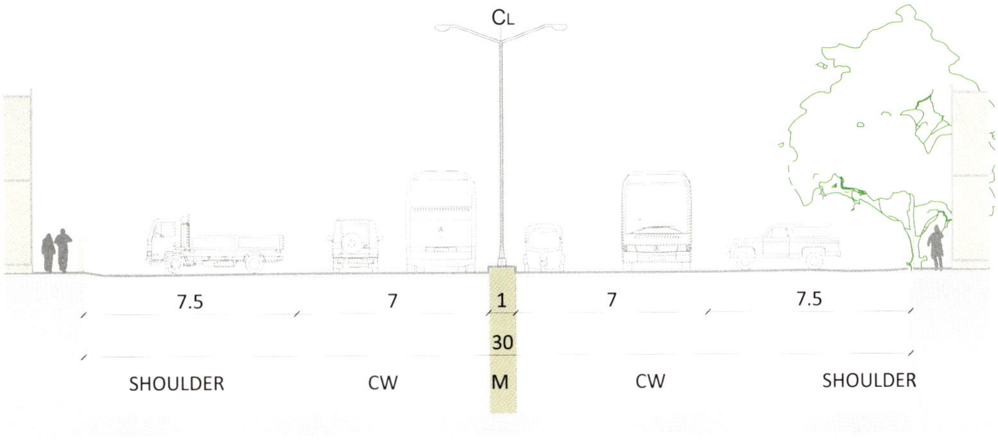

Earlier cross section of 30 m RoW: Phase II

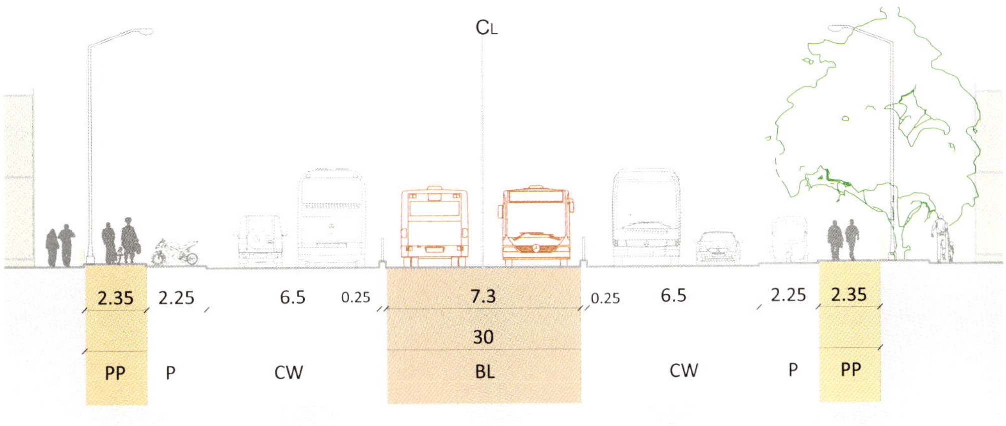

Existing typical cross section design of 30 m RoW: Phase II

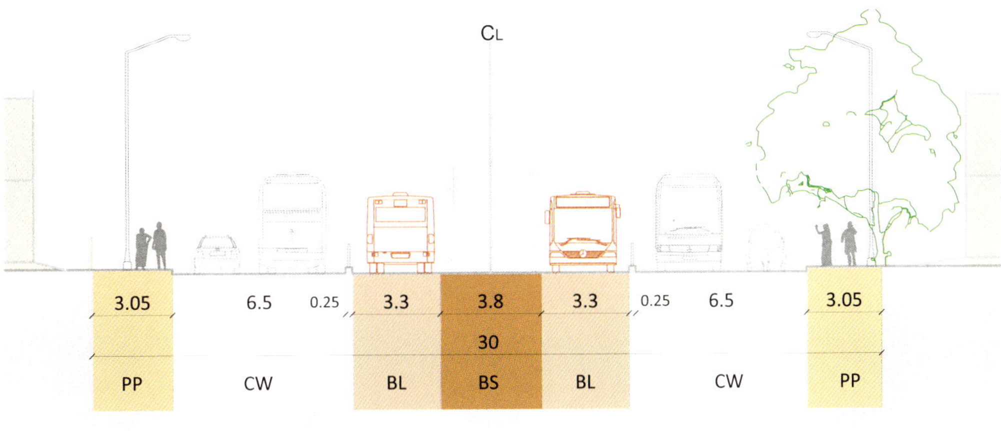

Existing typical cross section design at bus station location

Situation near Bhuyangdev before BRTS implementation

Situation near Bhuyangdev after BRTS implementation

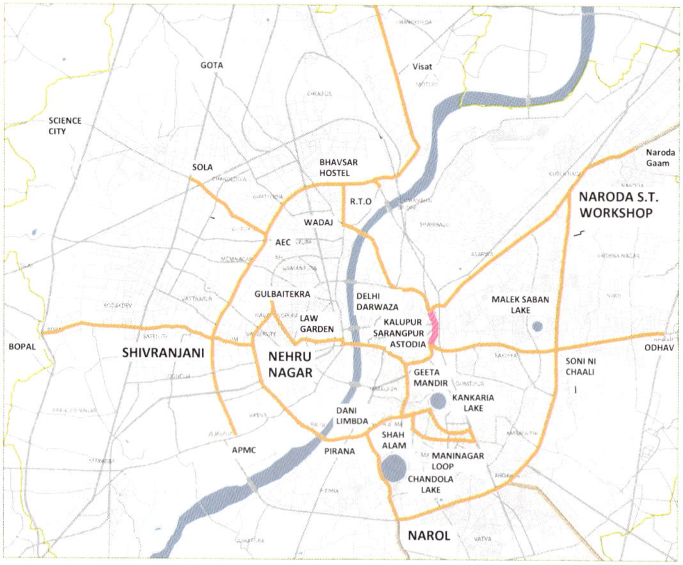

Location of Kalupur area in the BRTS network

Elevating BRTS

Space is the most important asset for any urban development project. In old cities it is always constrained. The area around the railway station in Ahmedabad is no exception. The traffic demand due to high concentration of activity far exceeds the capacity of the road segment serving this area. Linkages across the railway tracks, between areas on either side of the station are also inadequate.

The first option explored was an 'at grade' solution, i.e, segregated BRT lanes would be provided at road level itself. This would mean taking away road space from mixed traffic in an already congested street. Other solutions such as one-way streets for mixed traffic were explored.

The second option explored was an elevated corridor. Within this, two alternatives were mooted. In the first, an elevated road for mixed traffic was considered, while BRTS buses could ply below. The second envisaged the BRTS buses using the elevated corridor and mixed traffic below. The second alternative was explored further, with bus stations on top connected directly to the railway station foot over-bridges and access to the road below by staircases and elevators.

The elevated corridor was considered the better alternative. However, the National Monuments Authority advised against the proposal, as there are many ASI protected monuments in the vicinity. Therefore, an at-grade solution was finalised with one-way circulation for mixed traffic. Some area is proposed to be acquired from Kalupur railway station for the BRTS bus station.

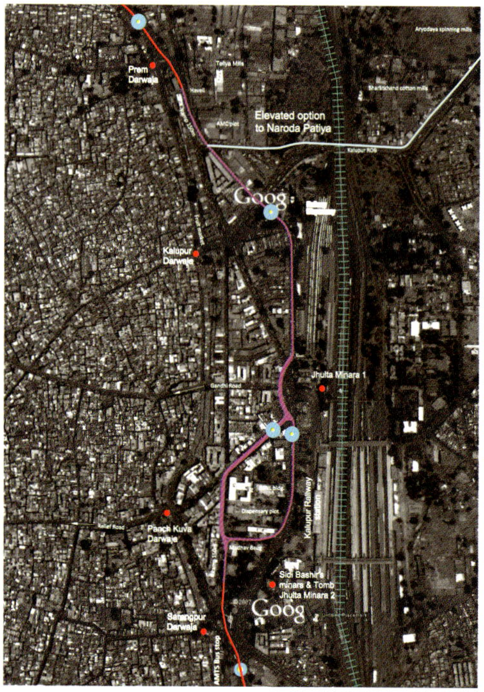

Google image of Kalupur station

Options for 18 m cross sections

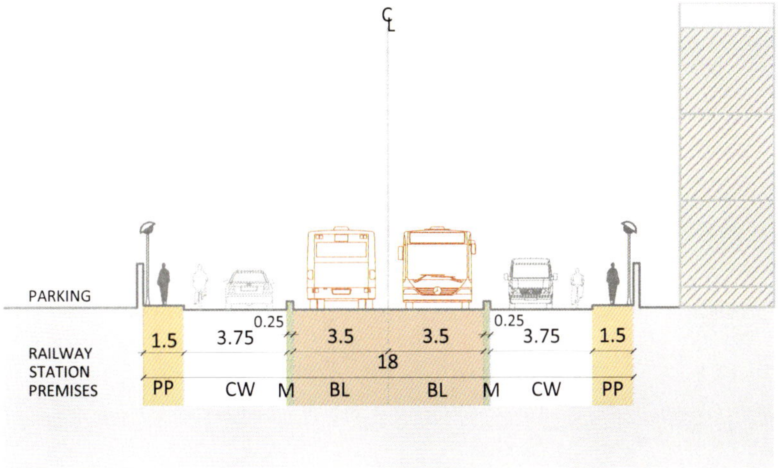

Option 1
At-grade BRTS and mixed traffic

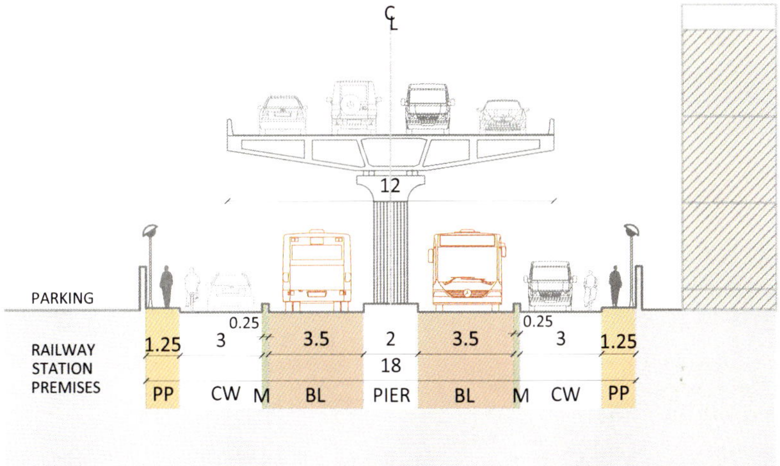

Option 2
At-grade BRTS and elevated mixed traffic

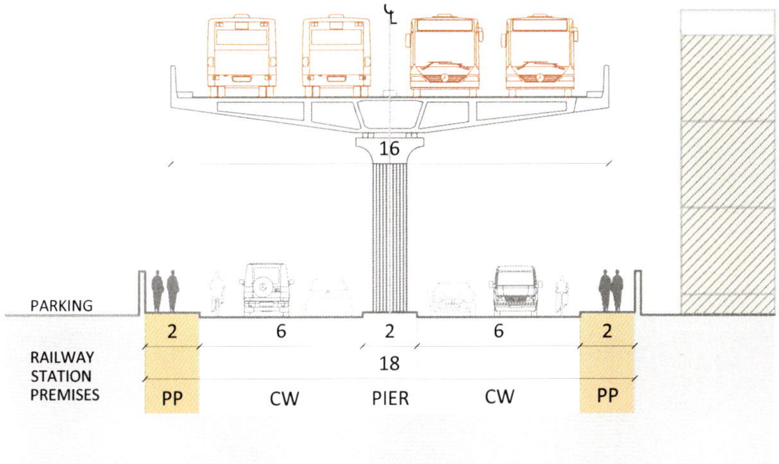

Option 3
Elevated BRTS and at-grade mixed traffic

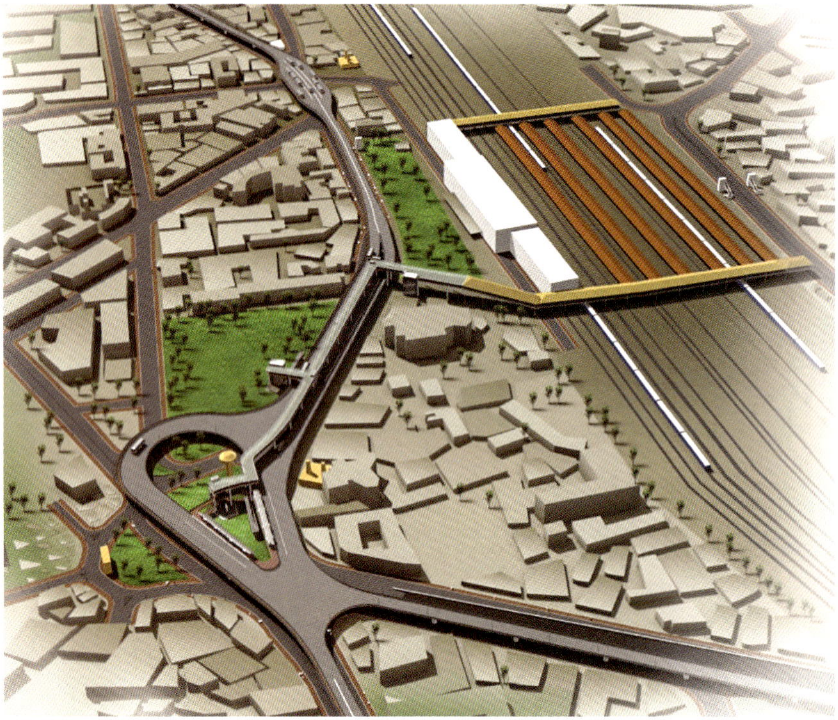

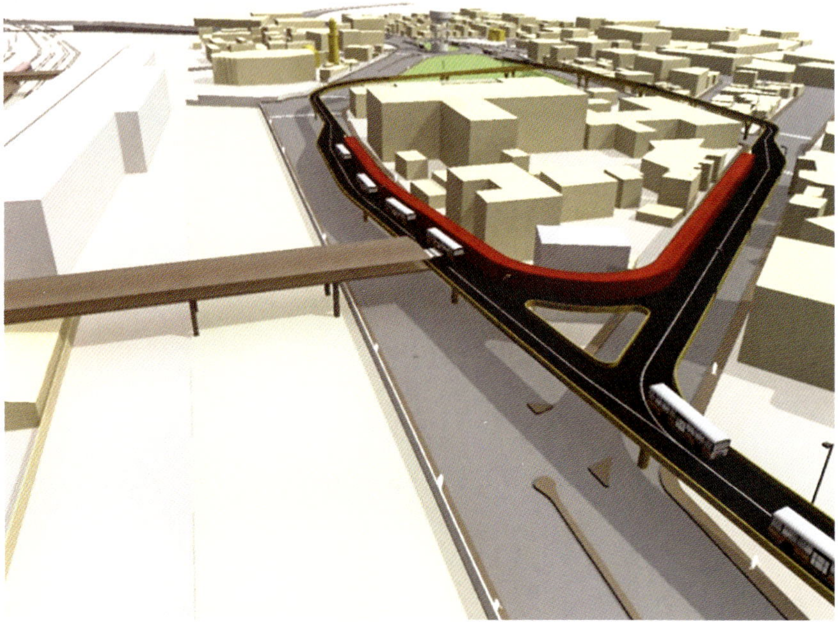

3D visuals showing elevated corridor alignment

At-Grade Turnaround

Turnarounds are needed to add flexibility to operations. Routes can be short terminated and returned based on demand. To facilitate this, the road design must allow space to build turnarounds. In the first phase, five turnarounds were built at junctions. In the second phase, these have been placed mid-block to avoid traffic congestion at junctions.

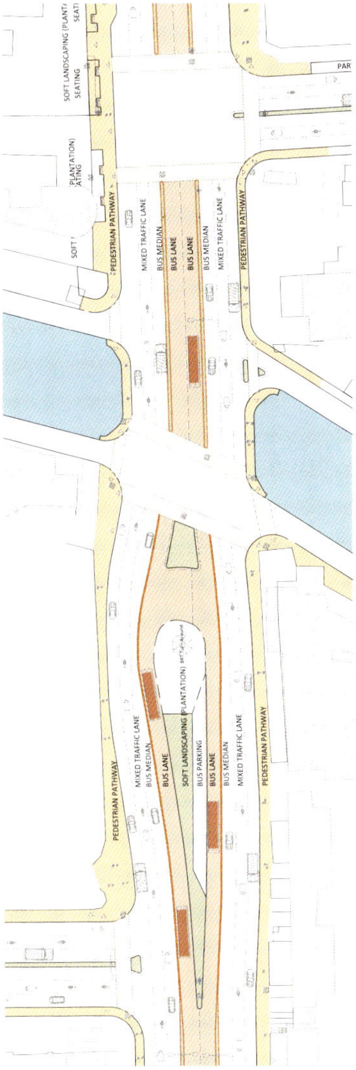

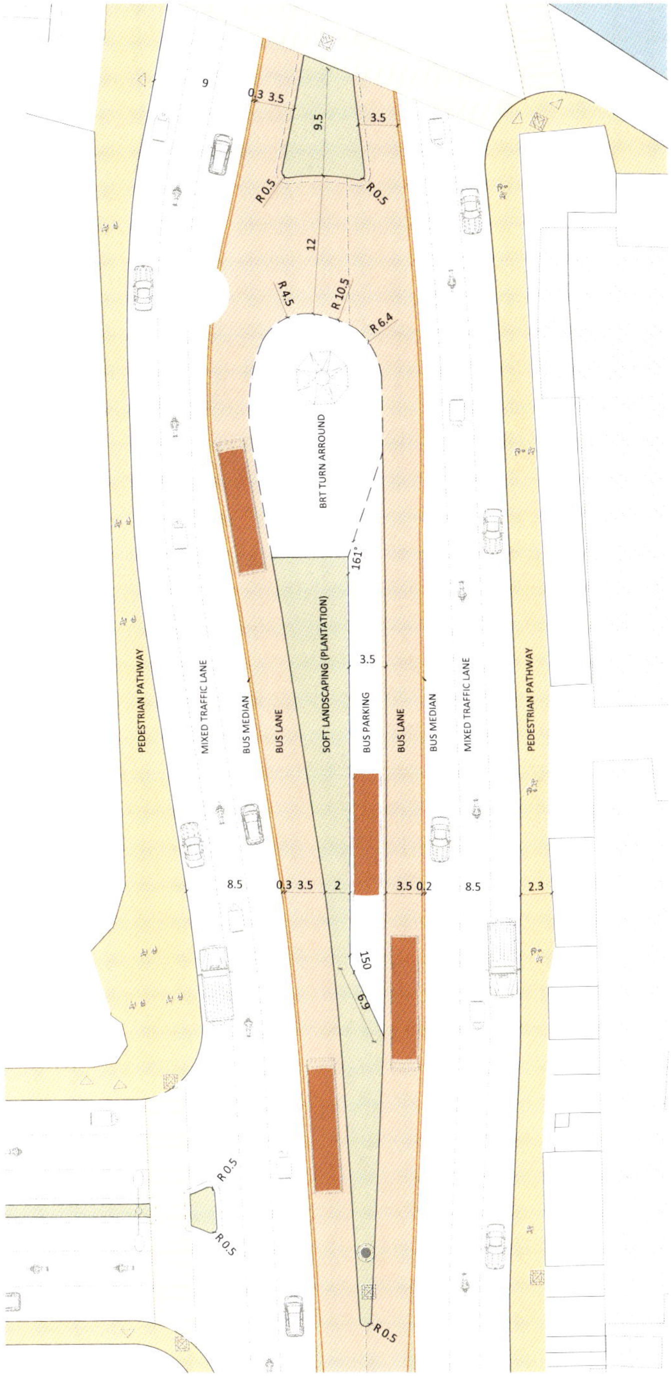

Plan showing at-grade turnaround at mid-block location on Odhav BRTS corridor

Turnaround locations on Janmarg

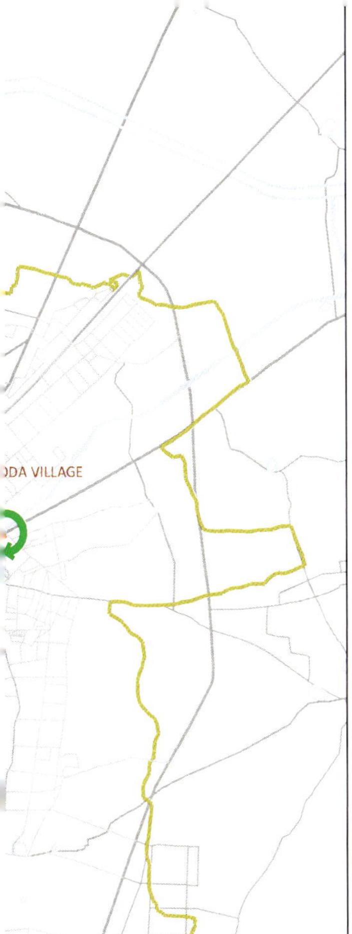

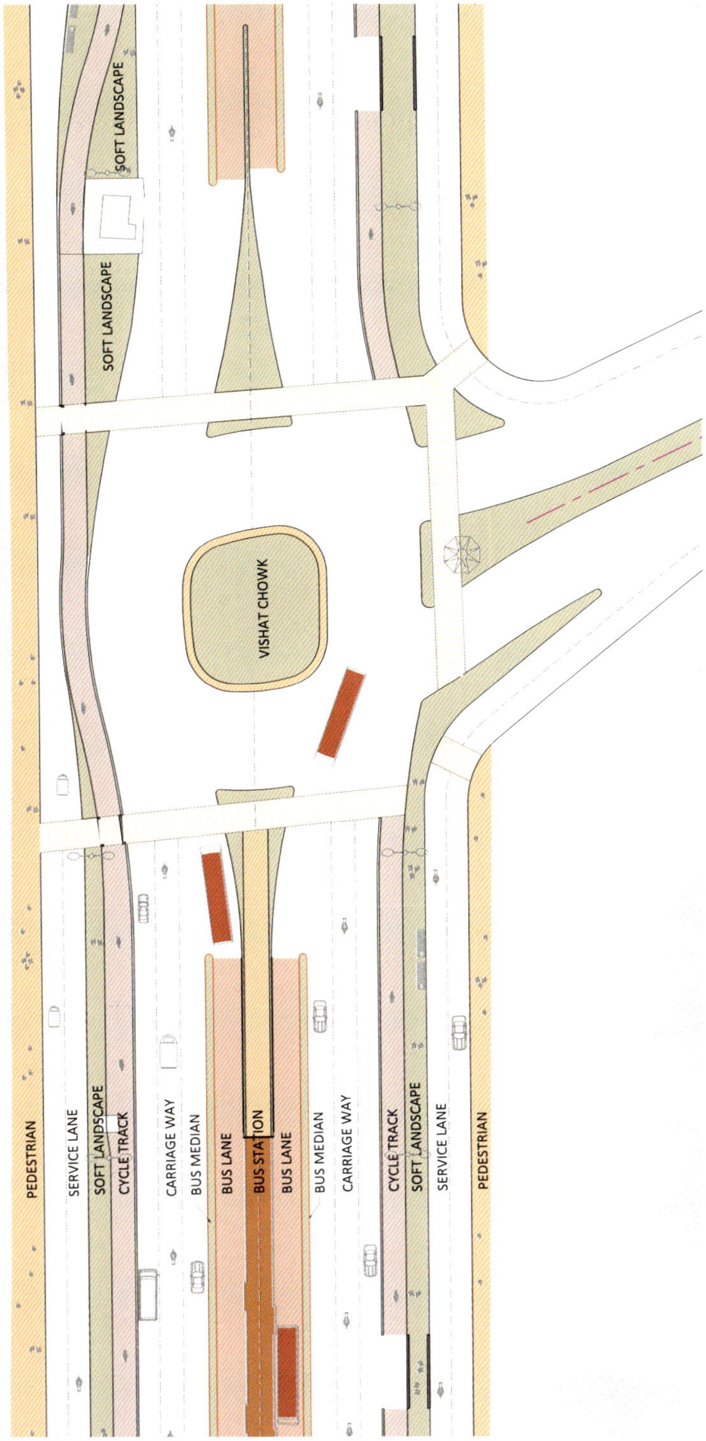

Plan showing at-grade turnaround at a junction near Visat on RTO–Chandkheda corridor

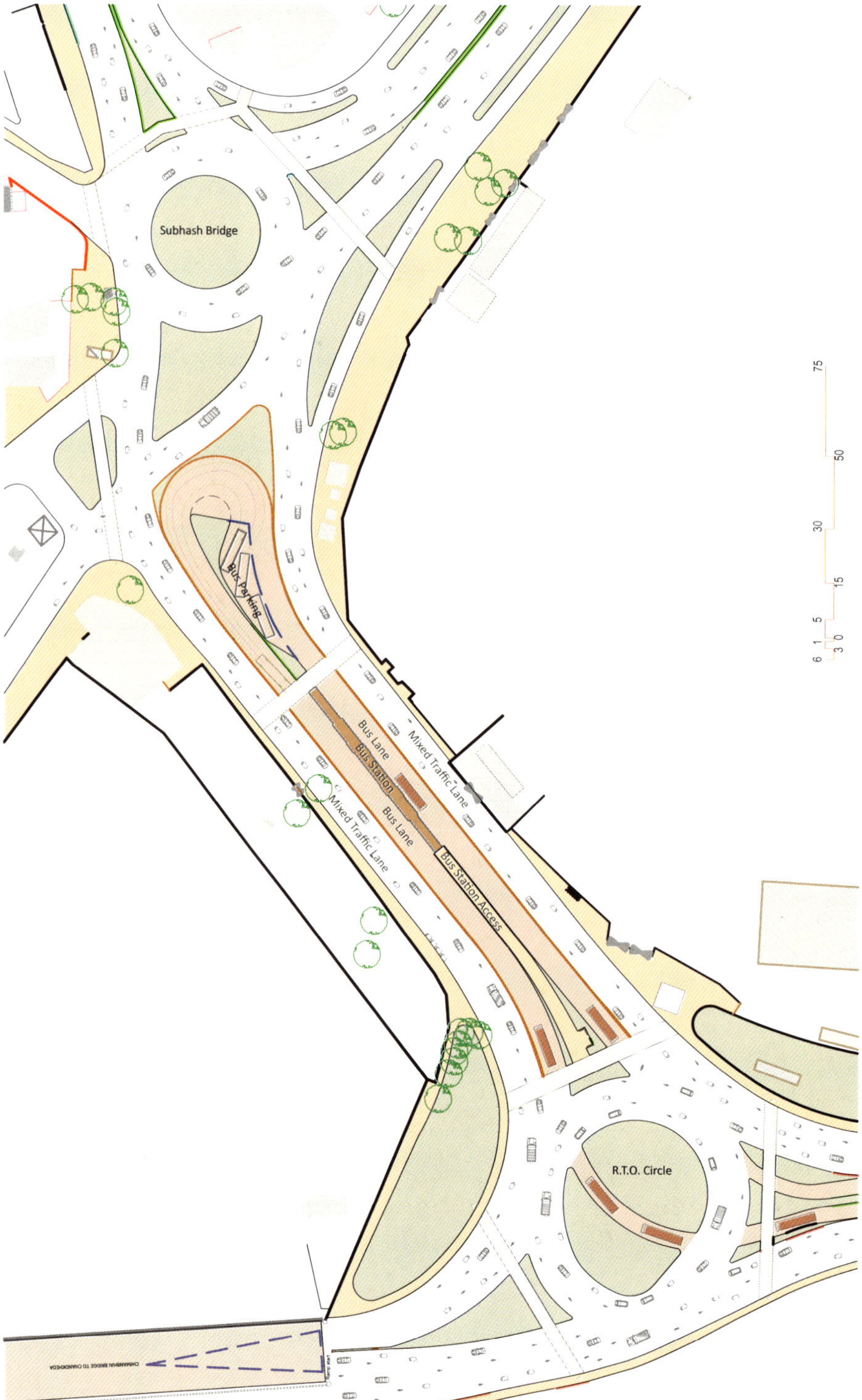

Plan showing proposed bus station and turnaround facility at RTO

View of turnaround at Anjali crossroads

BRT station at Jhansi ki Rani junction. This bus station is integrated with GSRTC buses.

BRTS Design

Junction Design

Junction design in a BRTS is one of the two critical factors (dwell time at bus stations being the other) that determine the speed of the system. Not only does the junction have to be efficient to clear all traffic, it needs to be designed in a manner that gives priority to buses and enables safe crossing for pedestrians and cyclists.

With a frequency as high as forty buses per hour, the junction design in Ahmedabad had to respond to a more or less constant flow of buses.

The following considerations are important while designing BRTS junctions:

- Physical character of the area
- Pedestrian flow
- Nature of traffic
- Modes of transport
- Possible directions of movement
- Existing/available RoWs

BRTS junction design involves various design components such as traffic signals, pedestrian (zebra) crossings, islands, appropriate signage and landscape. The design varies according to the on-site conditions, the nature of the existing junction on the corridor and BRTS design. The Ahmedabad BRTS corridor has diverse junction types: three-arm (T) to six-arm junctions, four-arm staggered junctions along with varying RoWs at each location and each arm.

All intersections along the BRTS corridor have signals at grade, designed with a view to minimise conflicts and improve traffic flow, with priority to BRTS bus flow. Traffic movements at the intersections are controlled through signal phasing.

The bicycle track ends 40 m before the junction and cyclists are allowed to merge with the mixed traffic. An additional lane is provided at intersections for mixed traffic. In case of wider RoW, i.e. 60 m, service lanes continue up to the intersection. However, only left turns are permitted from a service lane. All other turns are made from the main traffic lanes.

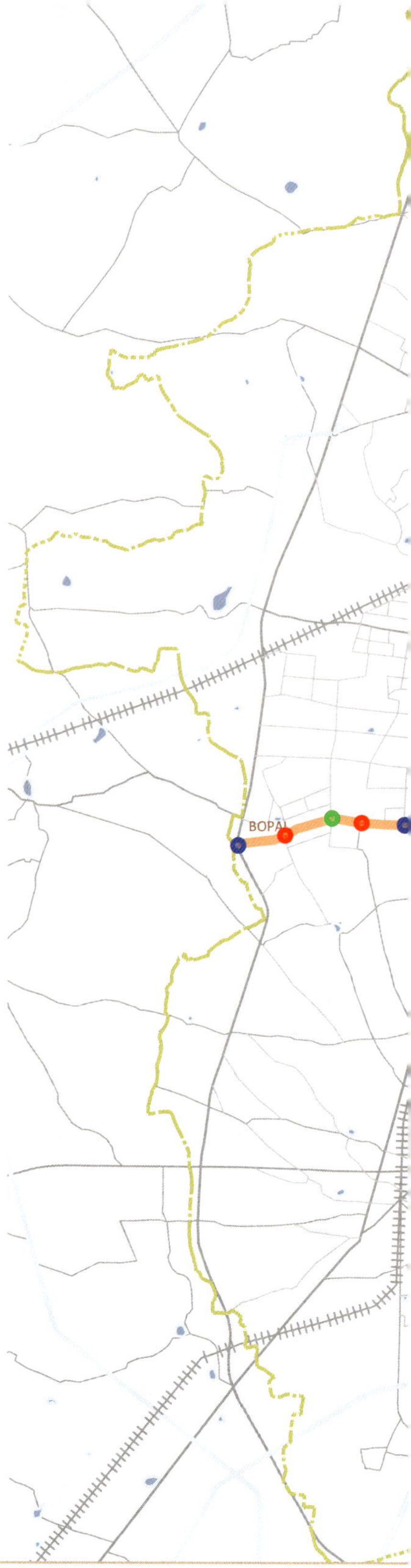

Junction typologies along BRTS network

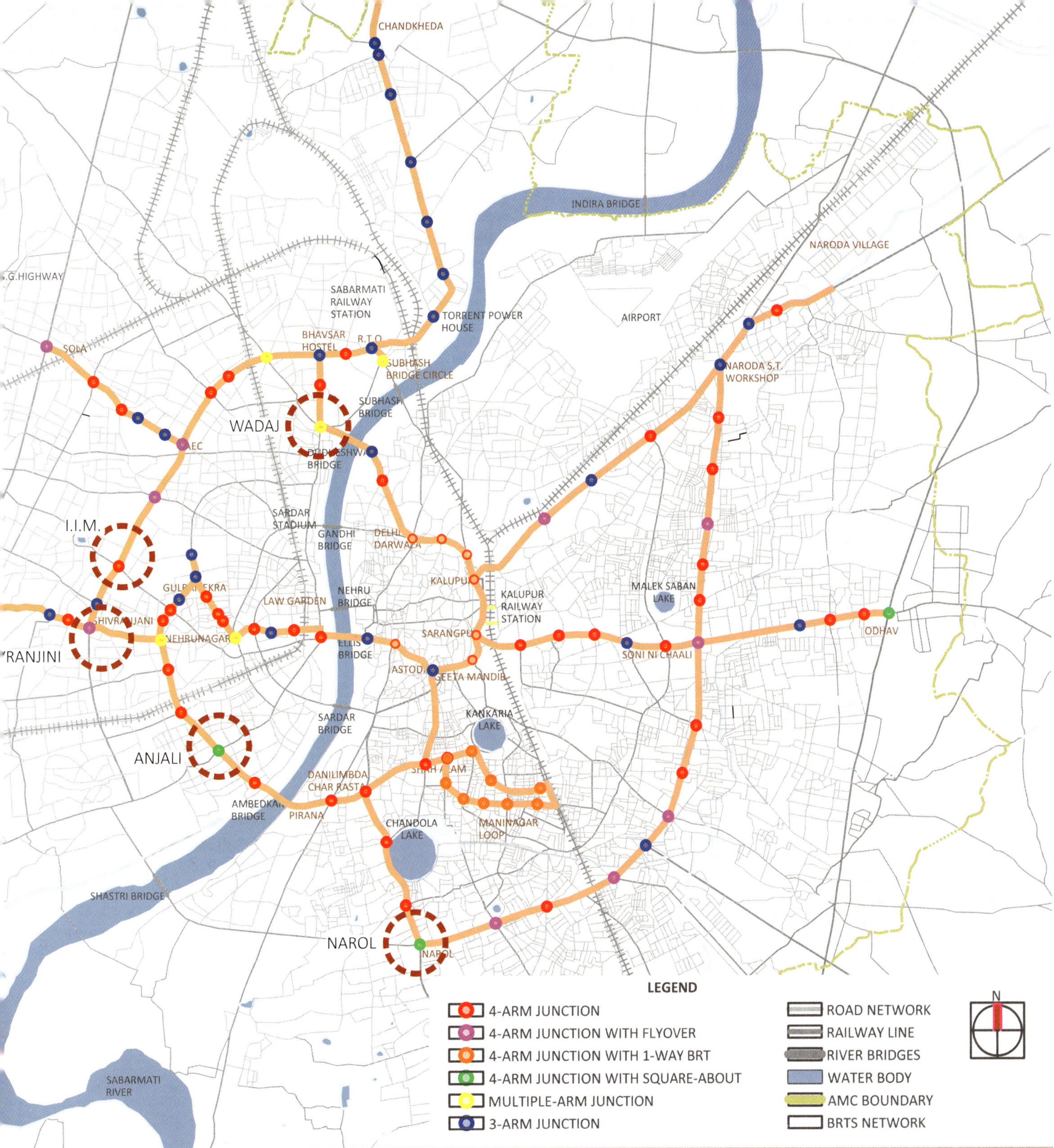
CHANDKHEDA
INDIRA BRIDGE
NARODA VILLAGE
S.G.HIGHWAY
SABARMATI RAILWAY STATION
TORRENT POWER HOUSE
AIRPORT
SOLA
BHAVSAR HOSTEL
R.T.O
SUBHASH BRIDGE CIRCLE
NARODA S.T. WORKSHOP
SUBHASH BRIDGE
WADAJ
AEC
DUDHESHWAR BRIDGE
SARDAR STADIUM
I.I.M.
GANDHI BRIDGE
DELHI DARWAZA
KALUPUR
MALEK SABAN LAKE
GULBAI TEKRA
NEHRU BRIDGE
LAW GARDEN
KALUPUR RAILWAY STATION
SHIVRANJANI
NEHRUNAGAR
ELLIS BRIDGE
SARANGPUR
ODHAV
SONI NI CHAALI
RANJINI
ASTODIA
GEETA MANDIR
SARDAR BRIDGE
KANKARIA LAKE
ANJALI
DANILIMBDA CHAR RASTA
SHAH ALAM
AMBEDKAR BRIDGE
PIRANA
CHANDOLA LAKE
MANINAGAR LOOP
SHASTRI BRIDGE
NAROL
NAROL
SABARMATI RIVER
LEGEND
4-ARM JUNCTION
4-ARM JUNCTION WITH FLYOVER
4-ARM JUNCTION WITH 1-WAY BRT
4-ARM JUNCTION WITH SQUARE-ABOUT
MULTIPLE-ARM JUNCTION
3-ARM JUNCTION
ROAD NETWORK
RAILWAY LINE
RIVER BRIDGES
WATER BODY
AMC BOUNDARY
BRTS NETWORK
N

Four-arm Junction with Two-way BRTS

A typical example of such a junction is at IIM crossroads. This is along a 40 m RoW BRT corridor intersected by a 30 m wide arterial. There is also a BRTS station near the junction, placed north of the intersection to be near the Blind People's Association.

The bus station is set back from the junction by 25 m to enable at least two buses to move ahead of the station and leave space for following buses. Free left turns are not allowed in order to provide safety for pedestrians, especially blind people when they cross the street. The cycle track is terminated 40 m before the junction to allow cyclists to merge with other traffic.

The signal cycle is designed to allow the BRTS bus two opportunities to cross during one cycle. At this four-arm junction, the signal phasing is in four cycles. The first phase of 45 seconds is in two cycles. The first cycle (A) allows straight movement along the BRT route and bus movement for 15 seconds. The second cycle (B) allows right and straight movement for the mixed traffic, holding up the BRTS movement.

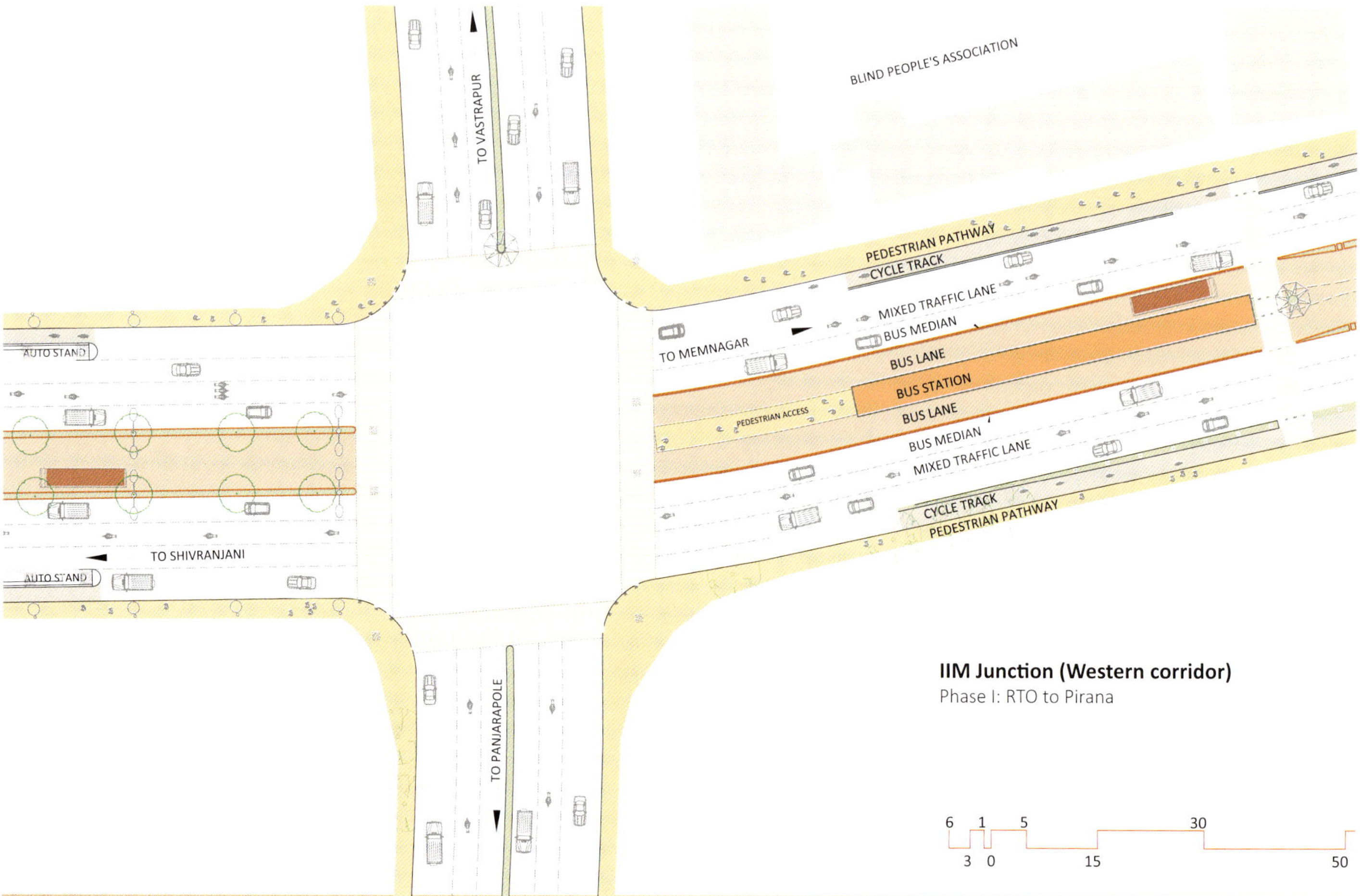

IIM Junction (Western corridor)
Phase I: RTO to Pirana

Signal Phasing

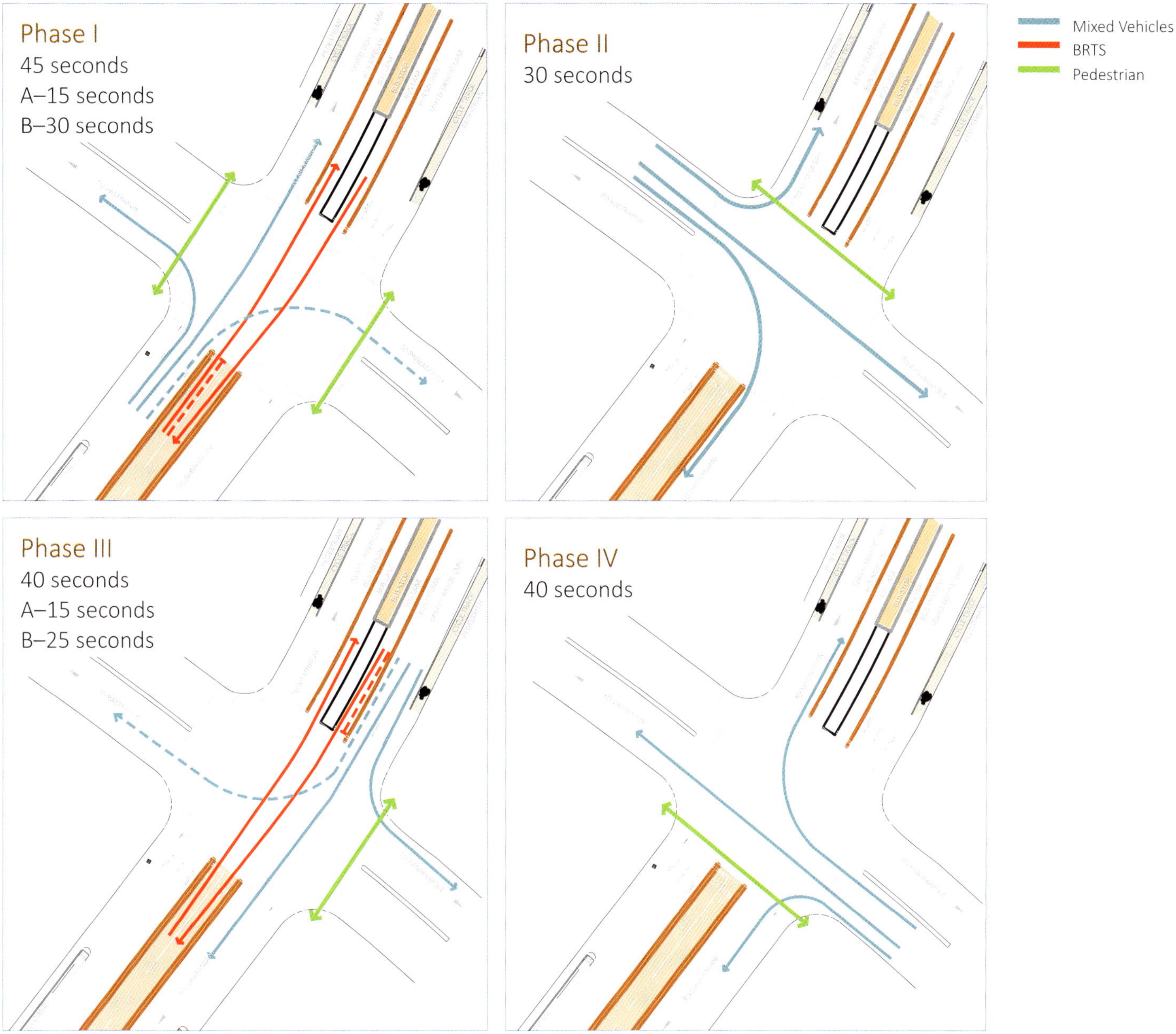

Four-arm Junction with Flyover

Another type of junction is a four-arm junction with a flyover. As previously discussed, the flyover is split, allowing buses to ply at grade. Owing to the flyover, the signal cycle is shorter than that at a normal four-arm junction. In a typical scenario, the BRTS corridor turns onto the intersecting arm of the junction.

In such a case, the buses from under the flyover have to turn left to the 'non-flyover' arm. In the signal cycle, this is achieved by synchronising this movement with the right turning movement towards the flyover from the 'non-flyover' arm.

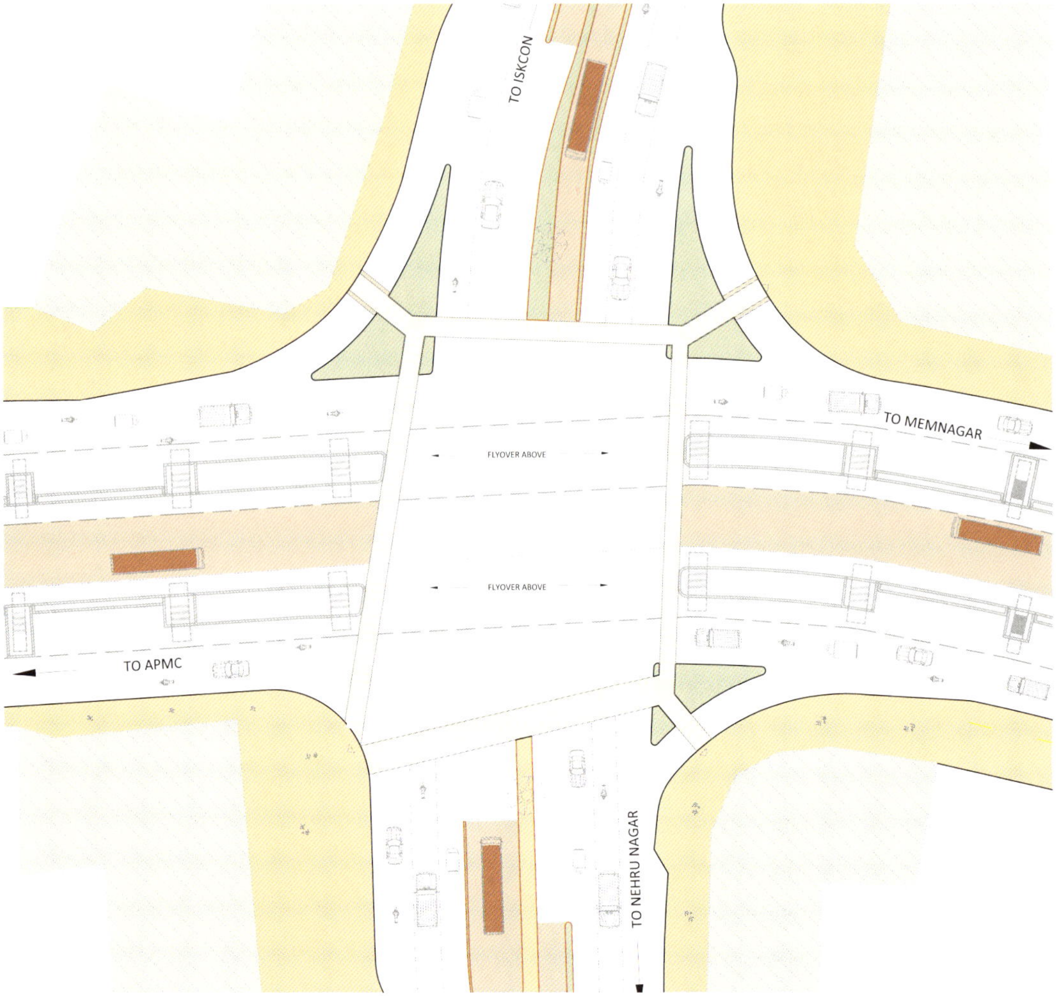

Shivranjini Junction (Western corridor)
Phase I: RTO to Pirana
Phase II: Shivranjini to Bopal
Phase III: Shivranjini to APMC

Signal Phasing

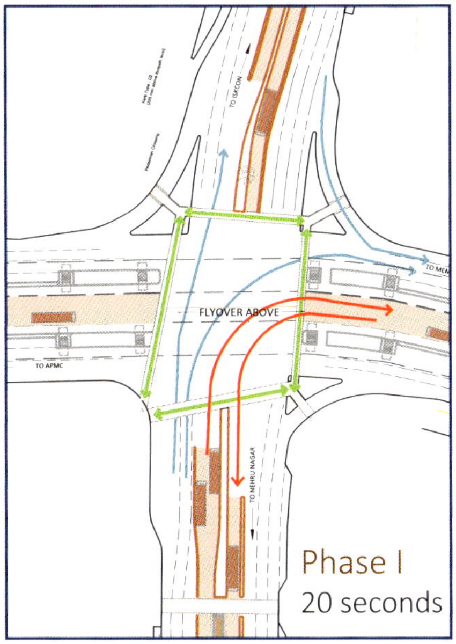

Phase I
20 seconds

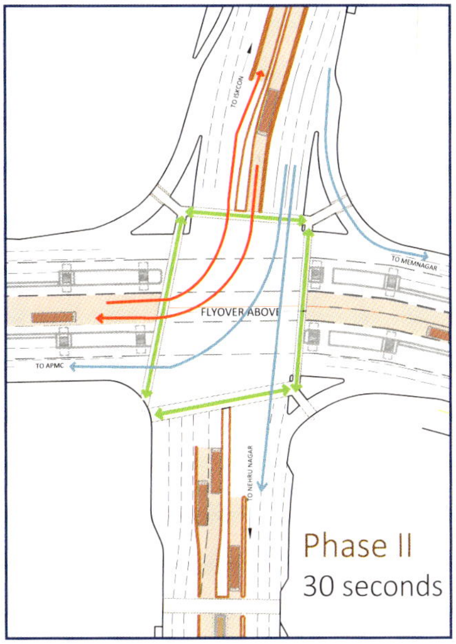

Phase II
30 seconds

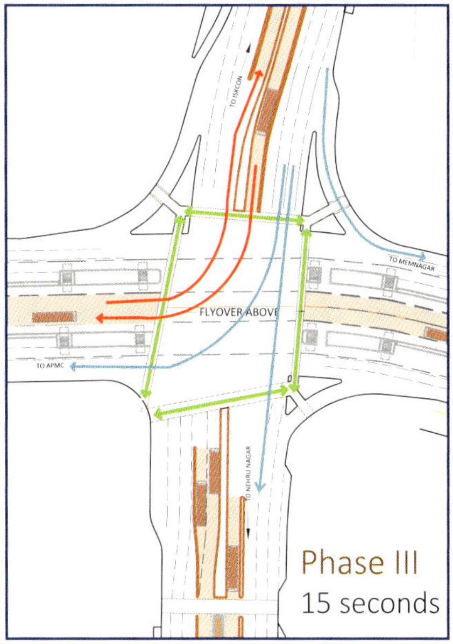

Phase III
15 seconds

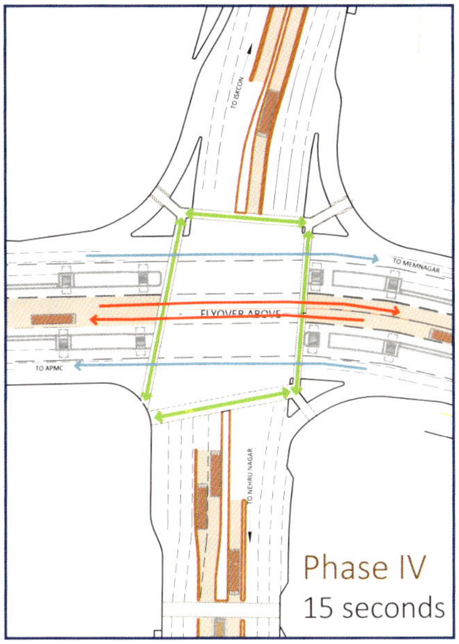

Phase IV
15 seconds

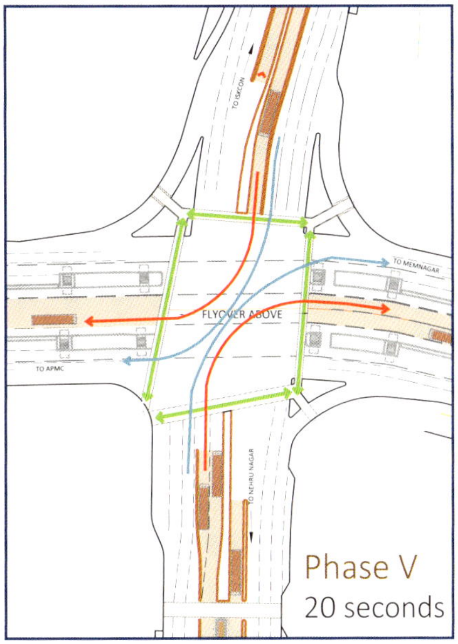

Phase V
20 seconds

Mixed vehicles
BRTS
Pedestrian

Four-arm Junction with Square about and Two-way BRTS

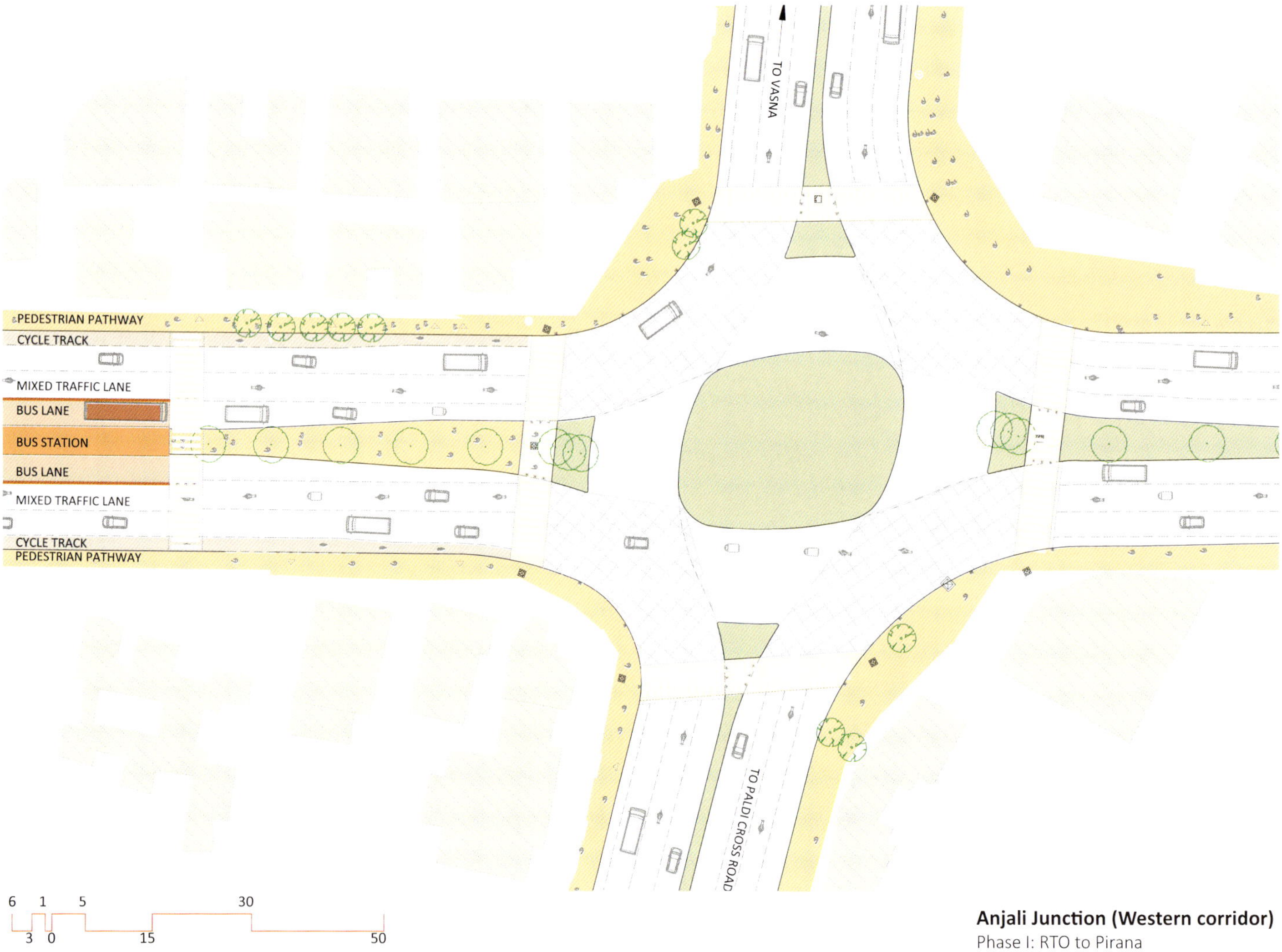

Anjali Junction (Western corridor)
Phase I: RTO to Pirana

Signal Phasing

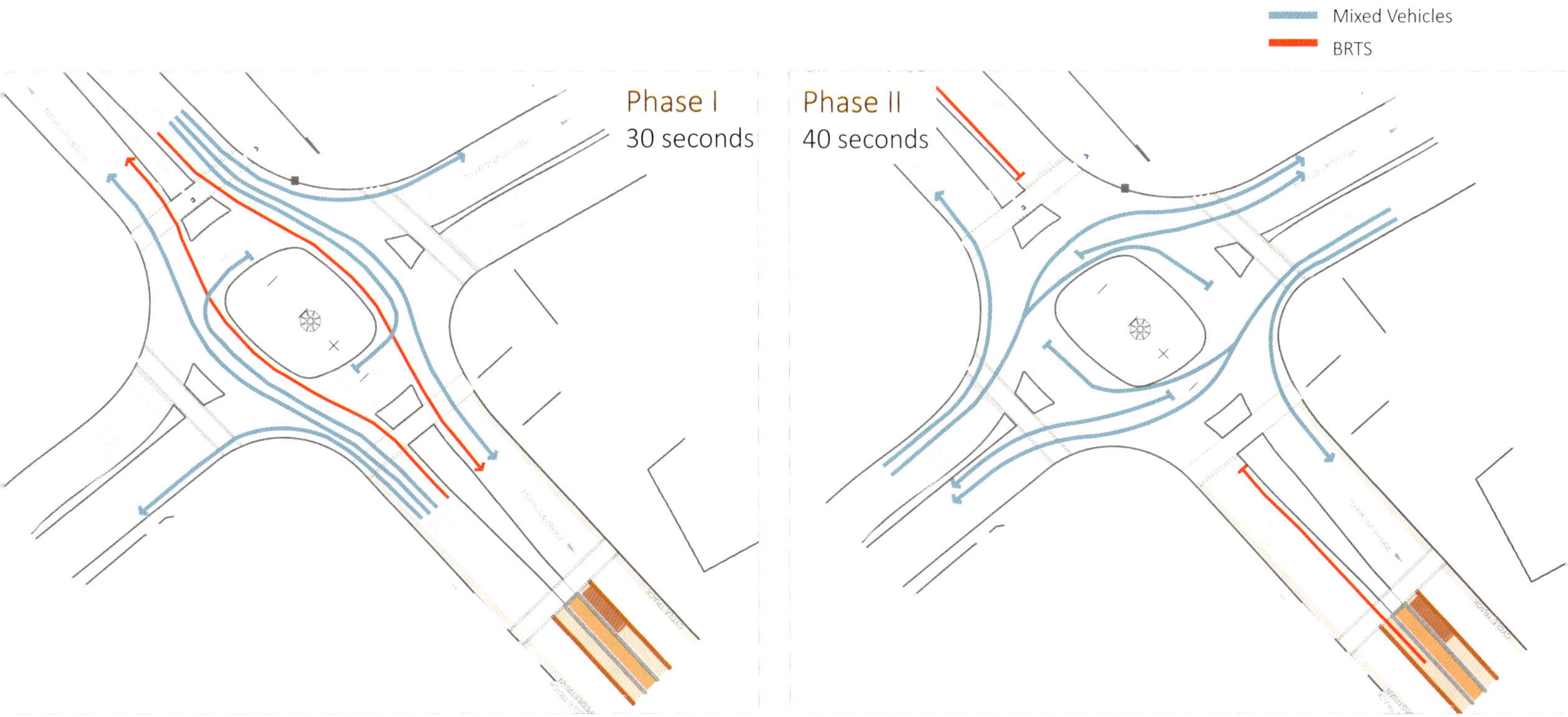

Signal phasing at this junction is broken down in two phases.

Another way of treating a four-arm junction is to reduce the signal cycle by providing a rotary. However, unlike a normal rotary, it is designed to allow for holding areas for vehicles inside the junction.

In the signal cycle design, straight and right turning movements from opposite directions are allowed in the same phase. The holding area inside the junction 'holds' the right turning traffic. In the second phase, straight and right turning movements from the other two arms are allowed with right turning vehicles stopping inside the junction. During this phase, the right turning vehicles from the first phase can now move in their intended direction. Thus, the entire junction is managed in two phases with all turning movements permitted.

An added advantage is that these junctions function as turnarounds for the BRTS. Buses can reverse direction, depending on the operational requirement. This builds flexibility in the system and allows Janmarg to plan schedules that respond to specific situations.

Before and after images of Anjali crossroads. The implementation of BRTS has also resulted in better pedestrian infrastructure.

Four-arm Junction with Square about and Bus Priority

This design is a variant of the earlier design. In this case, BRTS buses are given higher priority with dedicated lanes that cut across the rotary, while all other traffic has to move around the rotary. This saves about 45 seconds per bus negotiating the junction. This saves considerable operating time and helps achieve higher commercial speed.

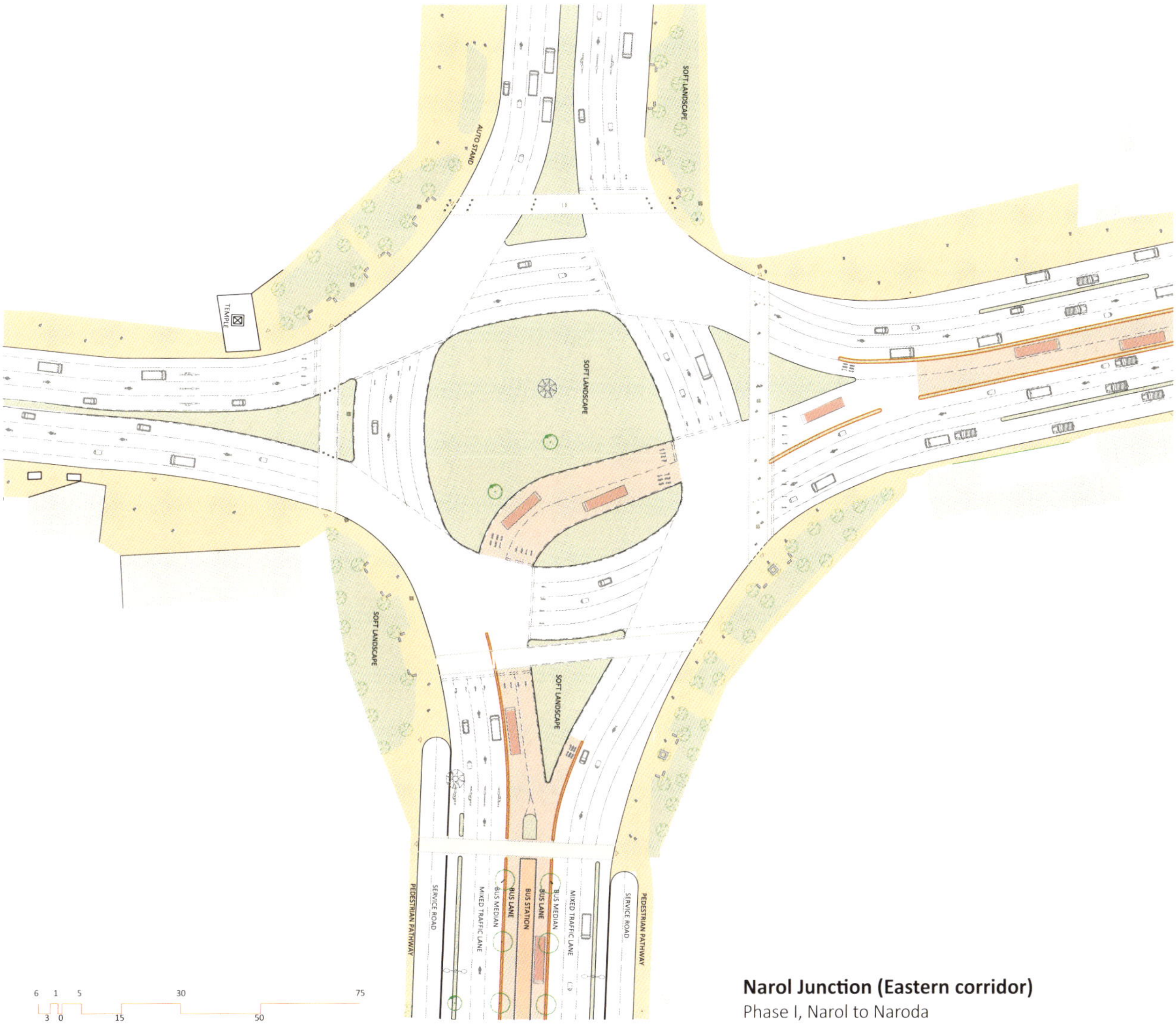

Narol Junction (Eastern corridor)
Phase I, Narol to Naroda

Signal Phasing

Mixed Vehicles
BRTS
Pedestrian

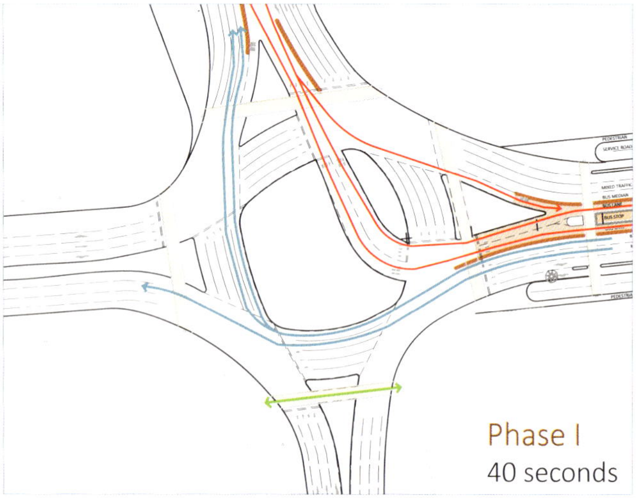

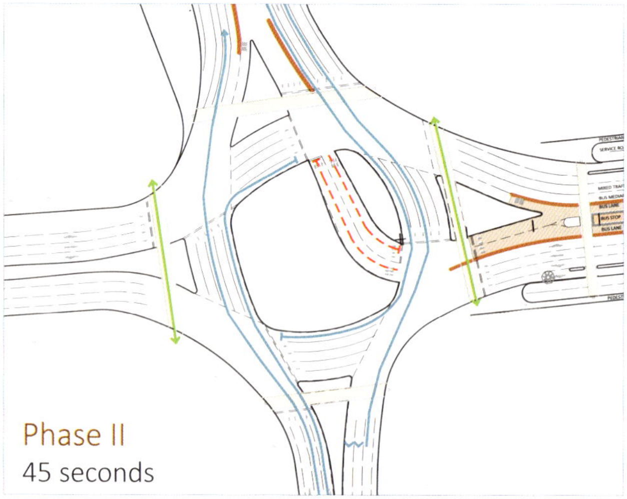

At Narol crossraods, bus lanes cut through the central island

BRTS Design

Placemaking

Street design for Janmarg does not focus only on the bus facility. One of the underlying premises in designing the entire RoW is that all modes of traffic should benefit. Also, the resulting street space quality should attract people.

Ahmedabad has always had a great street life characterised by places for shopping, meeting people, seeing and being seen. The BRTS design attempts to recreate many of these qualities. The footpaths are wide enough for comfortable walking and benches are provided at frequent intervals. Access to bus stations is designed to encourage users to pause, observe, sit and relax.

Various examples of public spaces on BRTS corridors. The system blends into the surrounding spaces.

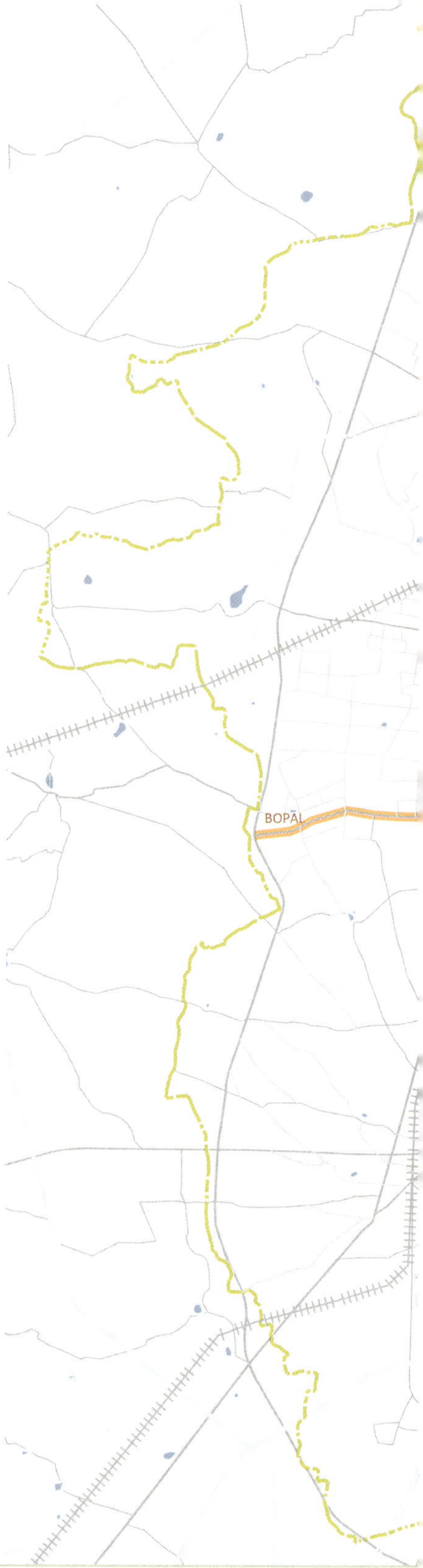

Public space design areas

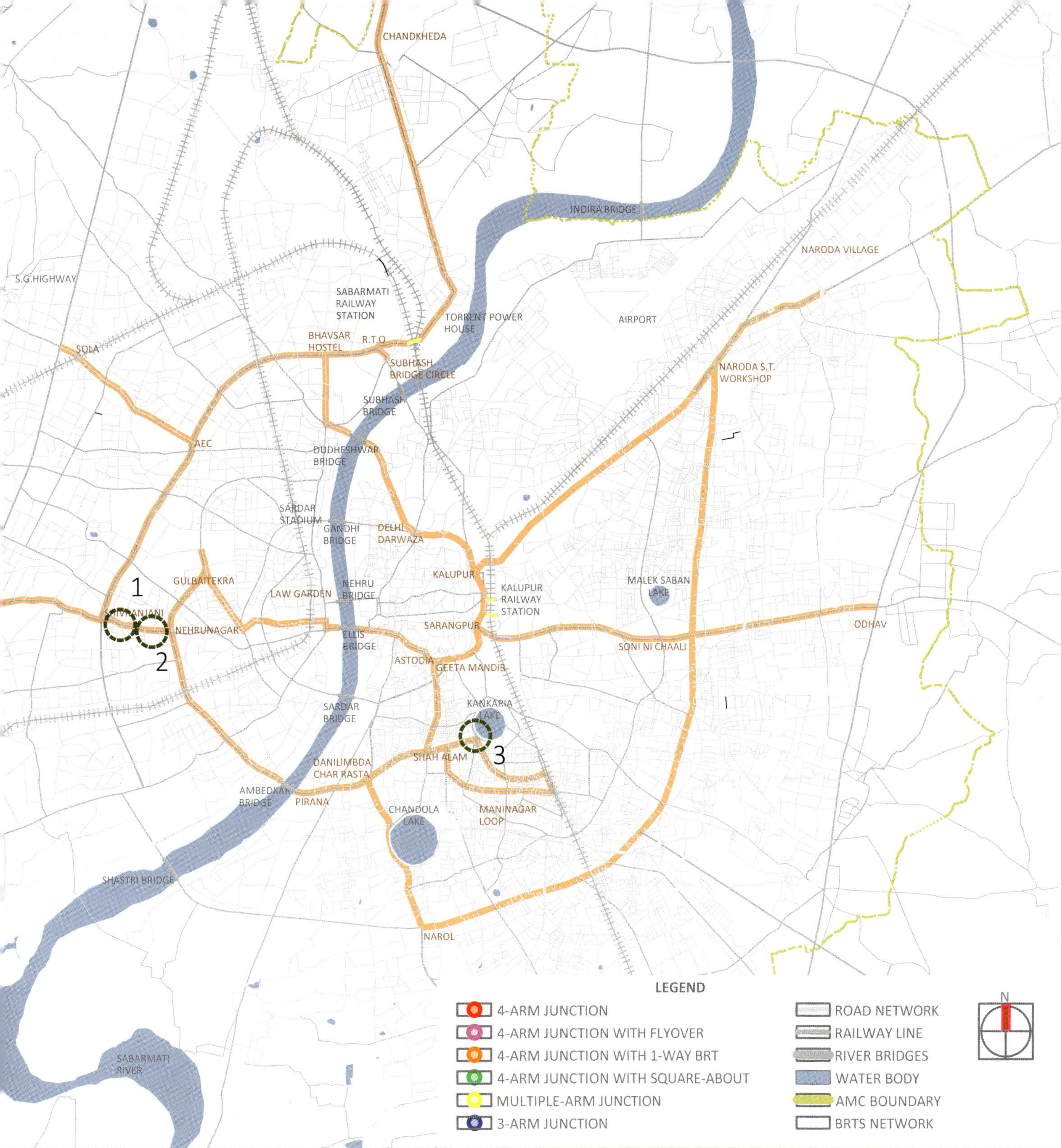
CHANDKHEDA
INDIRA BRIDGE
NARODA VILLAGE
S.G.HIGHWAY
SABARMATI RAILWAY STATION
TORRENT POWER HOUSE
AIRPORT
BHAVSAR HOSTEL
R.T.O.
SOLA
SUBHASH BRIDGE CIRCLE
NARODA S.T. WORKSHOP
SUBHASH BRIDGE
AEC
DUDHESHWAR BRIDGE
SARDAR STADIUM
GANDHI BRIDGE
DELHI DARWAZA
KALUPUR
1
GULBAITEKRA
LAW GARDEN
NEHRU BRIDGE
KALUPUR RAILWAY STATION
MALEK SABAN LAKE
SHIVRANJANI
NEHRUNAGAR
SARANGPUR
ODHAV
ELLIS BRIDGE
SONI NI CHAALI
2
ASTODIA
GEETA MANDIR
KANKARIA LAKE
SARDAR BRIDGE
3
SHAH ALAM
DANILIMBDA CHAR RASTA
AMBEDKAR BRIDGE
PIRANA
CHANDOLA LAKE
MANINAGAR LOOP
SHASTRI BRIDGE
NAROL
SABARMATI RIVER
LEGEND
4-ARM JUNCTION
4-ARM JUNCTION WITH FLYOVER
4-ARM JUNCTION WITH 1-WAY BRT
4-ARM JUNCTION WITH SQUARE-ABOUT
MULTIPLE-ARM JUNCTION
3-ARM JUNCTION
ROAD NETWORK
RAILWAY LINE
RIVER BRIDGES
WATER BODY
AMC BOUNDARY
BRTS NETWORK
N

Street Design

The Nehrunagar–Shivranjini stretch is characterised by the presence of a linear park, tree line, statues, pedestrian bazaar, hawkers and food joints. Many designs were worked out to preserve the tree line and the vibrancy of this stretch as a public space. The challenge was to accommodate all these existing features and enhance the public realm even though BRTS cross section demands more space.

The cross section has been designed incorporating local street activities, patterns of pedestrian movement and nearby land uses. Hawkers' area and extension of footpath accommodates vending activities by altering the cross section for the entire stretch. To preserve this quality extensive work has been done on small details.

BRTS stretch near Nehrunagar. The design has retained the informal shopping area along the street edge.

Tree line at Nehrunagar

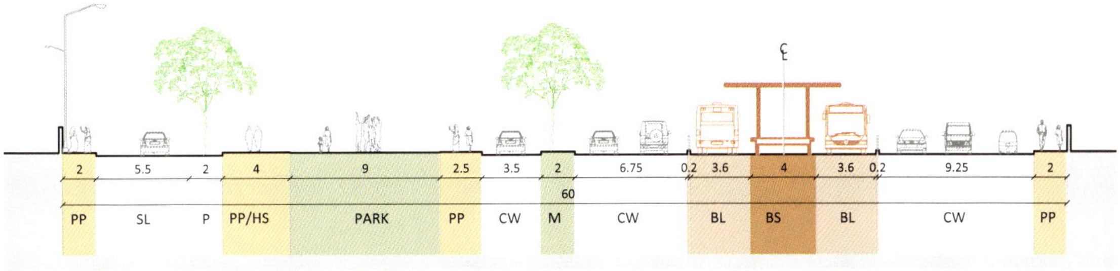

Existing cross section showing tree line incorporated in design

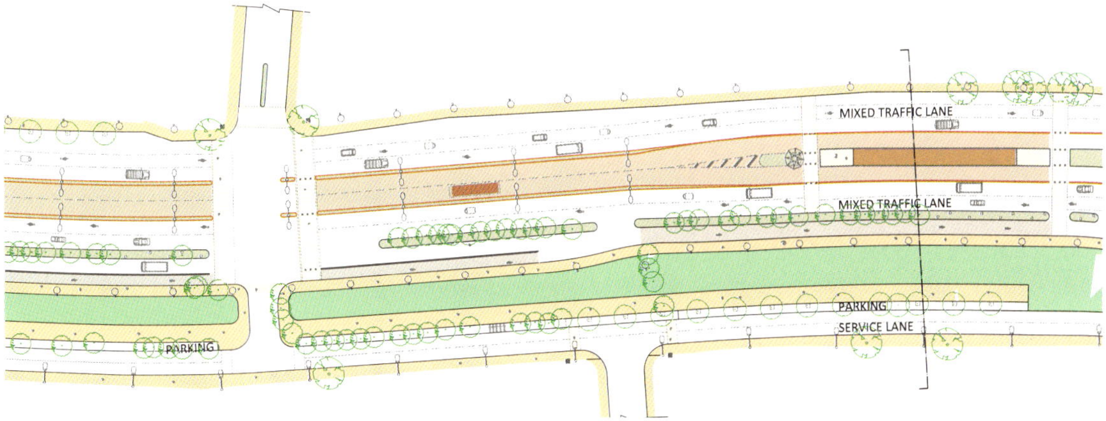

Part detail showing retained tree line near Nehrunagar circle

Considering the activity pattern and adjoining land uses, a context-sensitive approach was adopted. This resulted in a vibrant and successful street design, which retained and accommodated the existing tree line—an element that provides a comfortable and pleasant walking experience.

Retained tree line at Hutheesing ni Wadi near Bopal

Jhansi ki Rani Statue Area

The Jhansi ki Rani statue, a local landmark, has been retained in the design by modifying existing activities in the given space. A median park, in which the statue stands on one side of the BRTS lanes, is incorporated in the design. It also includes a regional interchange with GSRTC. Pedestrian connection to the park and interchange is by providing zebra crossings.

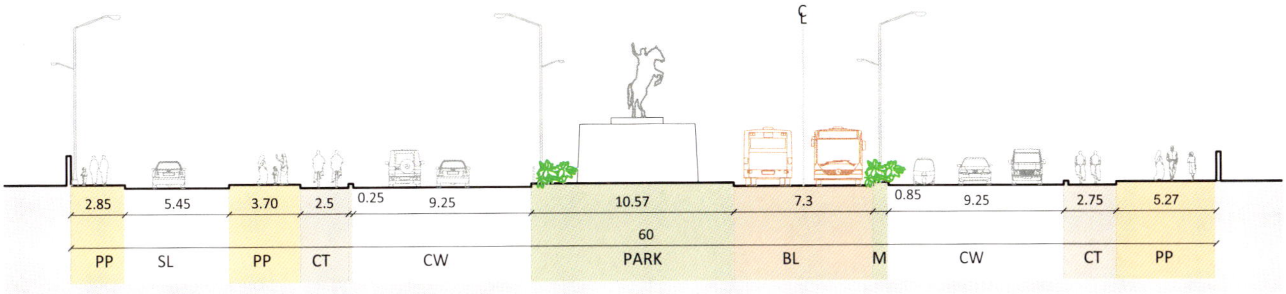

Existing cross section at Jhansi ki Rani statue area

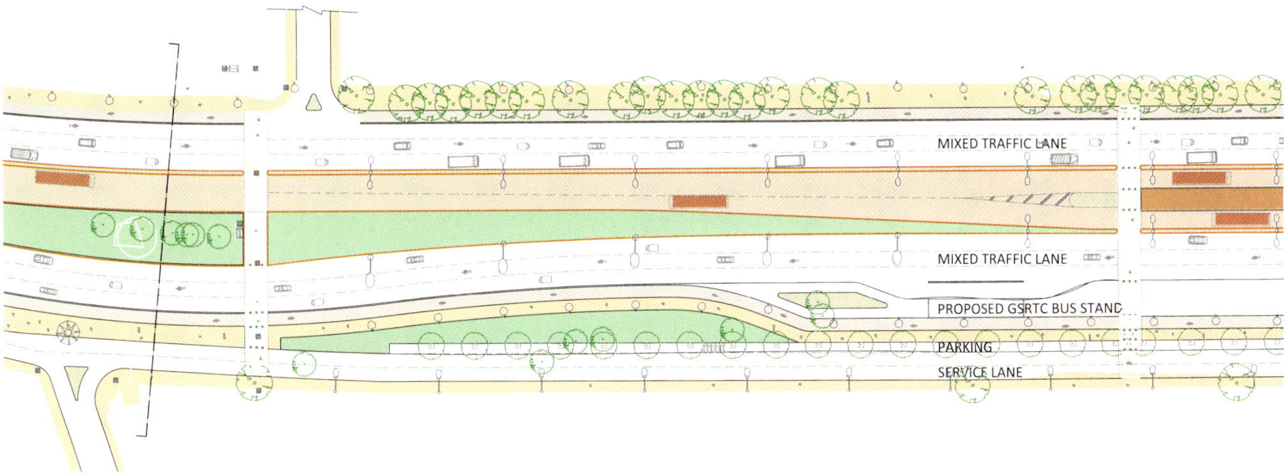

Part plan showing Jhansi ki Rani statue area

Placemaking

The Jhansi ki Rani statue watches over the BRTS corridor as other traffic passes through on the side.

PRESENTING
THE GRAND
NEW LINGO
PRESENTING
THE GRAND
NEW LINGO

Public Space Design

Kankaria Lake, with a circumference of approximately two kilometres, is the largest lake in the southeast quarter of Ahmedabad. It is located in Maninagar, one of the most densely populated areas of the city. Around the lake are many public places including the Zoo, Nagina Wadi, Balvatika, gardens and an aquarium. It is a popular and much-frequented place for yoga, walking, jogging, strolling, relaxing etc.

The Janmarg intervention in this area includes only BRTS and pedestrian access up to the entrance to the lakefront, to minimise walking distance and other vehicular movement, enabling safe and direct access. The specially designed bus station here has three bays and is longer and wider than the standard version, to cater to weekend and holiday demands. It integrates Kankaria Lake with the BRT system.

BRTS proposal in congruence with Kankaria Lakefront Development Project

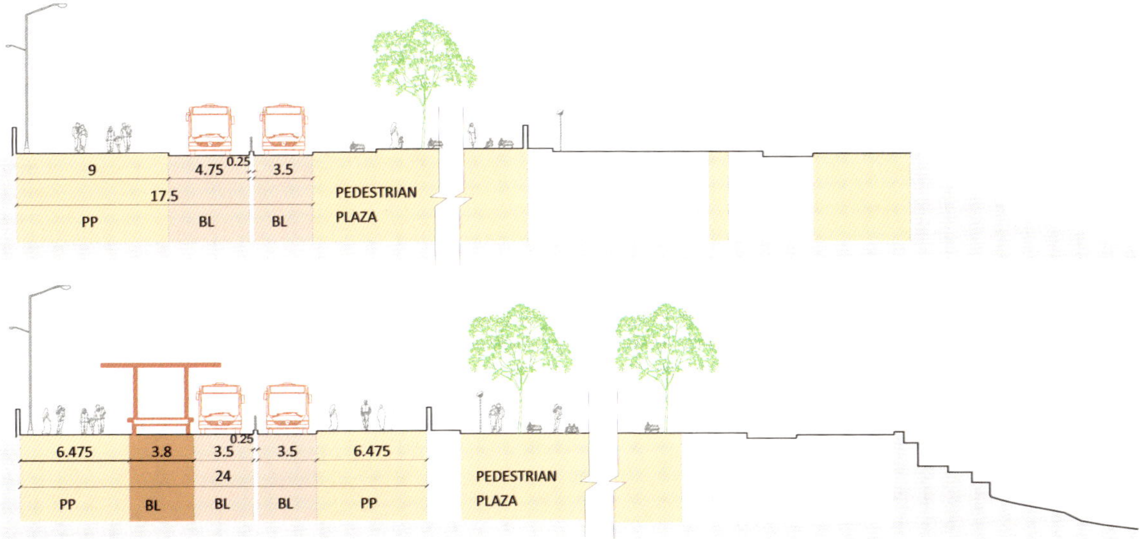

Cross section showing BRTS along Kankaria Lakefront

The wide and well-lit pedestrian space at Kankaria Lake BRT station

Provision of public seating areas, wide footpaths and a dedicated bus movement corridor creates a shared space and a multipurpose public place.

Bus station design integrates with public space

Access to Bus Station

The accesses to bus stations are made interesting and active by creating clusters of public seating areas along them at Anjali crossroads and Nehrunagar. These access areas have become active public places, especially in the evenings where senior citizens and children gather and watch the activities around them.

The access to bus station at Nehrunagar

A senior citizen couple exits the Kankaria Lake bus station

BRTS Design

Street Design Elements

Street furniture items, with typical details as illustrated, enhance design in the public domain. These are designed for ease of execution and maintenance desirable for public facilities.

Benches

The location of benches is determined by analysing public gathering areas, sun path, presence of trees, etc. The benches are placed near recreational areas with clusters. Generally, these have been placed at regular intervals of 200–300 m. Sometimes a cluster has been created to accommodate more people, depending on local context.

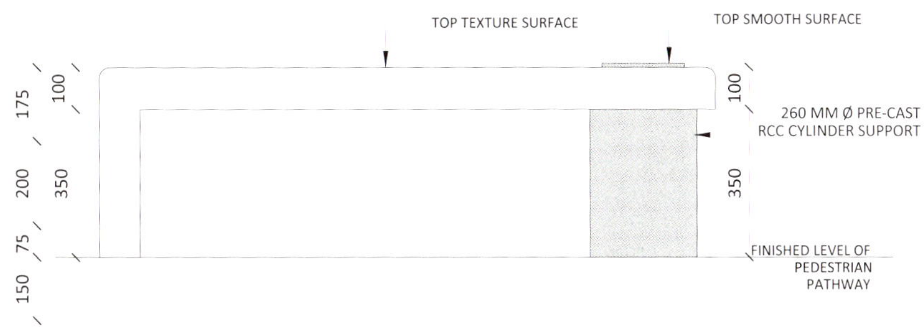

FRONT ELEVATION

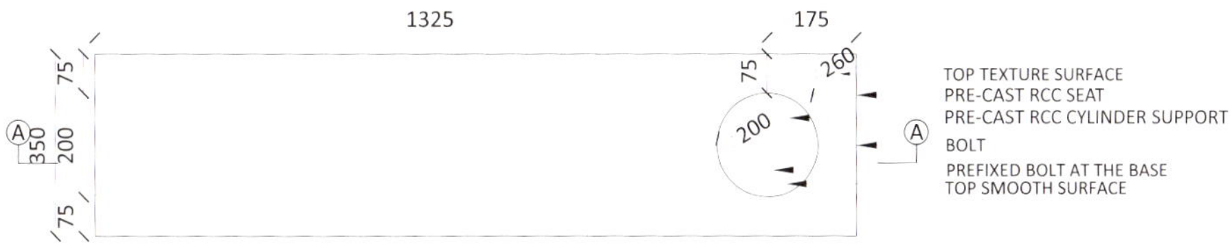

PLAN

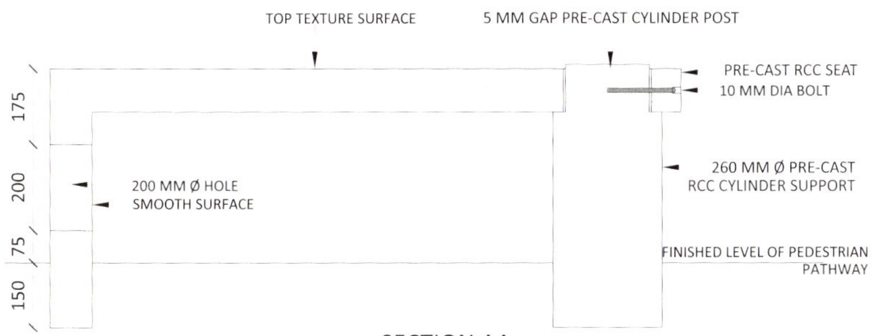

SECTION AA

Bollards

The earlier design of bollards in mild steel was changed to precast RCC, making them more aesthetically pleasing and amenable to multiple use in public areas. Their spacing at pedestrian crossings has been thoughtfully designed for the convenience of differently-abled people.

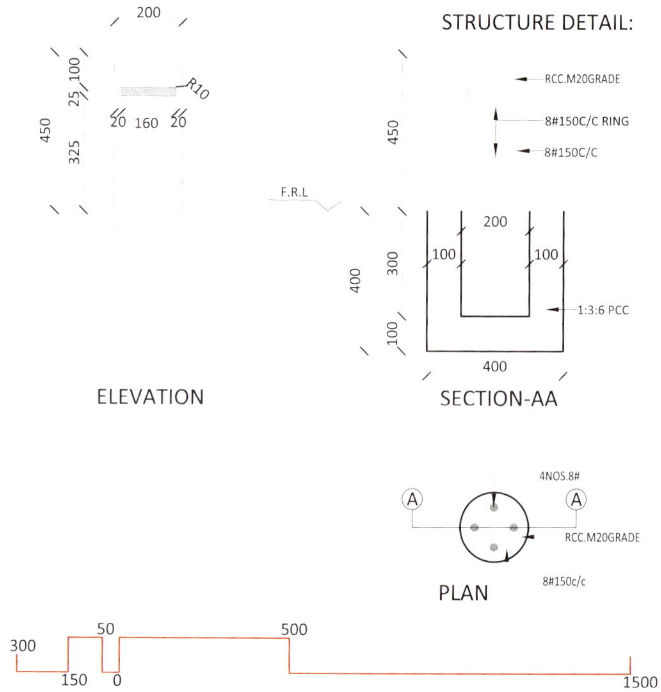

An elevated pedestrian crossing at Shivranjini

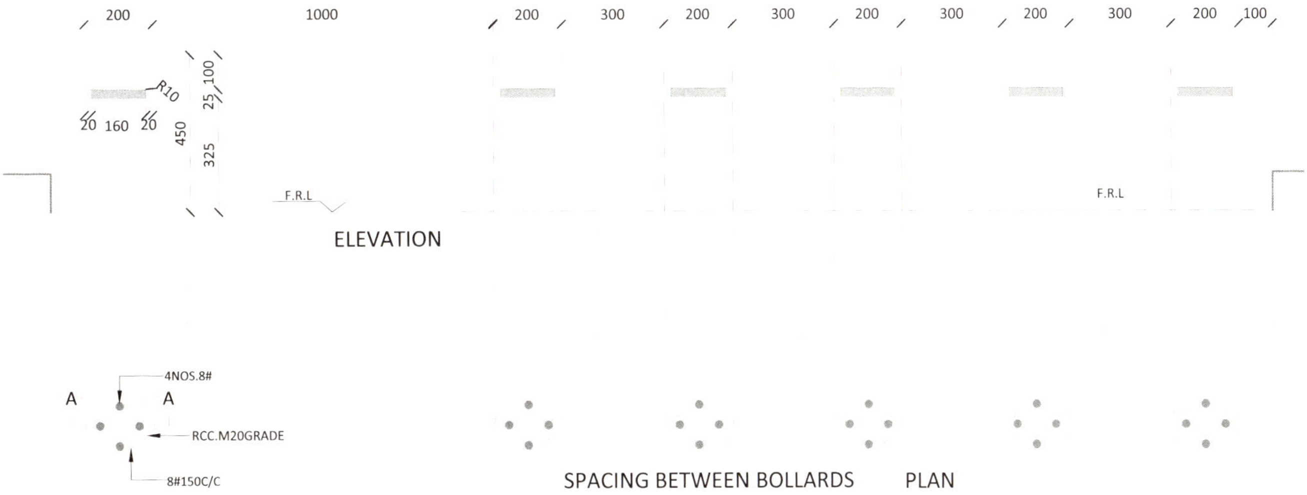

An innovative use of bollards. A senior citizen sits on the bollards as he awaits an opportunity to cross the road.

Railings

Railings along the corridor define the extent of BRTS territory. These were necessary to prevent pedestrians from carelessly crossing it.

Drawing of BRTS median and railing

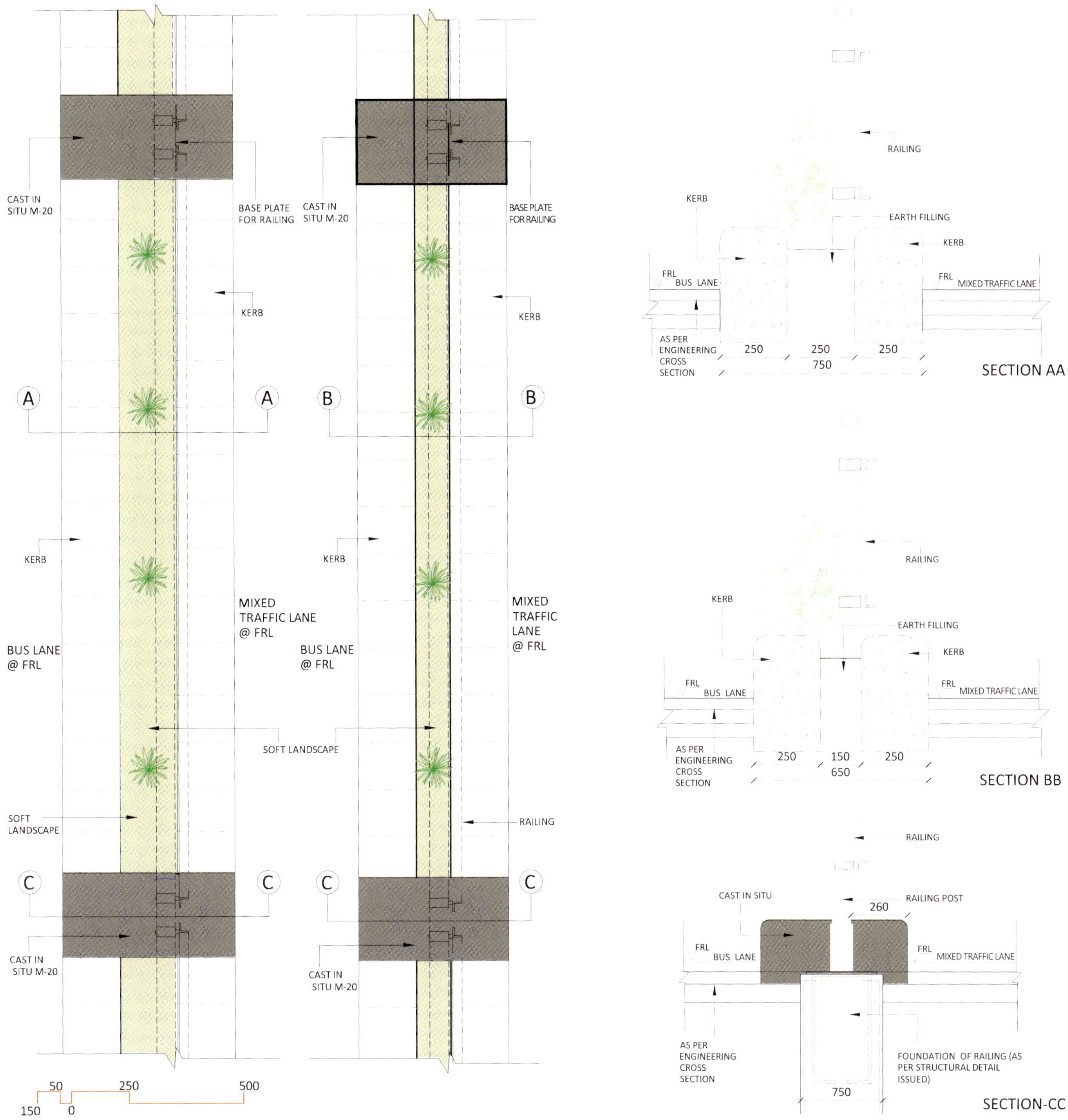

Kerb Cuts

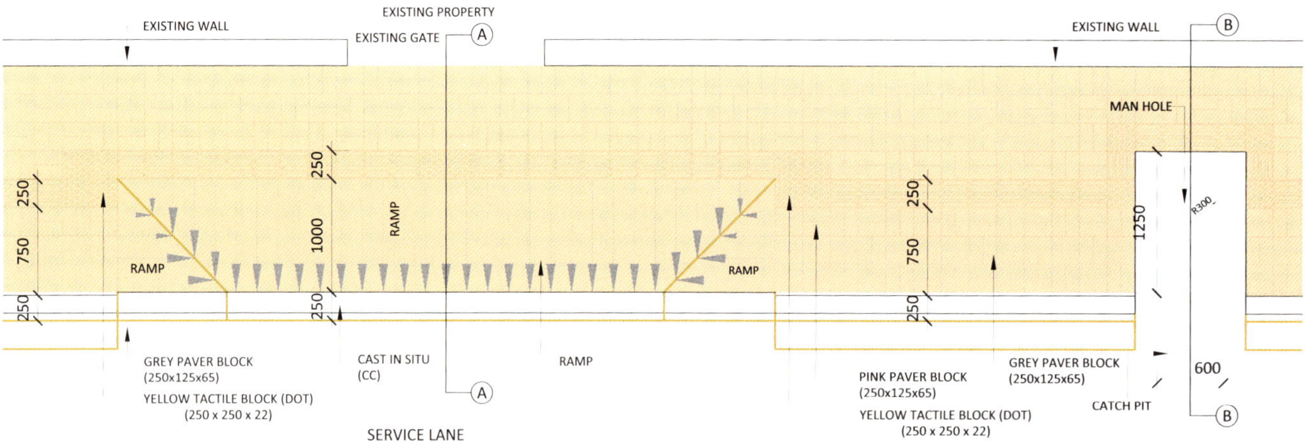

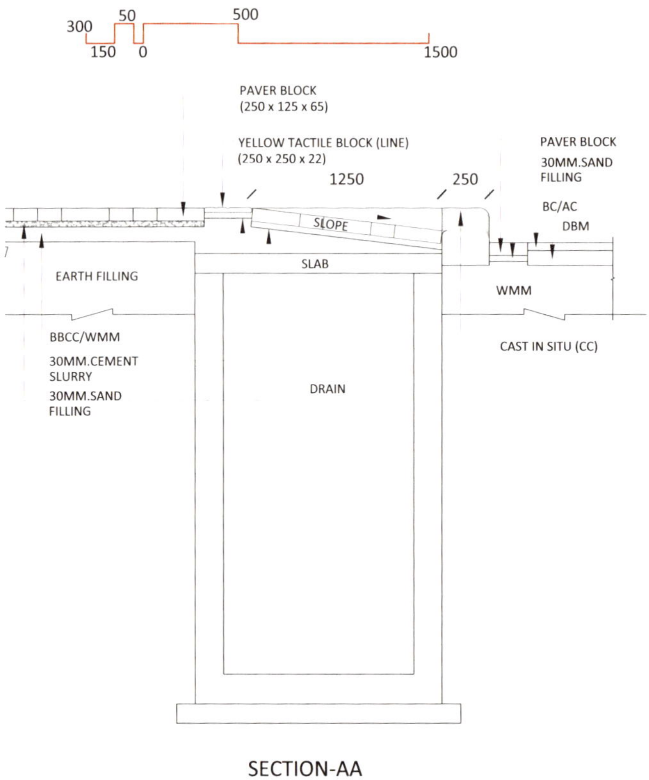

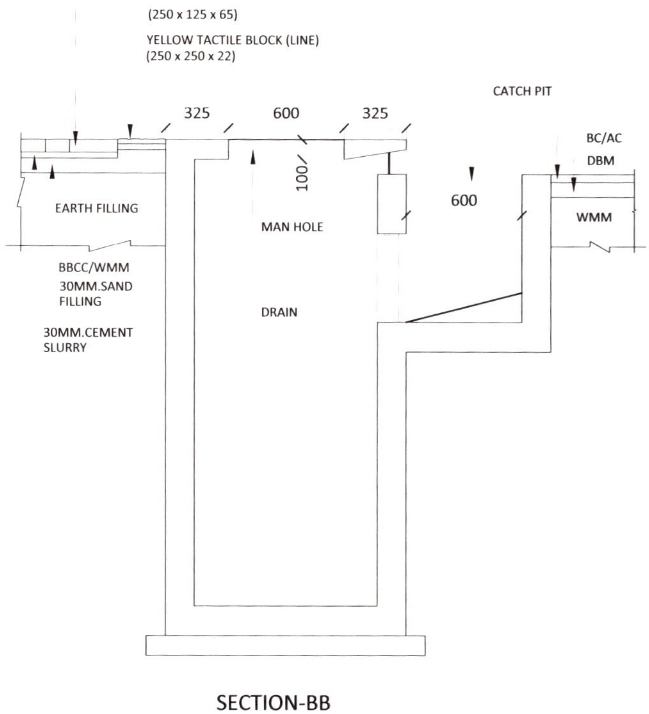

Plan and sections of typical details for access to private property. These are provided to enable vehicular entry to the adjoining properties.

Footpaths are lowered towards access points to private properties.

Raised Pedestrian Crossing at Bus Stations

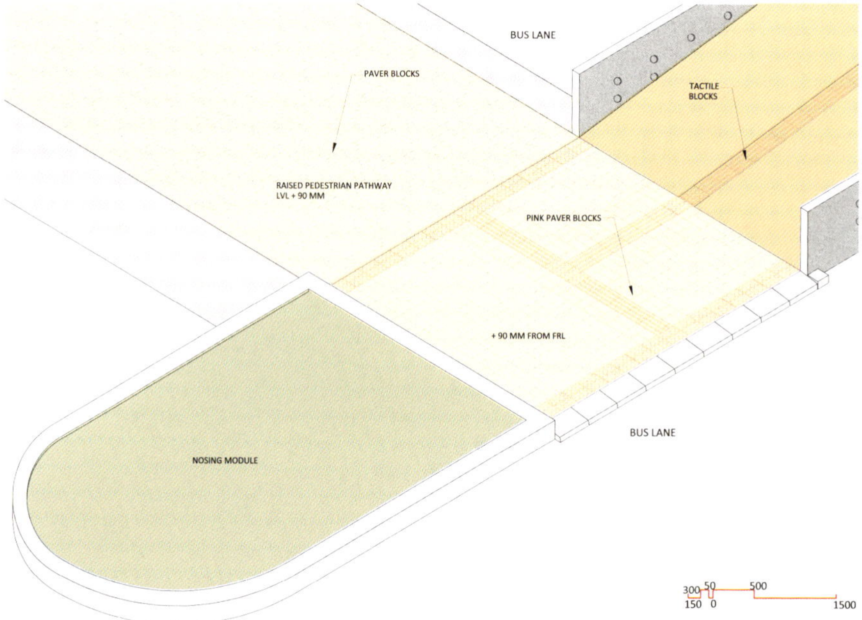

At locations with high-speed vehicular movement, pedestrian crossings raised 100 mm above FRL are recommended to reduce the speeds of approaching vehicles, thereby ensuring pedestrian safety.

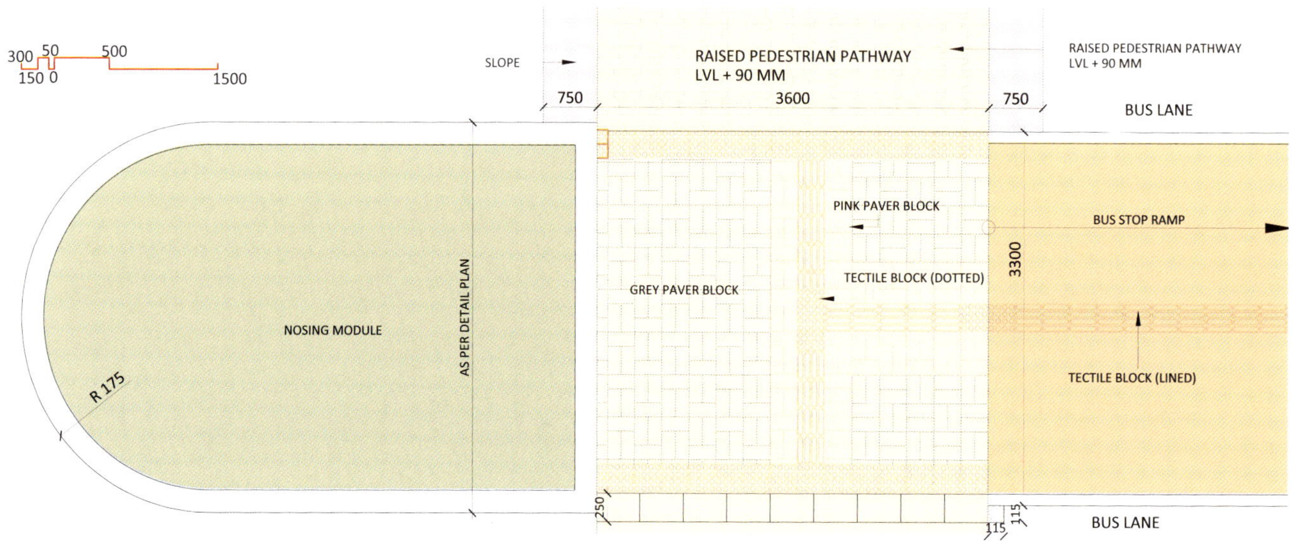

Parking Module and Tree-pit Cover

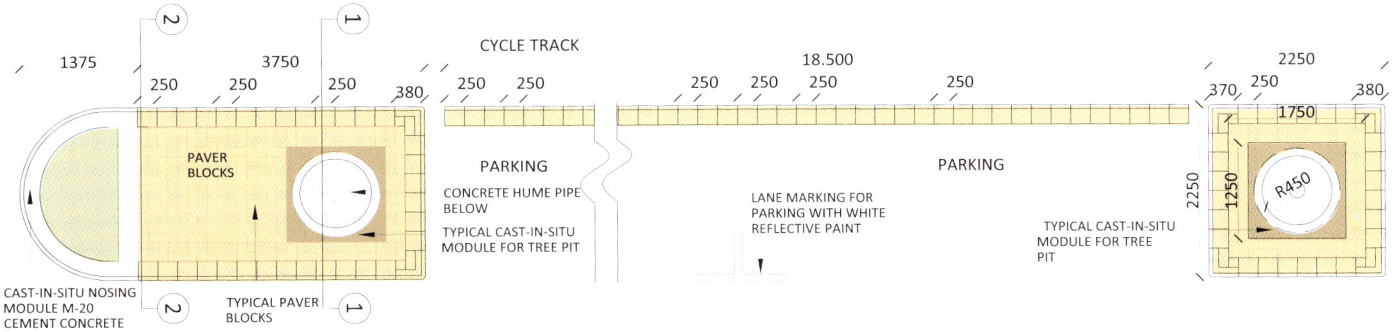

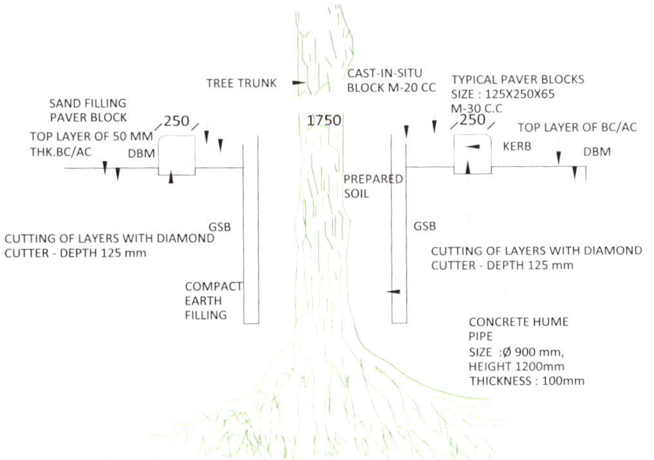

TYPICAL TREE PIT SECTION 2-2

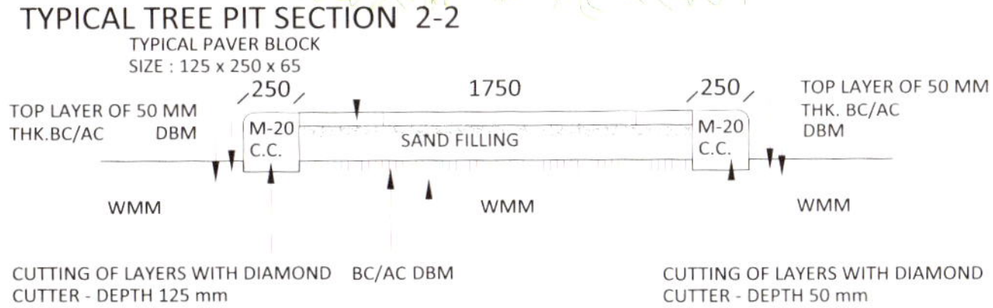

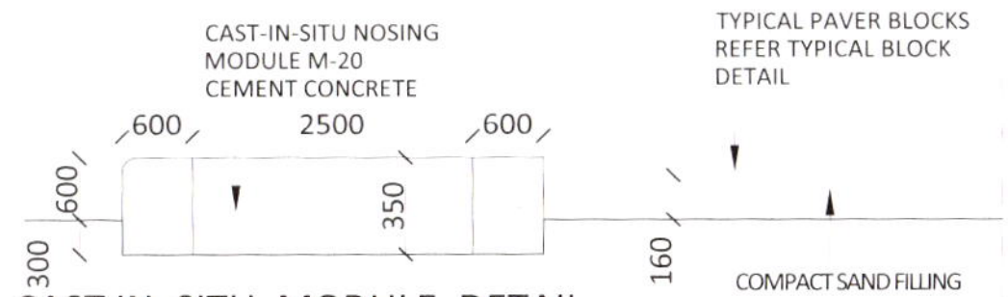

CAST IN SITU MODULE DETAIL

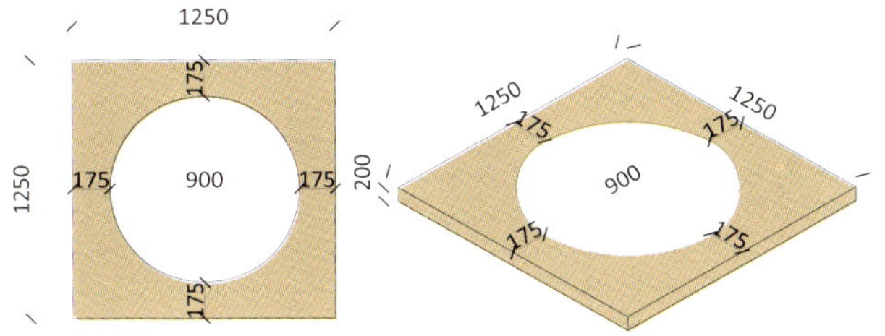

PLAN

ISOMETRIC VIEW
CAST-IN-SITU MODULE
FOR TREE PIT

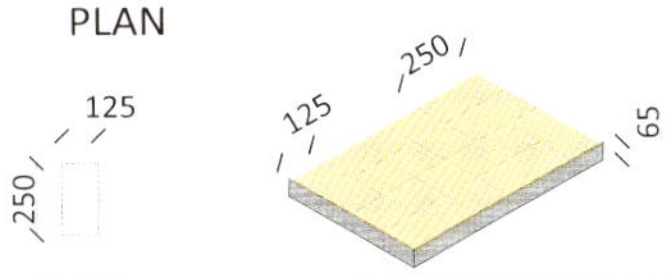

PLAN

ISOMETRIC VIEW

N.T.S

Tree-pit Cover Details

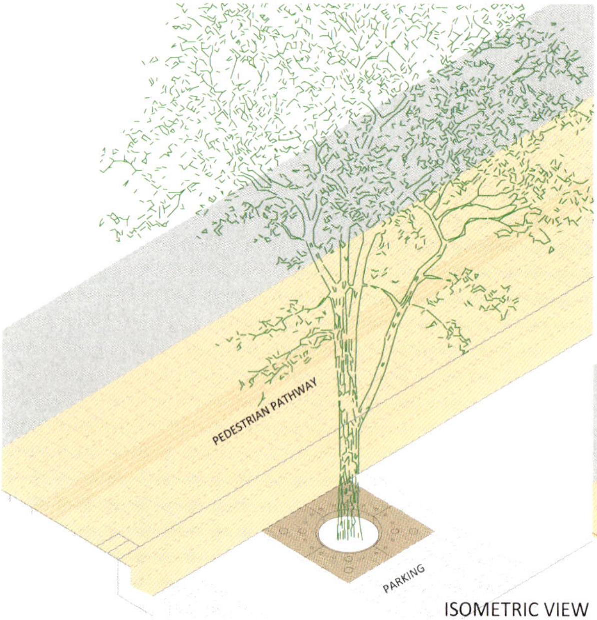

ISOMETRIC VIEW

ISOMETRIC VIEW

TREE-PIT COVER DETAIL (PRE-CAST)

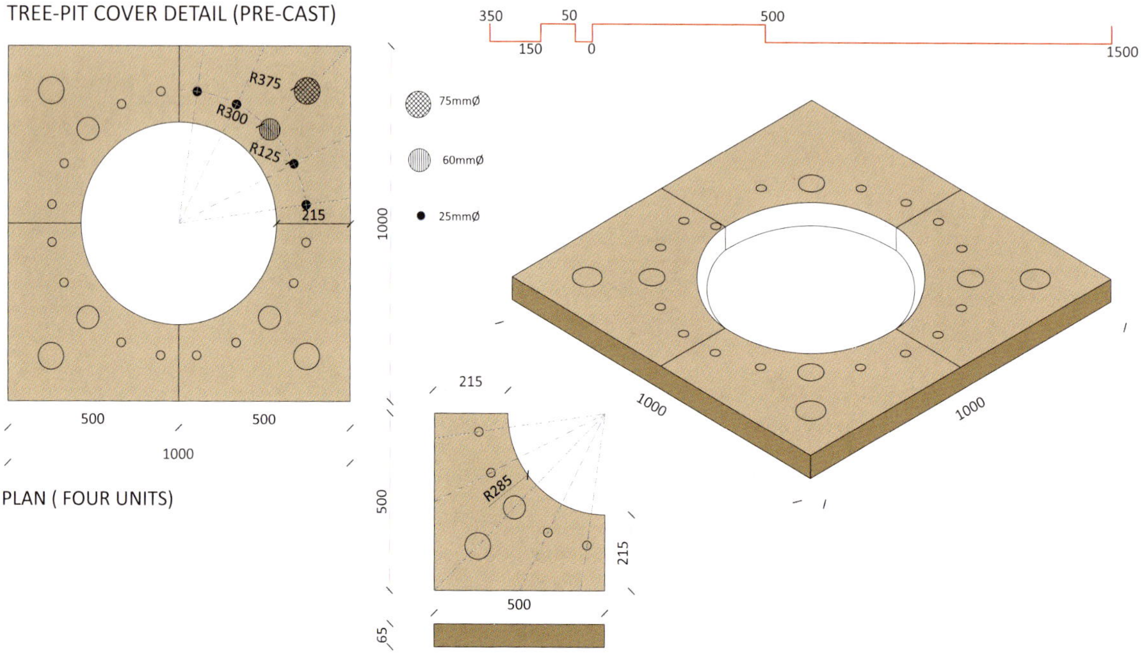

Typical drawings for tree-pit cover

Existing trees are protected by providing well-designed tree pits.

At-grade pedestrian access to bus stations has proven to be extremely safe and convenient for all.

BRTS Design

Transit Infrastructure System

Transit facilities can be of two kinds—public interface or exclusively for BRTS use. The former include facilities such as bus stations, interchanges and their precincts, which form the direct link between commuters and the BRTS. The latter provide places for vehicle parking and maintenance, such as workshops, depots and terminals.

Bus stations give the system its identity. They are the first interface between commuters and the BRTS. They should enable precise docking of buses, so that commuters can enter and exit safely and quickly. Some seating area may be provided for senior citizens and people with disabilities, along with facilities such as ticketing, automatic doors, announcements, space for queuing etc.

Interchanges are the transit points between Janmarg and other modes of public transport. These stations are developed for smooth, fast and effective transfer of the passengers including those with disabilities or encumbered with luggage.

Bus depots are facilities for parking and maintaining buses. At the end of a shift involving several trips along a route, the driver has to bring the vehicle back to an operations base. The base serves a number of functions such as fare deposit, recording passenger activity, rest facilities for drivers, cleaning and refuelling vehicles, and parking buses until the next run or overnight.

The workshop facility is meant for inspection, repair and routine maintenance of the buses. In addition to facilities available at bus depots, workshops handle motor servicing, engine rebuild, transmission shop and body component area for major repairs.

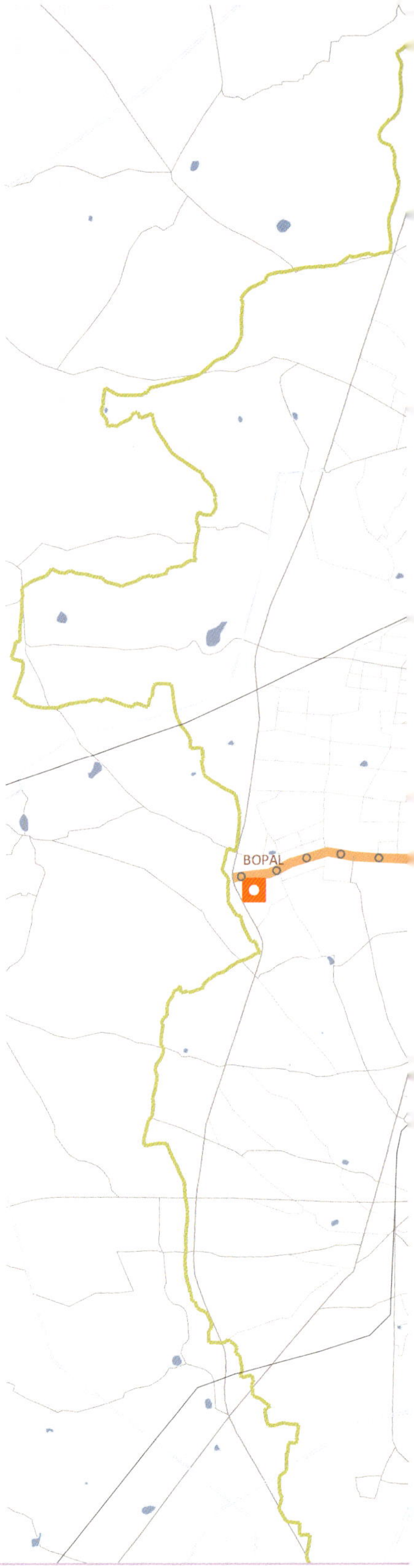

Transit infrastructure system of Janmarg

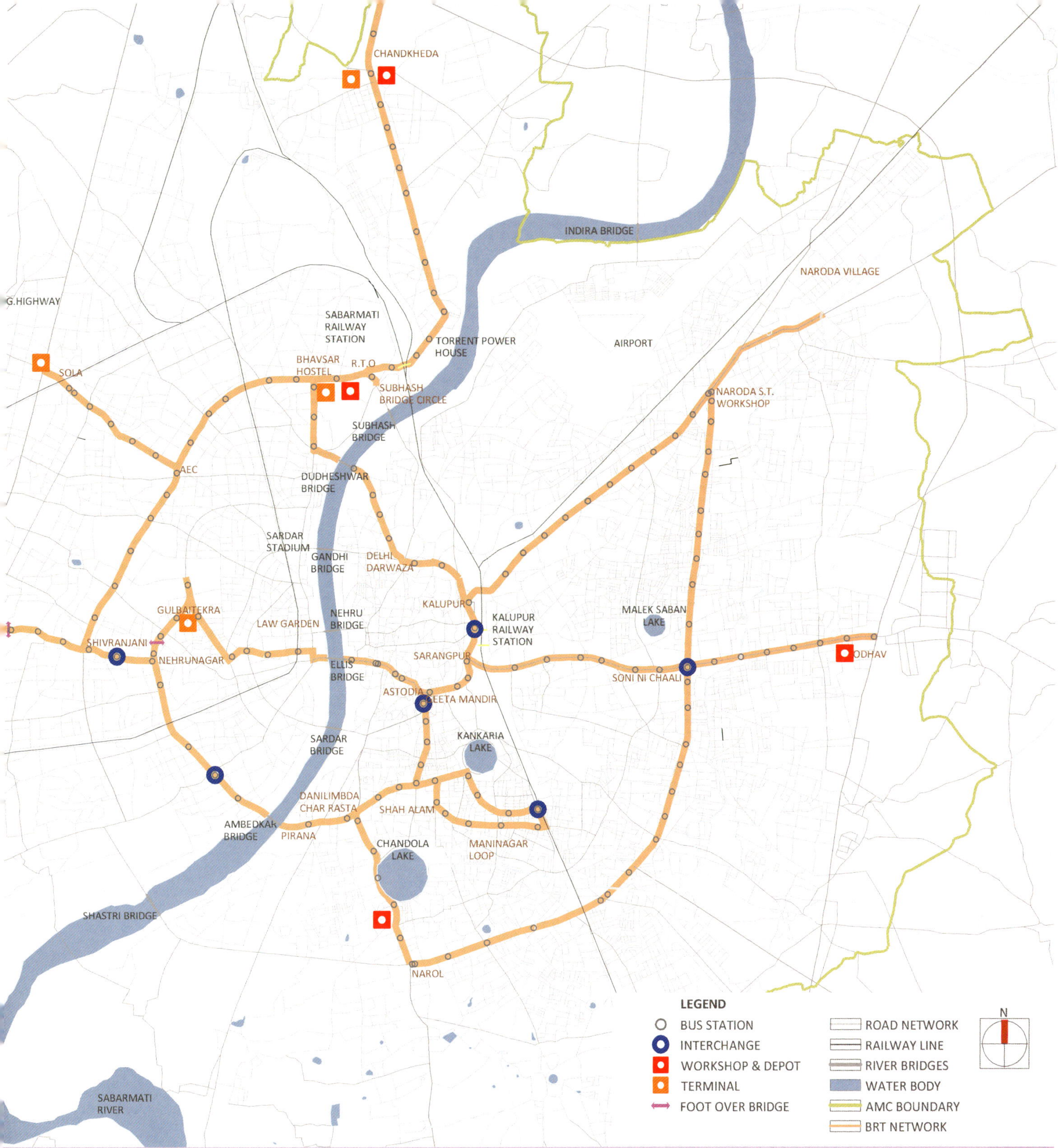
CHANDKHEDA
INDIRA BRIDGE
NARODA VILLAGE
G.HIGHWAY
SABARMATI
RAILWAY
STATION
TORRENT POWER
HOUSE
AIRPORT
BHAVSAR
HOSTEL
R.T.O
SOLA
SUBHASH
BRIDGE CIRCLE
NARODA S.T.
WORKSHOP
SUBHASH
BRIDGE
AEC
DUDHESHWAR
BRIDGE
SARDAR
STADIUM
GANDHI
BRIDGE
DELHI
DARWAZA
GULBAI TEKRA
KALUPUR
NEHRU
BRIDGE
KALUPUR
RAILWAY
STATION
MALEK SABAN
LAKE
LAW GARDEN
SHIVRANJANI
NEHRUNAGAR
SARANGPUR
ODHAV
ELLIS
BRIDGE
SONI NI CHAALI
ASTODIA
GEETA MANDIR
KANKARIA
LAKE
SARDAR
BRIDGE
DANILIMBDA
CHAR RASTA
SHAH ALAM
AMBEDKAR
BRIDGE
PIRANA
CHANDOLA
LAKE
MANINAGAR
LOOP
SHASTRI BRIDGE
NAROL
SABARMATI
RIVER
LEGEND
BUS STATION
INTERCHANGE
WORKSHOP & DEPOT
TERMINAL
FOOT OVER BRIDGE
ROAD NETWORK
RAILWAY LINE
RIVER BRIDGES
WATER BODY
AMC BOUNDARY
BRT NETWORK
N

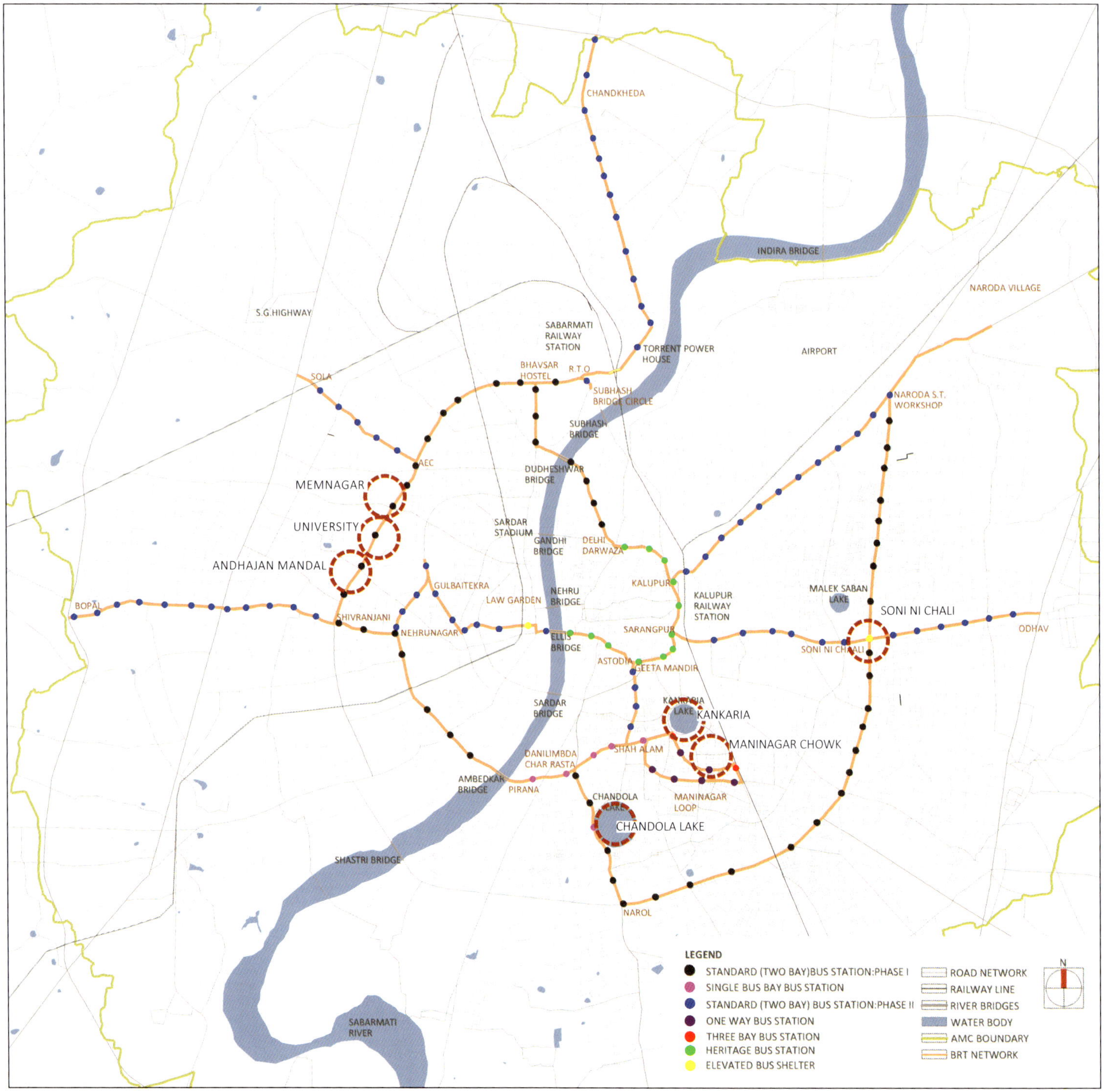

Bus station design types for Janmarg

Bus Stations

A typical BRTS station in Ahmedabad

Bus stations, the first interface between the people and Janmarg, are designated halts along the corridor for passengers to board and alight. As the first interface between the people and Janmarg, they have to serve a large number of people with ease and efficiency. Therefore, they are designed with seating, ticketing and electronic passenger information system.

The design of bus stations hinges on two important considerations: 1) to engage and attract the people of the city towards public transport, stressing the value of the bus system as a core of the transit options in the city; 2) to provide a comfortable, durable and safe 'place' for the transit.

For success, especially in the public realm, any new system must gain acceptance. To this end, a strong public image is necessary.

The bus stations, as the transition spaces between the people and Janmarg, must be universally accessible and welcoming to the commuter. These stations reflect the aspirations of the city, both physically and psychologically. They are the face of the system with all the implied characteristic features of its architecture.

The bus stations project the philosophy of Janmarg to provide reliable, fast and safe public transport to the people. Hence, they have an obstacle-free movement, with transparency for safety and provide a protected, climatically comfortable place for the users. Along with this, durability and low maintenance are essential. To this end, the structures use energy minimally, relying largely on natural light and ventilation.

Access to Bus Stations

Access to the bus stations is via zebra crossings from both ends of the bus stations. In Phase II, in order to provide convenient access to commuters, flat-topped humps at the same level as footpaths are proposed at the entry, and bollards are placed between mixed traffic lanes and bus lanes to prevent other traffic from intruding. An option for grade separation at the crossing has been designed at some bus stations with high densities of pedestrian crossing. Access is devised to ensure safe and convenient movement of passengers. Ramps at the station entrances, leading to boarding platforms level with the bus floors, are designed with tactile blocks, to provide obstacle-free access to differently-abled people and senior citizens. The beginning of the ramp is identified by twelve small LED lights that glow at night to caution users. The bus station signal phase is synchronised with the junction signal phase to enable safe pedestrian crossing.

At-grade pedestrian crossing at Shastrinagar BRTS station

Access from Junction

Bus station near Anjali Junction

Bus station near Blind People's Association, IIM Junction

Bus stations accessible from junctions are located at a minimum distance of 25 m from them, leaving waiting space for two buses when the signal is red. Safe access from the median is provided.

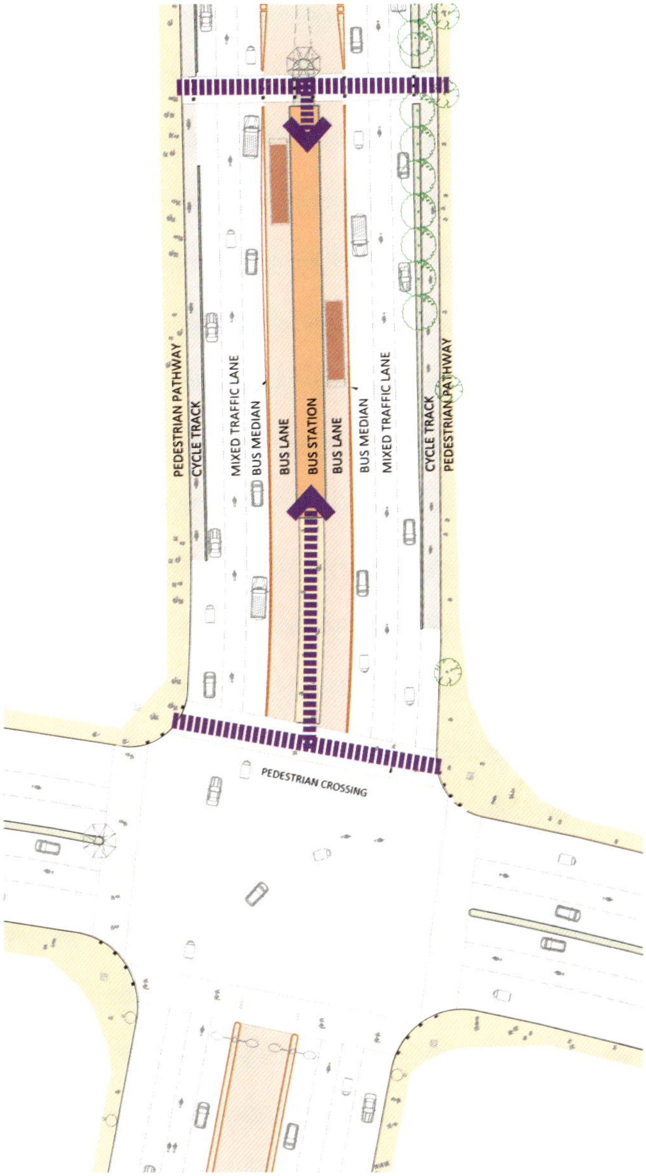

Pedestrian access
BRTS bus station near Blind People's Association, IIM Junction

Access from Mid-block

Vaalinath Chowk bus station

Himmatlal Park bus station

Bus stations located at mid-block are accessible from pedestrian crossings at both ends. Pedestrian signals have been installed for ensuring safety of passengers. At locations with high-speed vehicular movement, raised pedestrian crossings are recommended with 100 mm rise from FRL. This would reduce the speeds of approaching vehicles, thereby enhancing pedestrian safety.

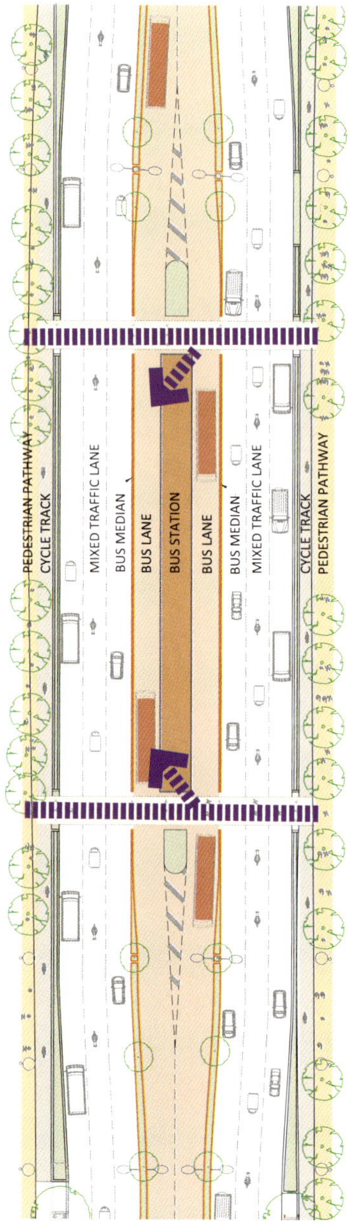

Pedestrian access at BRT bus station near Gujarat University

Access below Flyover

Special split flyovers have been designed to allow the BRTS buses to move in the designated lane at grade. This is particularly important at critical traffic intersections to keep the bus accessible to passengers.

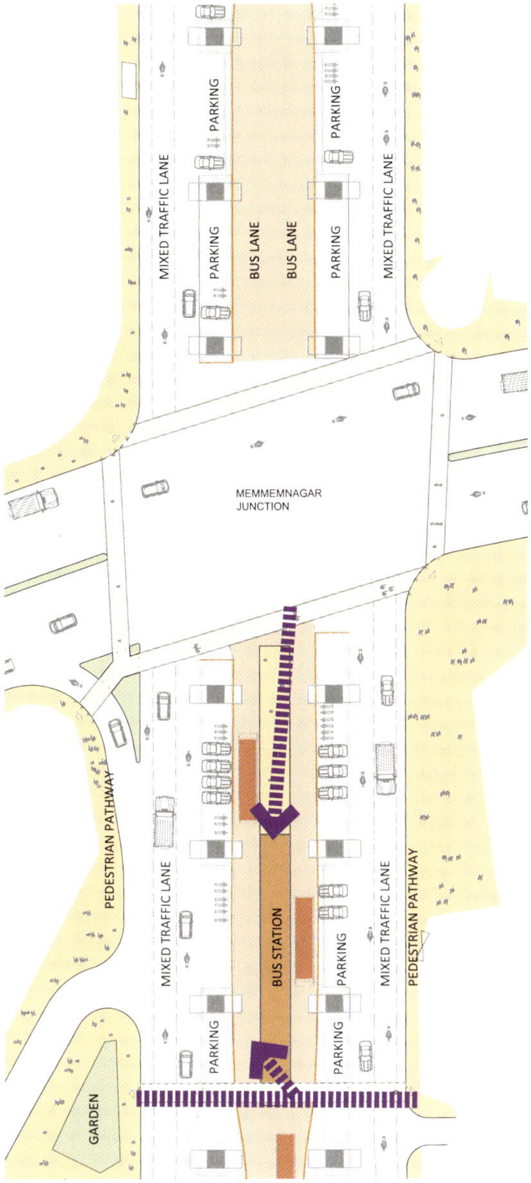

Pedestrian access at Memnagar BRT bus station

Level Alighting and Boarding

The platforms of Janmarg bus stations are designed to be level with the bus floors. This is a critical element in design as it reduces the boarding and alighting time of passengers and increases the efficiency of the system.

Level alighting and boarding enables universal and safe access.

Architectural Details

A combination of 'cool' and 'warm' elements defines various spaces in bus stations. This also makes travelling a 'tactile' experience.

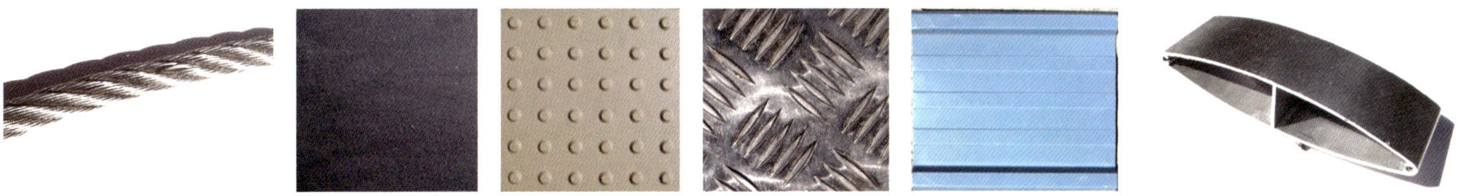

Innovative use of various materials enhances the overall experience of bus stations.

Phase I: Bus Station Design *TWO-BUS BAYS*

This is a standard bus station module used for all Phase I corridors. These are designed to dock two buses in either direction. Ticket counters separate the entry and exit points for passengers.

Typical two-bus bays stations on Janmarg: University bus station (top) and Viratnagar bus station (above)

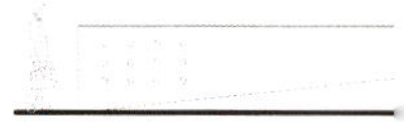

Elevation 1

Section A - A

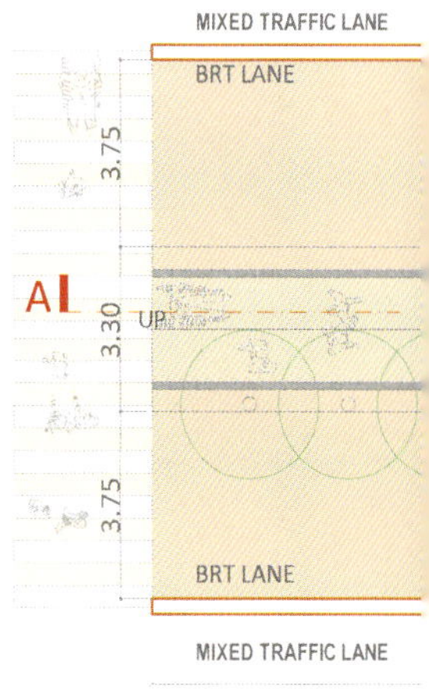

Plan

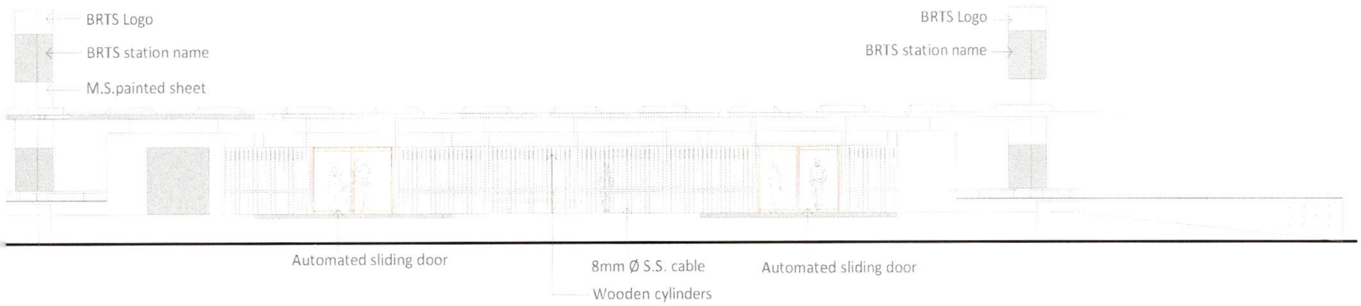
BRTS Logo
BRTS station name
M.S.painted sheet
BRTS Logo
BRTS station name
Automated sliding door
8mm Ø S.S. cable
Wooden cylinders
Automated sliding door

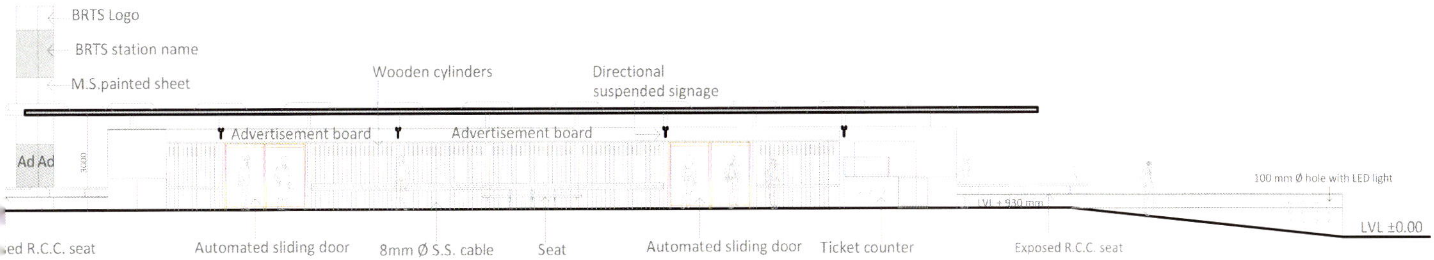
BRTS Logo
BRTS station name
M.S.painted sheet
Wooden cylinders
Directional suspended signage
Advertisement board
Advertisement board
Ad Ad
100 mm Ø hole with LED light
LVL ±0.00
ed R.C.C. seat
Automated sliding door
8mm Ø S.S. cable
Seat
Automated sliding door
Ticket counter
Exposed R.C.C. seat

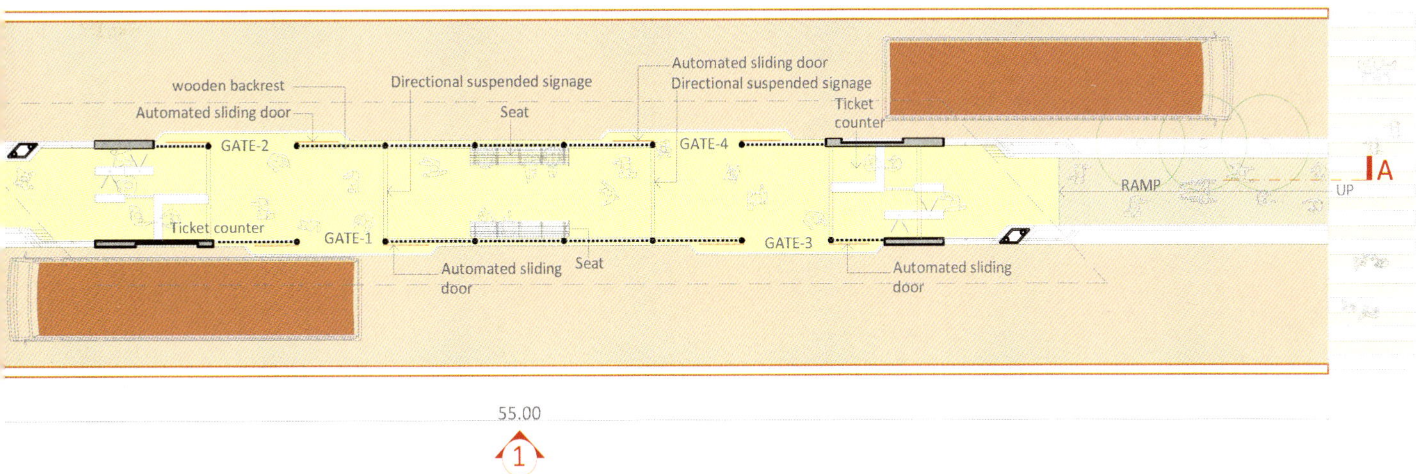
wooden backrest
Automated sliding door
Directional suspended signage
Seat
Automated sliding door
Directional suspended signage
Ticket counter
GATE-2
GATE-4
RAMP
UP
A
Ticket counter
GATE-1
GATE-3
Automated sliding door
Seat
Automated sliding door
55.00
1

Janmarg's stations are designed to have restricted access, yet the design manages to be transparent and they have become symbols of accessibility across the city.

Phase I: Special Bus Station Design *SINGLE-BUS BAY*

These stations are built at locations where demand is low. In some cases, they are built to counter unsuitable soil conditions caused due to massive excavation works in the past. The roof is fabricated and access is from one side only. Space has been kept in the design to add another bus bay in future.

Chandola Lake bus station

The single-bay bus stations retain most of the elements of the original design.

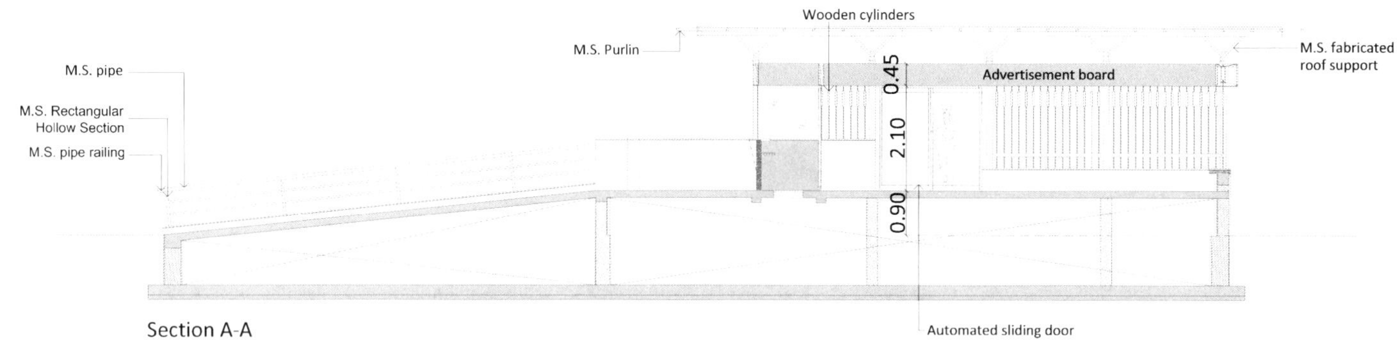

Section A-A

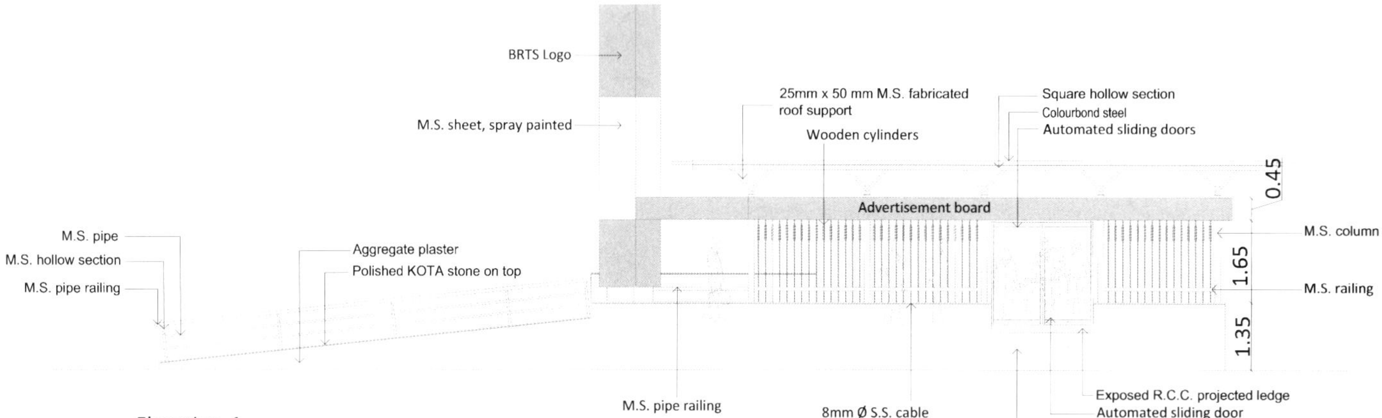

Elevation 1

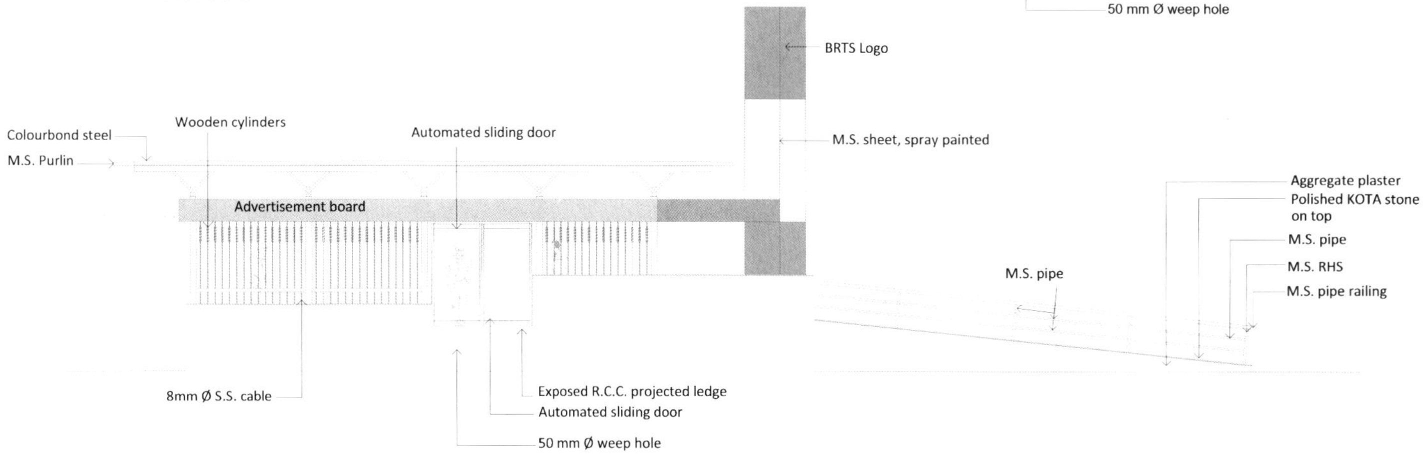

Elevation 2

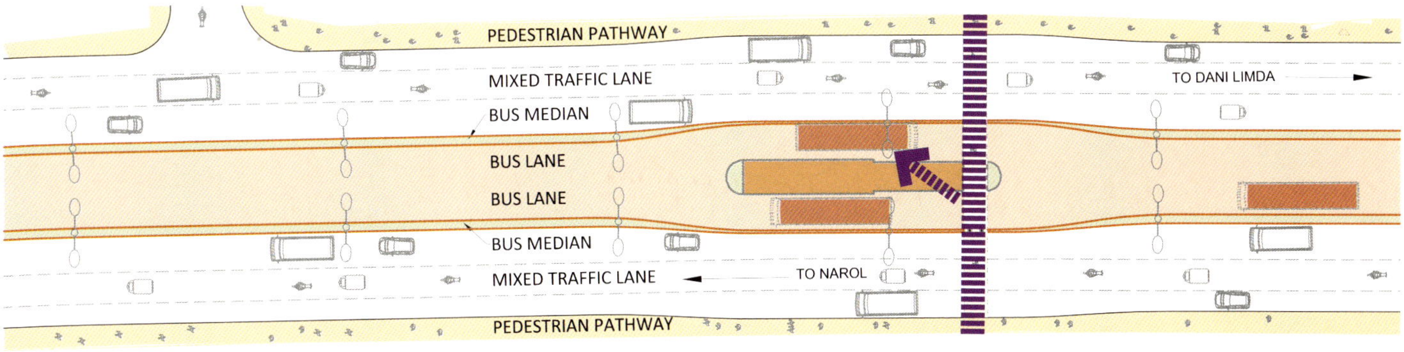
PEDESTRIAN PATHWAY
MIXED TRAFFIC LANE
TO DANI LIMDA
BUS MEDIAN
BUS LANE
BUS LANE
BUS MEDIAN
MIXED TRAFFIC LANE
TO NAROL
PEDESTRIAN PATHWAY

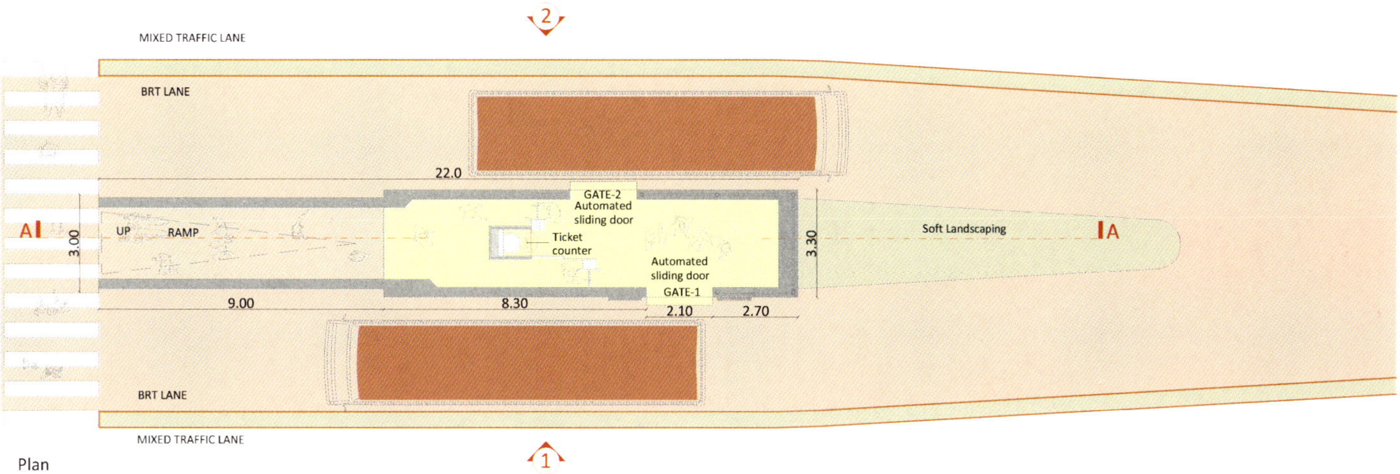
2
MIXED TRAFFIC LANE
BRT LANE
22.0
GATE-2
Automated sliding door
A
3.00
UP
RAMP
Ticket counter
Automated sliding door
GATE-1
3.30
Soft Landscaping
A
9.00
8.30
2.10
2.70
BRT LANE
MIXED TRAFFIC LANE
1

Plan

Phase I: Special Bus Station Design *THREE-BUS BAYS*

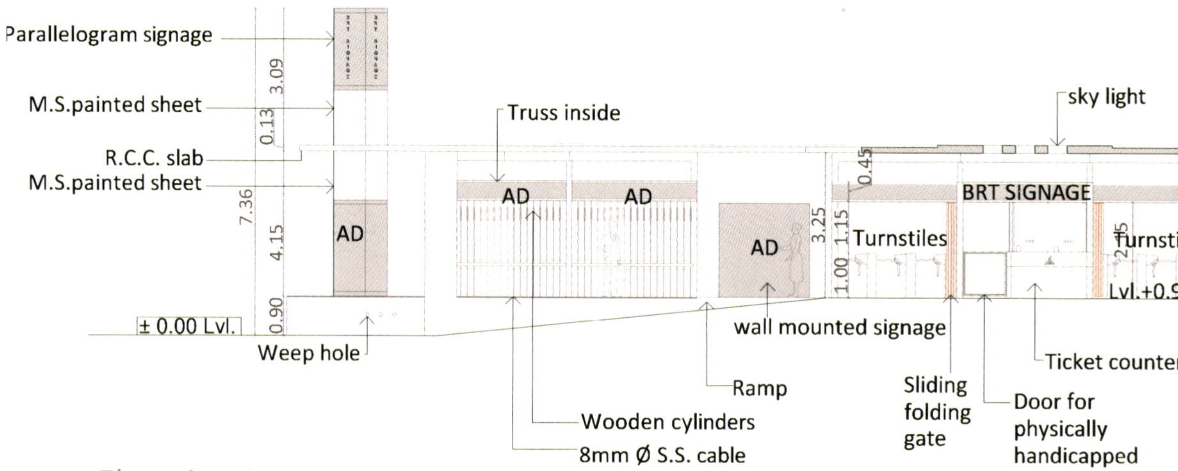

Elevation 1

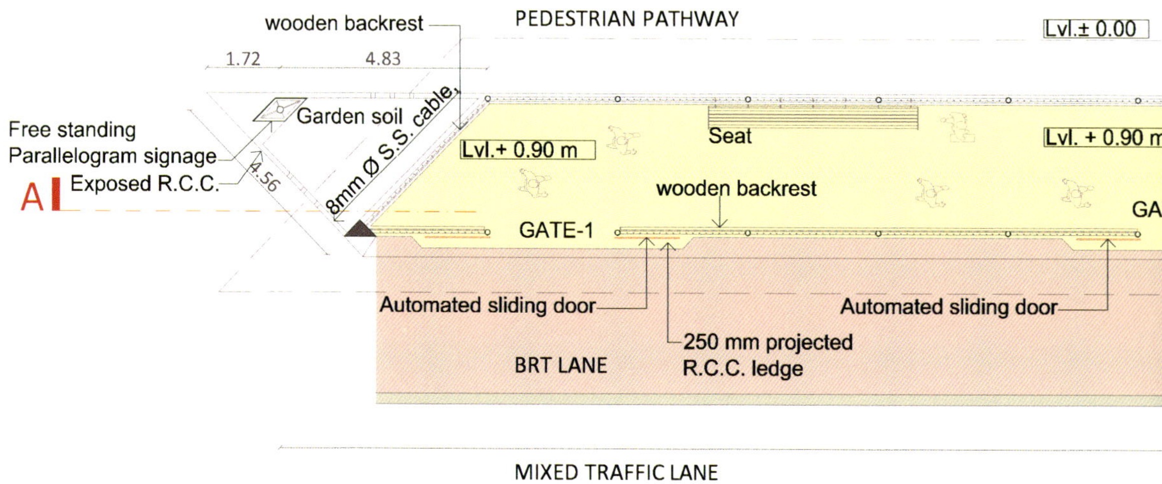

Plan

This station is designed for places with higher-than-normal passenger demand. It enables three buses to dock, and is designed to cater to the most frequently visited public places in the city. There are only two such stations built—at Kankaria and Maninagar.

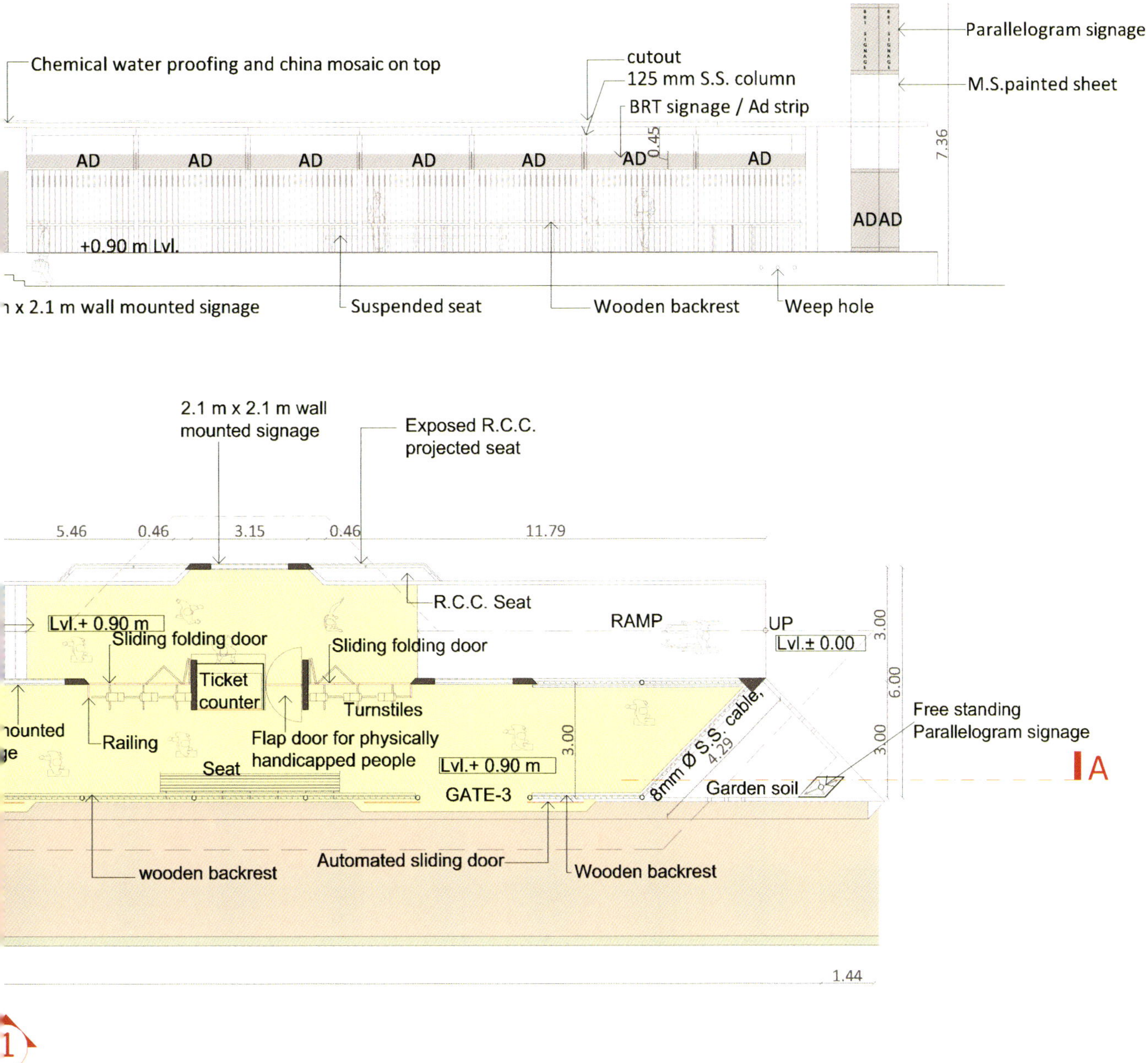

Plan and section of three-bus bays station at Kankaria Lake

Kankaria Lake BRTS station with three-bus bays

KANKARIA LAKEFRONT DEVELOPMENT

Phase I: Special Bus Station Design *ONE-WAY BUS STATION*

In the one-way corridor mentioned earlier, special bus stations, with boarding from one side only, are designed to cater to this condition. The non-boarding side has louvers for cross-ventilation and to adjust light.

One-way bus station in Maninagar

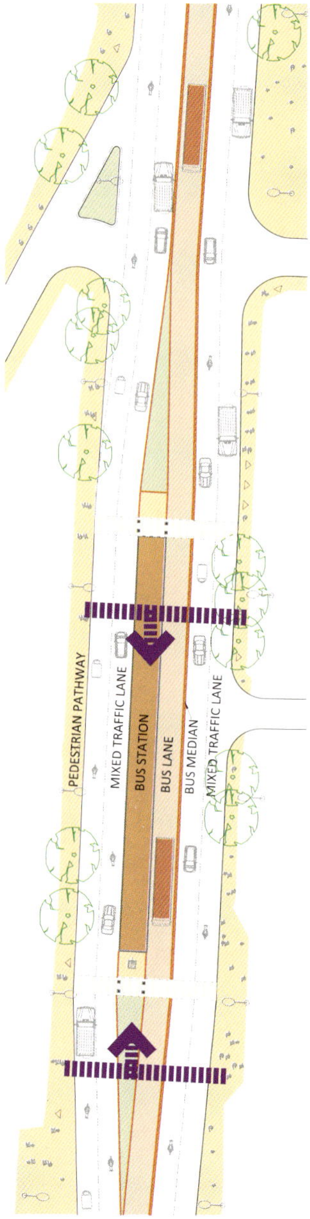

Plan for one-way bus stations

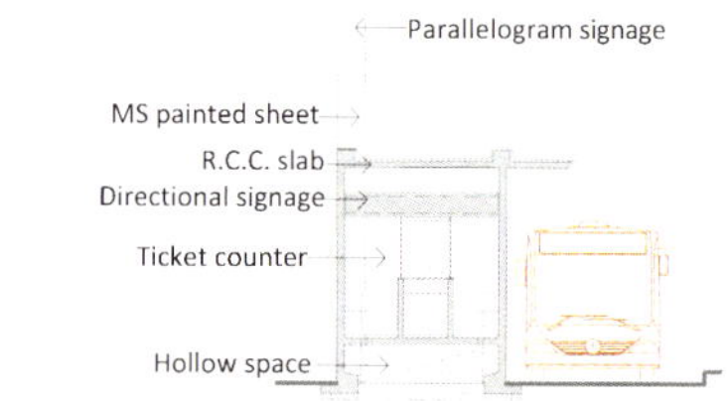

Section A - A

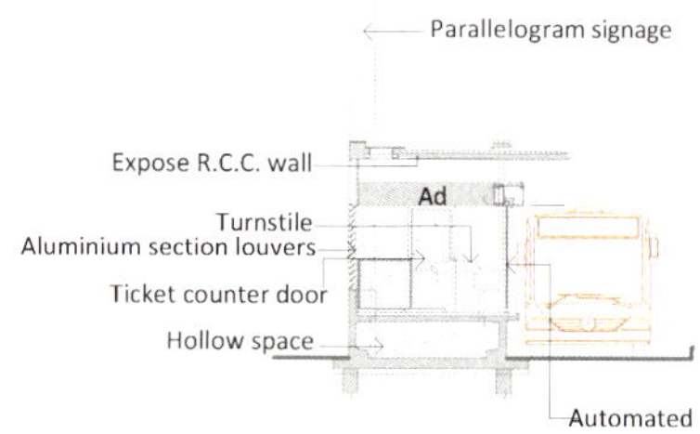

Section B - B

Plan, section and elevation for one-way bus station

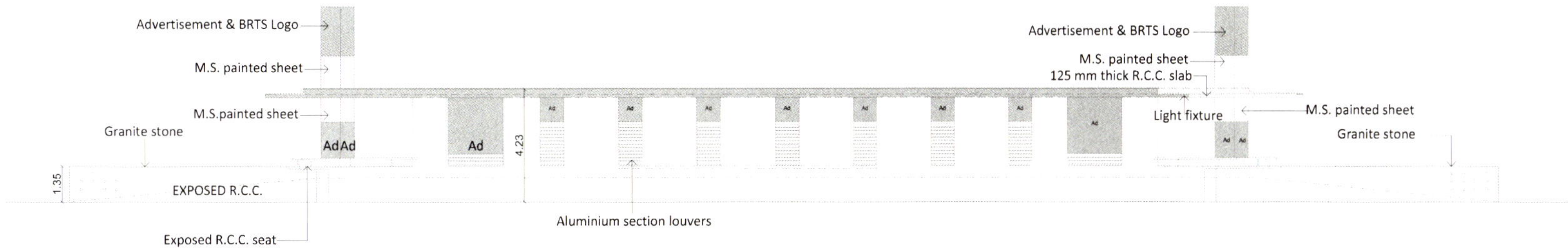

evation 1

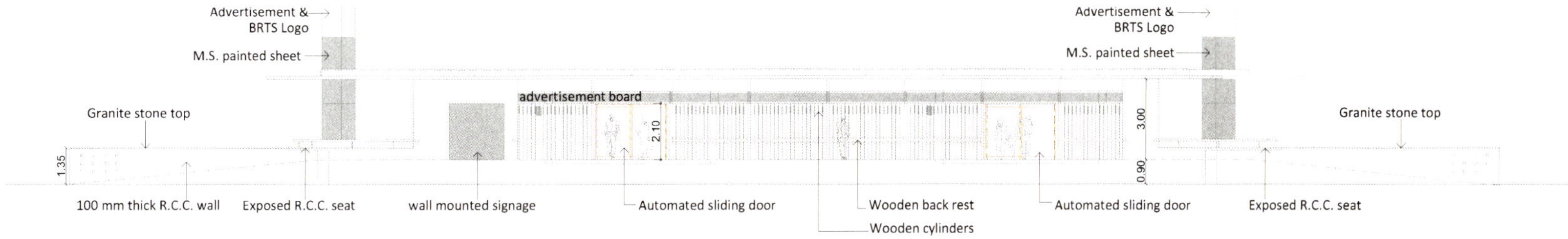

evation 2

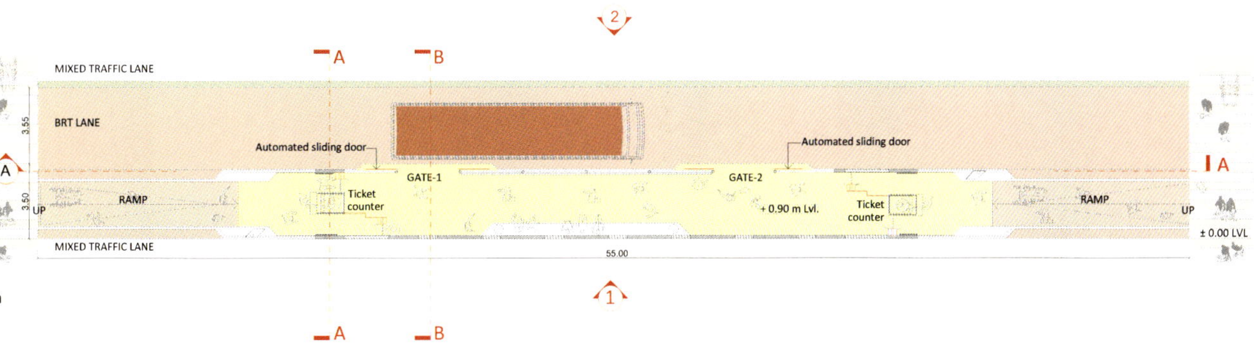

Plan

Phase II: Heritage Bus Station Design

These are specially designed bus stations within the walled city. They respond to the art and architecture of old Ahmedabad. Instead of glass and concrete, these stations are treated with local stone cladding and wooden ceiling with fabricated roof. However, the new treatment does not make them radically different from the earlier stations.

Heritage bus stations have a fabricated roof and stone cladding to reflect the surrounding heritage.

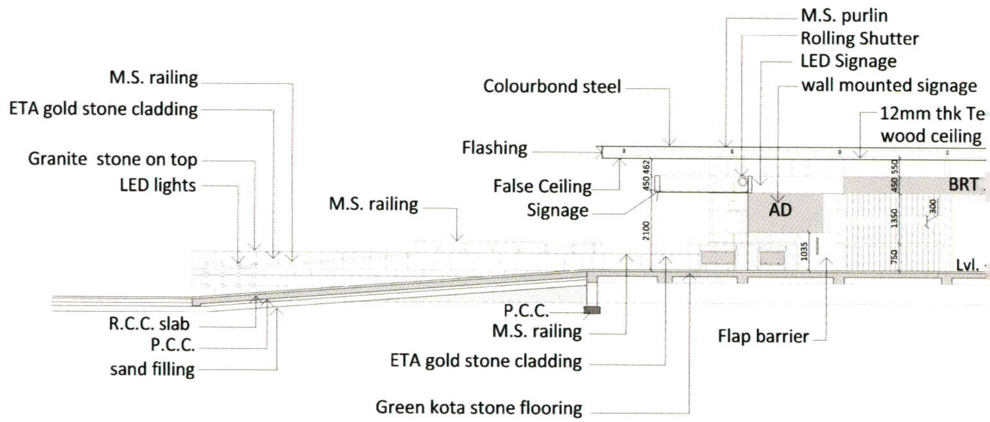

Section A-A

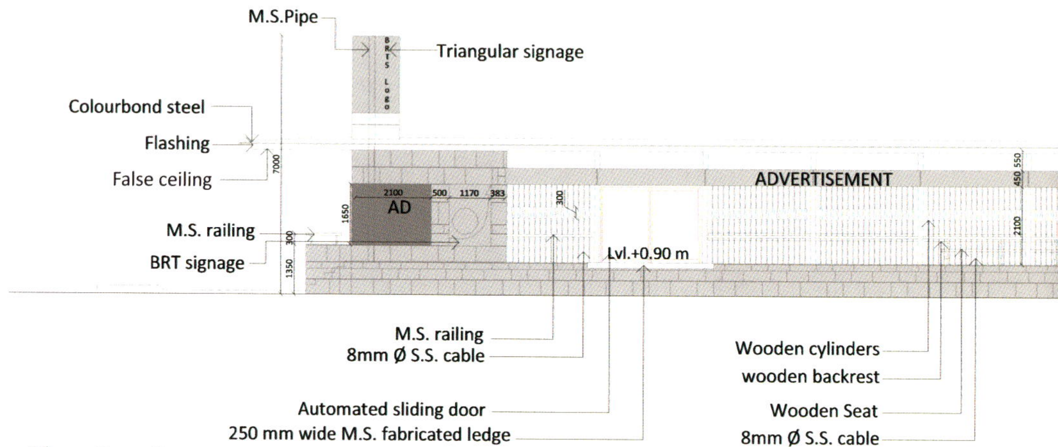

Elevation 1

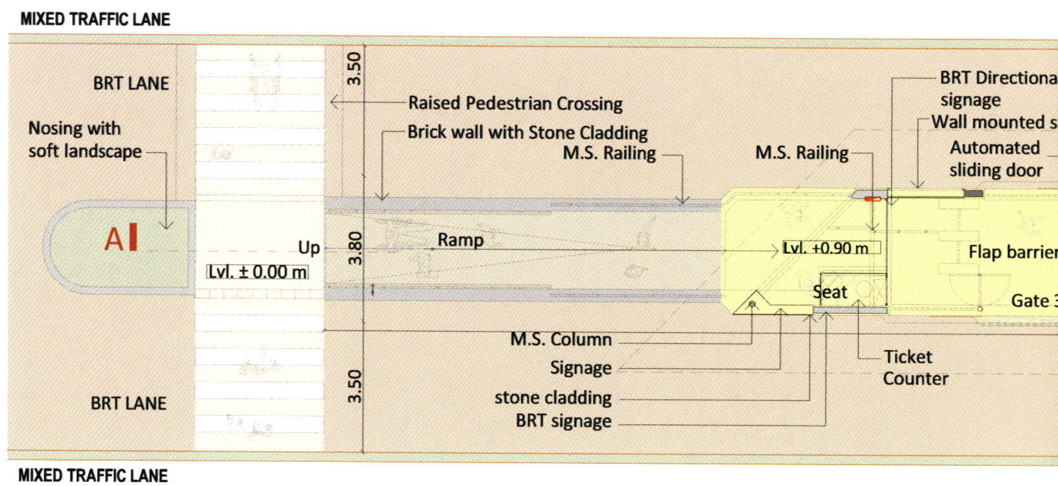

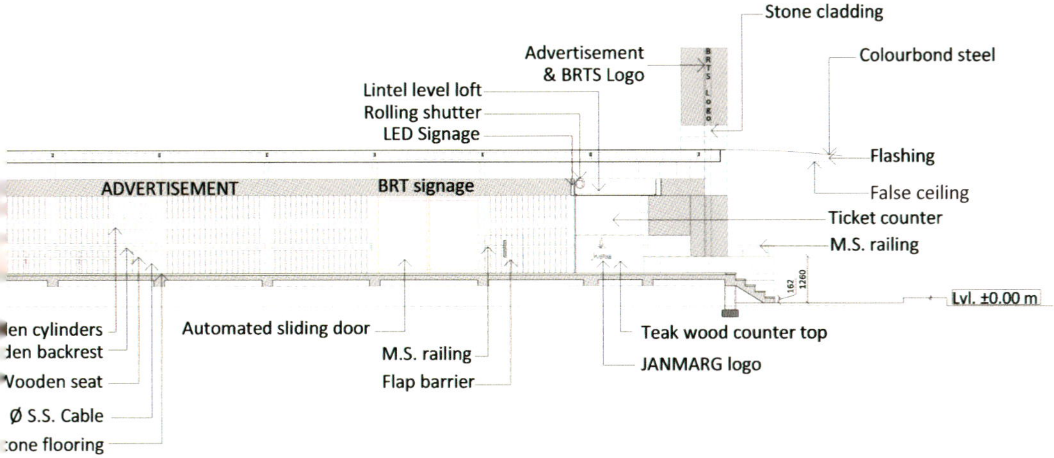

Stone cladding
Colourbond steel
Advertisement
& BRTS Logo
Lintel level loft
Rolling shutter
LED Signage
Flashing
False ceiling
Ticket counter
M.S. railing
ADVERTISEMENT
BRT signage
Lvl. ±0.00 m
len cylinders
len backrest
Vooden seat
Ø S.S. Cable
one flooring
Automated sliding door
M.S. railing
Flap barrier
Teak wood counter top
JANMARG logo

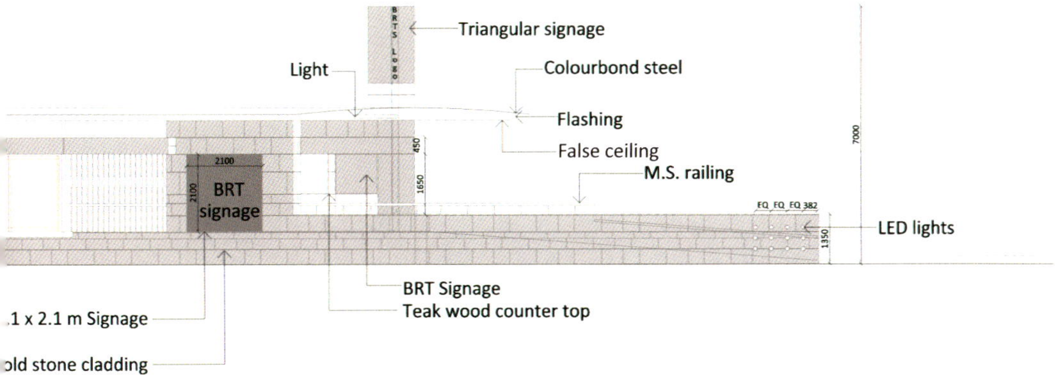

Triangular signage
Light
Colourbond steel
Flashing
False ceiling
M.S. railing
BRT
signage
LED lights
BRT Signage
Teak wood counter top
.1 x 2.1 m Signage
old stone cladding

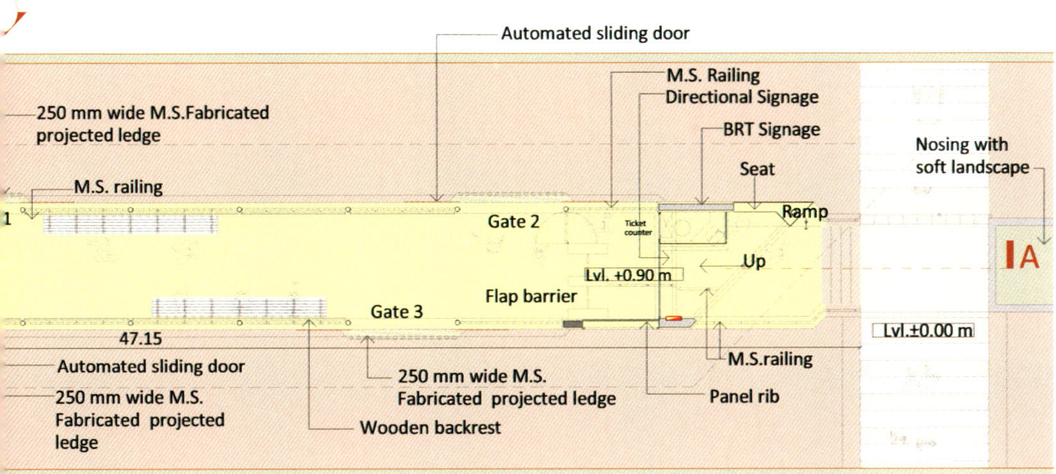

Automated sliding door
M.S. Railing
Directional Signage
BRT Signage
Seat
Ramp
250 mm wide M.S.Fabricated
projected ledge
M.S. railing
Nosing with
soft landscape
Gate 2
Up
Lvl. +0.90 m
Flap barrier
Gate 3
47.15
Lvl.±0.00 m
M.S.railing
Automated sliding door
250 mm wide M.S.
Fabricated projected ledge
Panel rib
250 mm wide M.S.
Fabricated projected
ledge
Wooden backrest

Interchanges

Consistent with the principle of providing safe and easy passenger transfers between two different public transport modes, interchange facilities have been developed as part of the design of Janmarg. This happens at six locations—all of them part of Phase I. Of these, the Jhansi ki Rani station acts as an interchange between Janmarg and GSRTC with at-grade pedestrian access. The Anjali station enables transfer between two BRT routes. The Maninagar Railway Station interchange conveys passengers from Janmarg to the railway system by means of an over-bridge. The Geeta Mandir station provides access to the GSRTC terminal through pedestrian connectivity at grade. Soni ni Chali is a specially designed grade-separated interchange between two BRT corridors crossing at this junction.

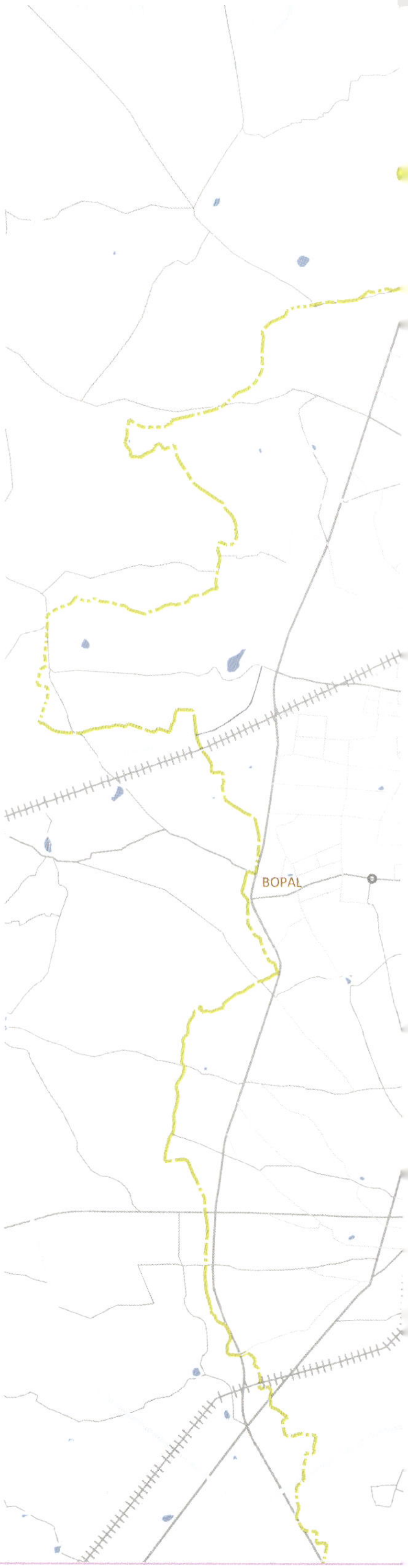

Interchanges along Janmarg

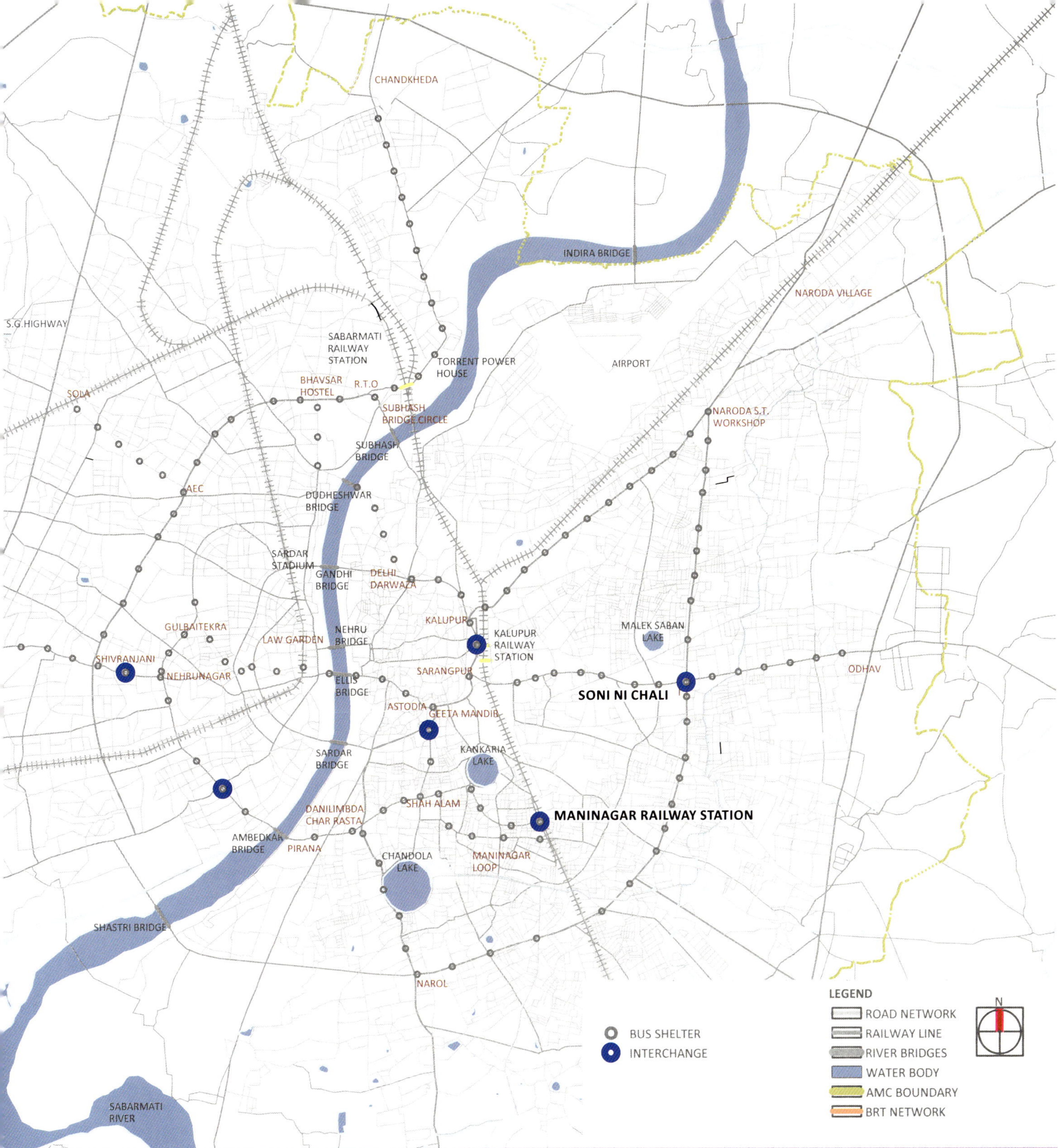
CHANDKHEDA
INDIRA BRIDGE
NARODA VILLAGE
S.G.HIGHWAY
SABARMATI RAILWAY STATION
TORRENT POWER HOUSE
AIRPORT
BHAVSAR HOSTEL
R.T.O
SOLA
SUBHASH BRIDGE CIRCLE
NARODA S.T. WORKSHOP
SUBHASH BRIDGE
AEC
DUDHESHWAR BRIDGE
SARDAR STADIUM
GANDHI BRIDGE
DELHI DARWAZA
KALUPUR
GULBAITEKRA
KALUPUR RAILWAY STATION
MALEK SABAN LAKE
LAW GARDEN
NEHRU BRIDGE
SHIVRANJANI
NEHRUNAGAR
SARANGPUR
ODHAV
ELLIS BRIDGE
SONI NI CHALI
ASTODIA
GEETA MANDIR
KANKARIA LAKE
SARDAR BRIDGE
SHAH ALAM
MANINAGAR RAILWAY STATION
DANILIMBDA CHAR RASTA
AMBEDKAR BRIDGE
PIRANA
CHANDOLA LAKE
MANINAGAR LOOP
SHASTRI BRIDGE
NAROL
BUS SHELTER
INTERCHANGE
LEGEND
ROAD NETWORK
RAILWAY LINE
RIVER BRIDGES
WATER BODY
AMC BOUNDARY
BRT NETWORK
N
SABARMATI RIVER

Janmarg to Regional Rail

The BRTS network connects with the regional railway station at Maninagar in Phase I. A foot overbridge joins the two stations. Pedestrians can directly transfer from one mode to the other without encountering vehicular traffic on the way. The junction development also incorporates existing conditions and activities such as street vending, city bus terminal, walking areas, etc., along with station area development.

Foot overbridge at Maninagar Railway Station

Maninagar Railway Station precinct

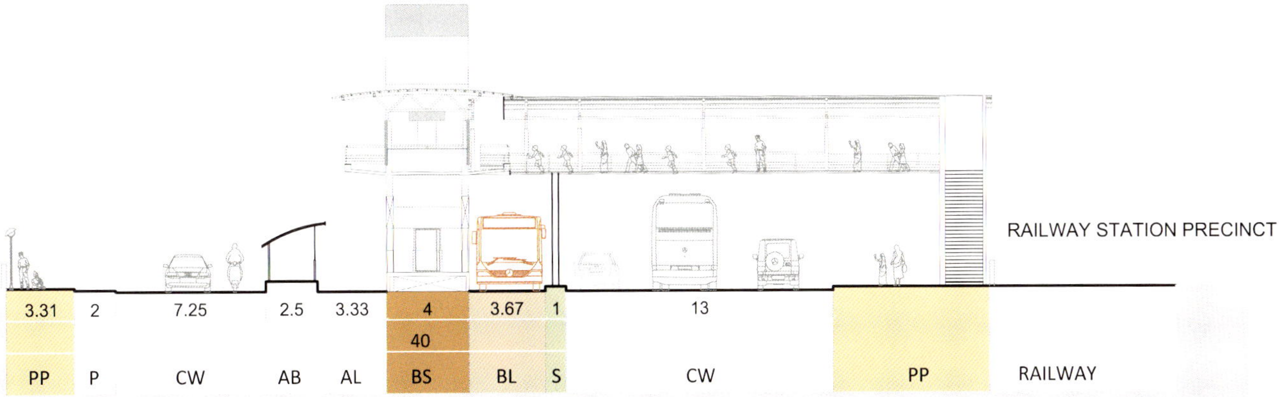
RAILWAY STATION PRECINCT
3.31
2
7.25
2.5
3.33
4
3.67
1
13
40
PP
P
CW
AB
AL
BS
BL
S
CW
PP
RAILWAY

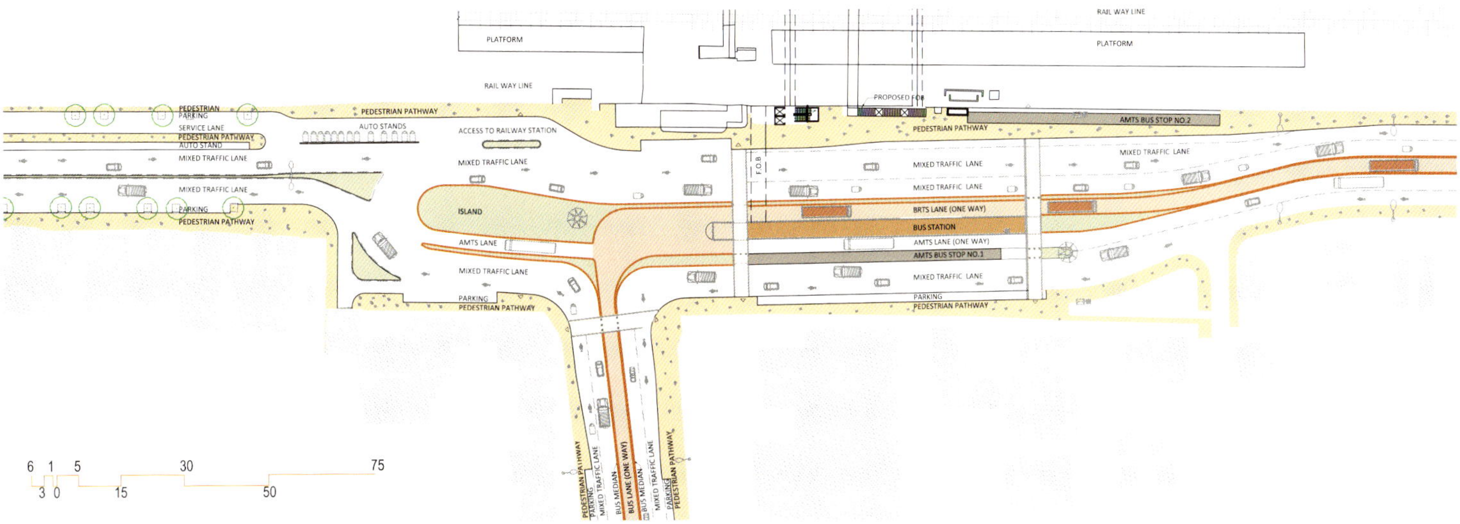
RAIL WAY LINE
PLATFORM
PLATFORM
RAIL WAY LINE
PROPOSED FOB
PEDESTRIAN PATHWAY
AUTO STANDS
ACCESS TO RAILWAY STATION
AMTS BUS STOP NO.2
PEDESTRIAN PATHWAY
MIXED TRAFFIC LANE
MIXED TRAFFIC LANE
MIXED TRAFFIC LANE
MIXED TRAFFIC LANE
ISLAND
BRTS LANE (ONE WAY)
BUS STATION
AMTS LANE
AMTS LANE (ONE WAY)
AMTS BUS STOP NO.1
MIXED TRAFFIC LANE
MIXED TRAFFIC LANE
PARKING
PEDESTRIAN PATHWAY
PARKING
PEDESTRIAN PATHWAY
F.O.B
6 1 5 30 75
3 0 15 50

Janmarg to Janmarg *DOUBLE DECKER BUS STATION*

An interesting innovation is created where two BRTS corridors intersect. Soni ni Chali junction is grade-separated for mixed traffic by means of a flyover. Demand data revealed that this junction would have many people changing from one route to the other. Therefore, stations on the two routes had to be close to each other.

In the final design, the bus stations are at two different levels and connected by a staircase and elevators. The station below is located at the centre of the junction and all right turns are through U-turns located further down the road.

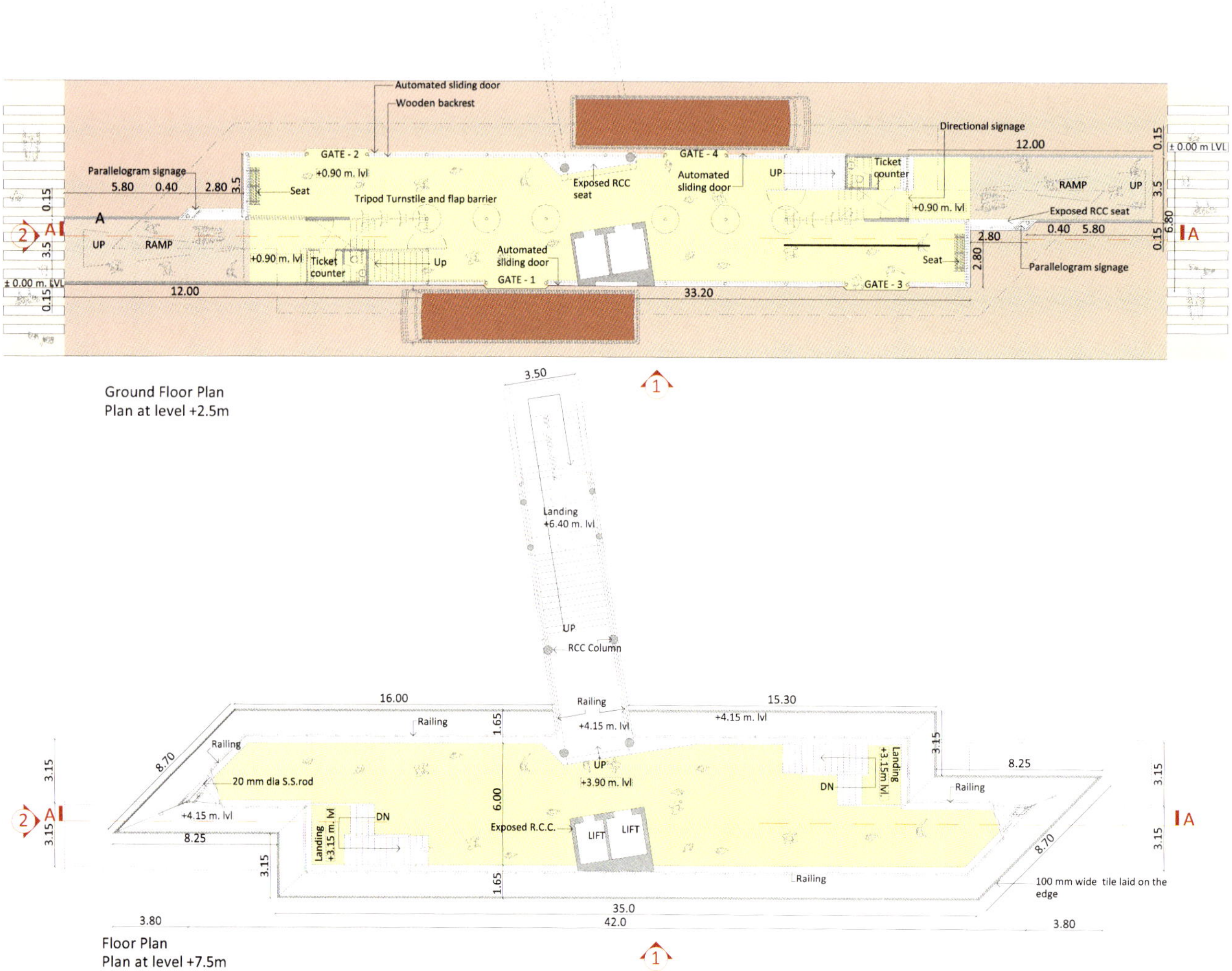

Architectural drawings for double decker bus stations

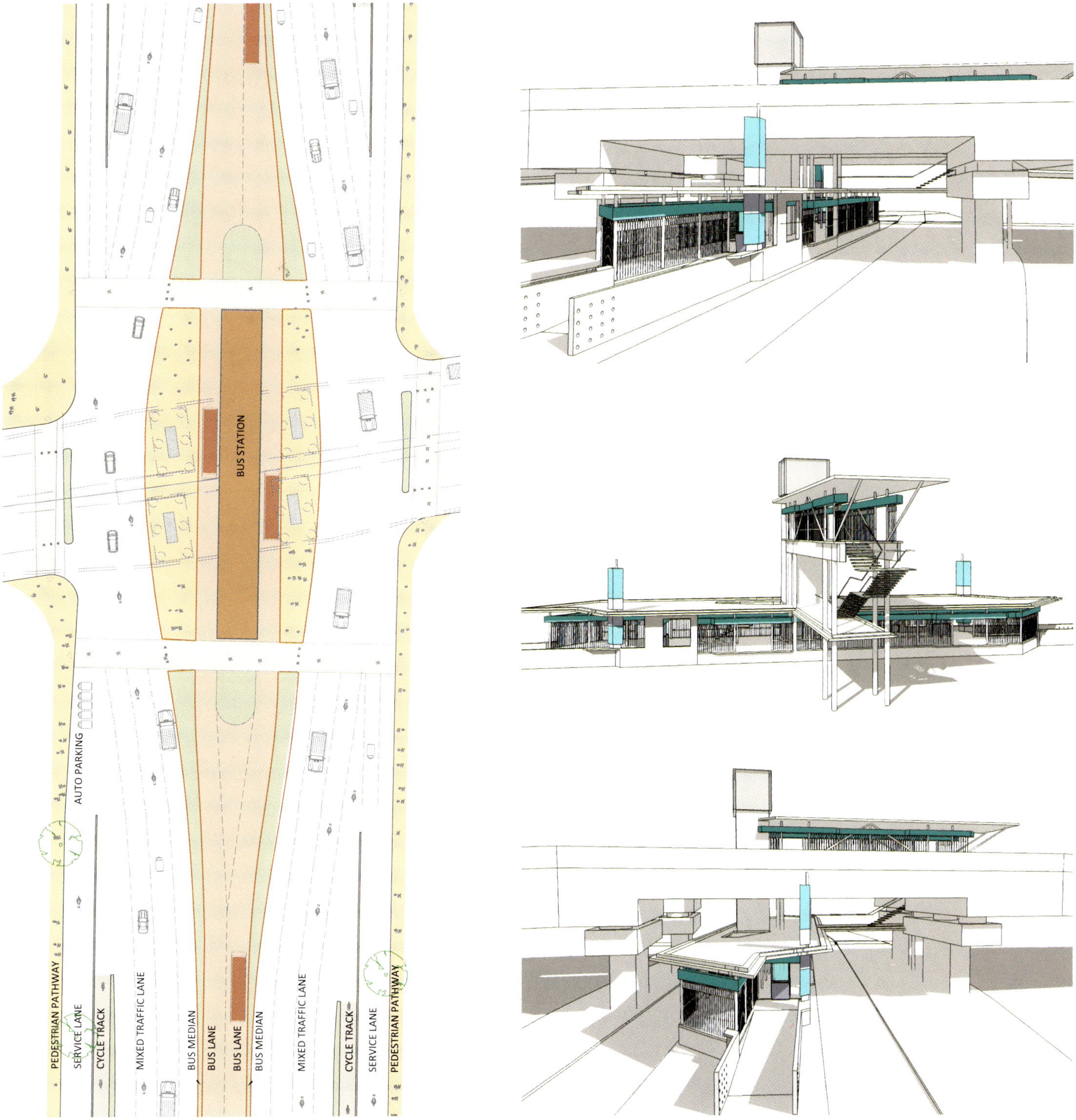

Bus station design at grade separated location: Soni ni Chali

Soni ni Chali bus station with two levels

Soni ni Chali BRT station. The staircase enables transfer to the upper level station.

Workshops

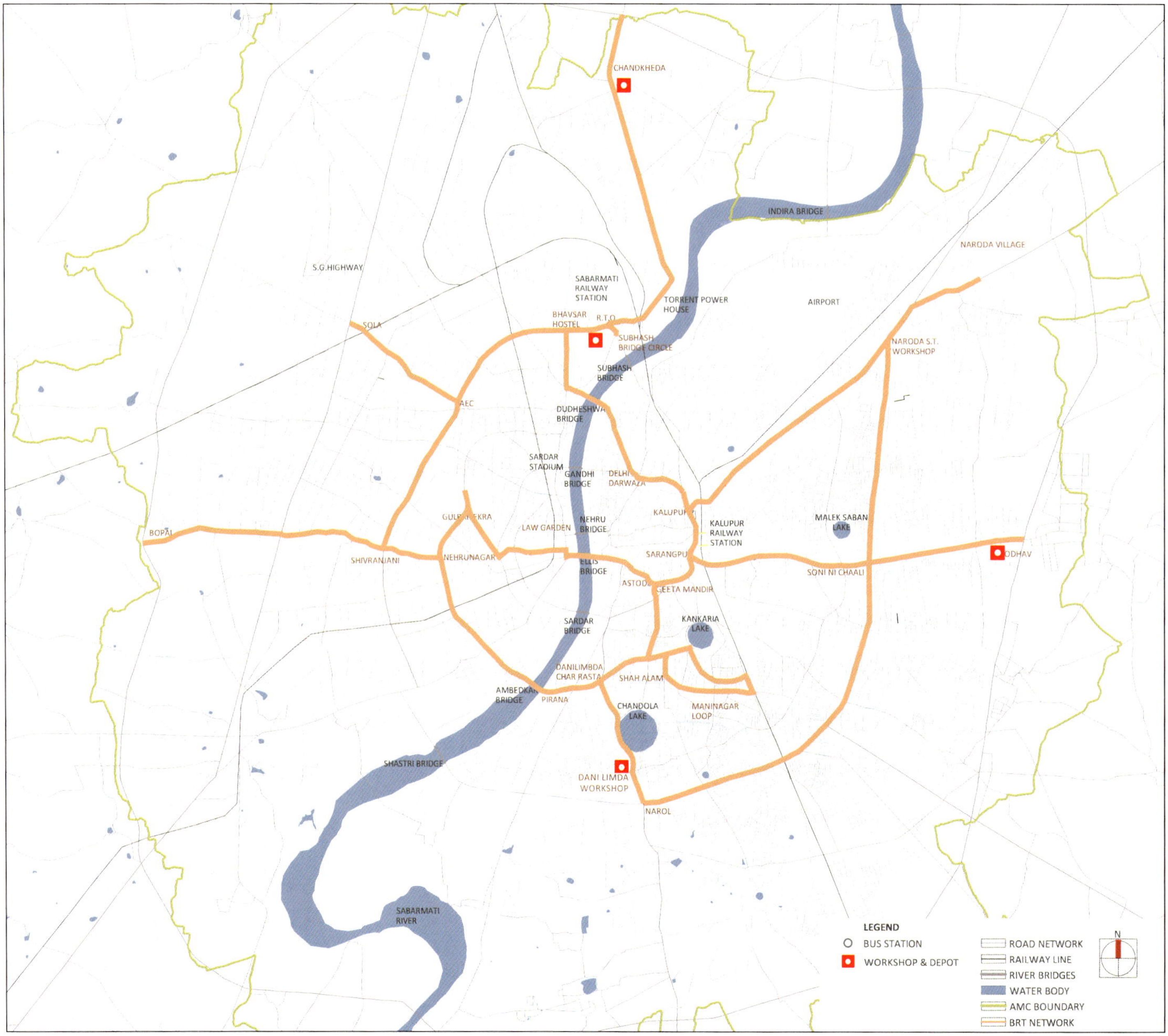

Workshop and depot for Janmarg

Phases I and II have four depots and workshops identified, with each depot accommodating an average of 60–70 buses. Of these, one workshop and depot is operational near Chandola Lake and a second is proposed at Odhav. Bus operators operate and manage this facility provided by Janmarg. This ensures daily maintenance and upkeep of the buses.

The workshop and depot is designed with state-of-the-art facilities that include maintenance pits, washing and cleaning yards, denting and painting facility, bus parking areas and CNG/ diesel station. Apart from administrative offices, rest rooms and dining facilities are also provided for the staff.

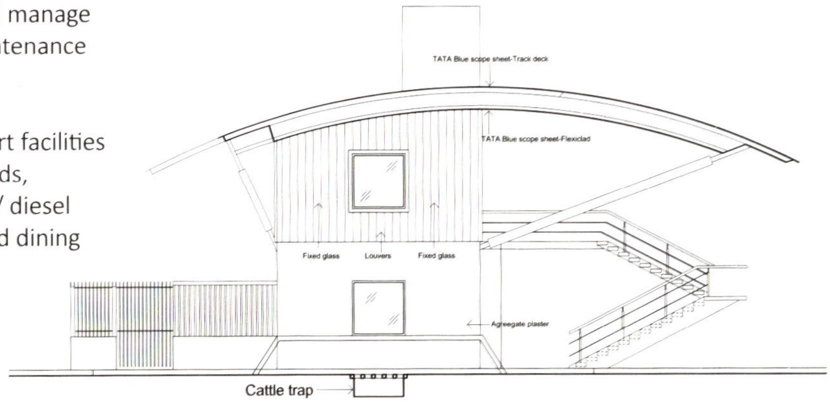

Plan and section of workshop near Chandola Lake

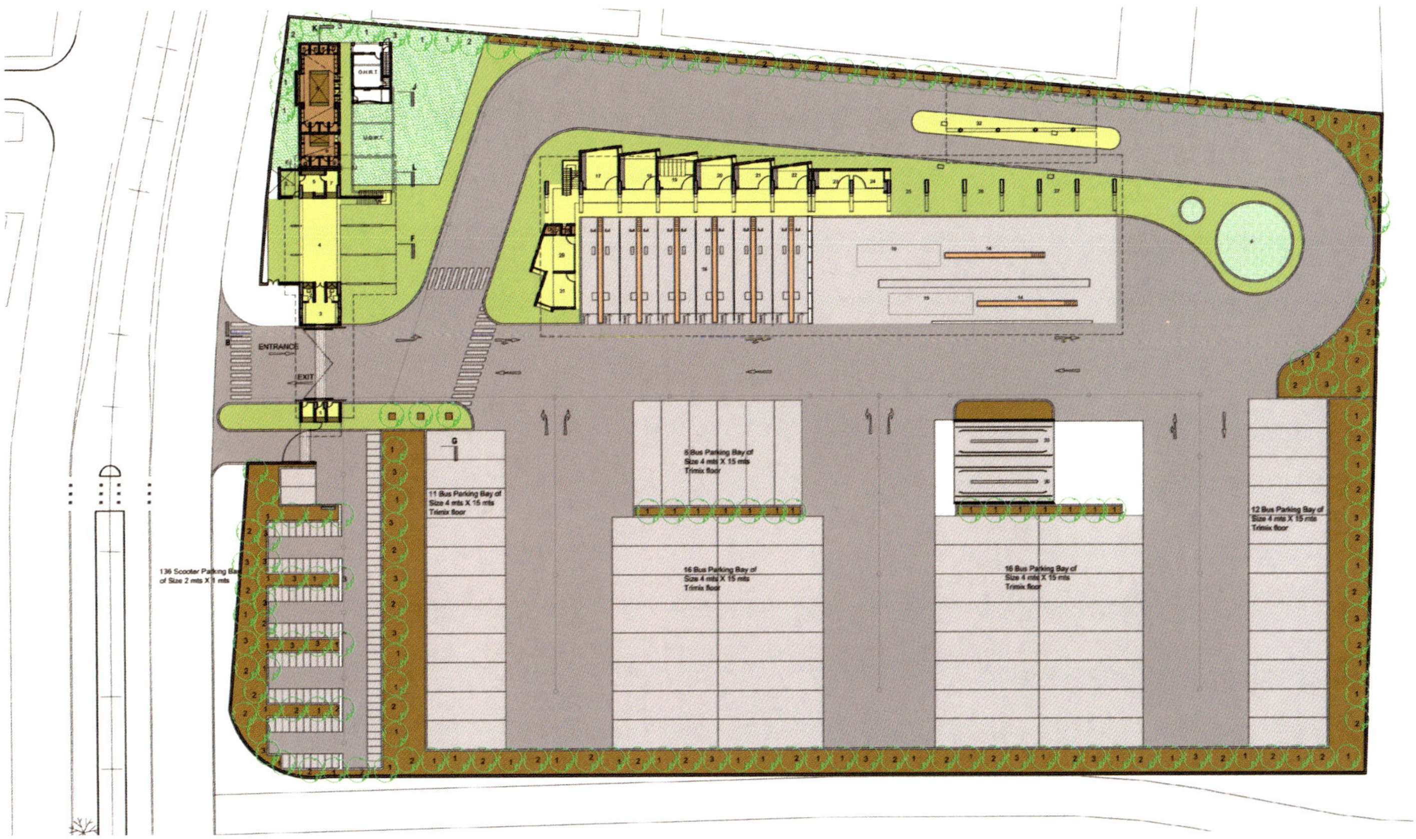

Program For Bus Depot Facilities

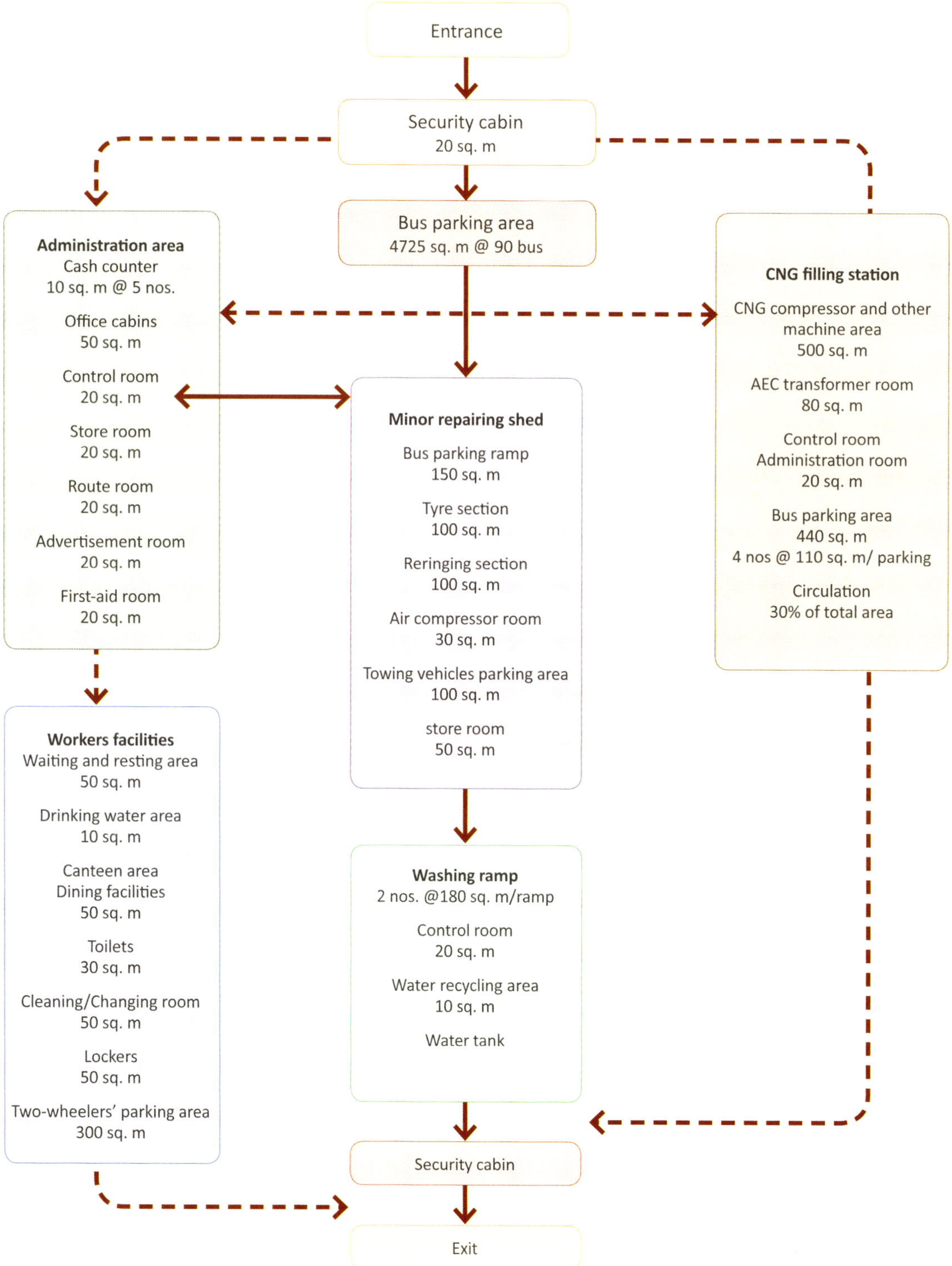

Buses parked at workshop near Chandola Lake

Janmarg currently has 150 buses. These include AC and non-AC buses.

BRTS Design

Ideas for Future

Drivers' Facility

The well-being of drivers is critical for passenger safety and an important aspect of BRTS operations. Driving for long durations in complex urban traffic conditions is often stressful. Hence, the provision of rest and refreshment facilities for drivers is necessary at the start or end of a trip. These are identified along the network where routes terminate or change. The facilities are incorporated in the design of the relevant stations. The proposal is consciously prepared to meet the need for consistency with the design language adopted. In all, ten such locations have been identified along the Phase I and Phase II corridors.

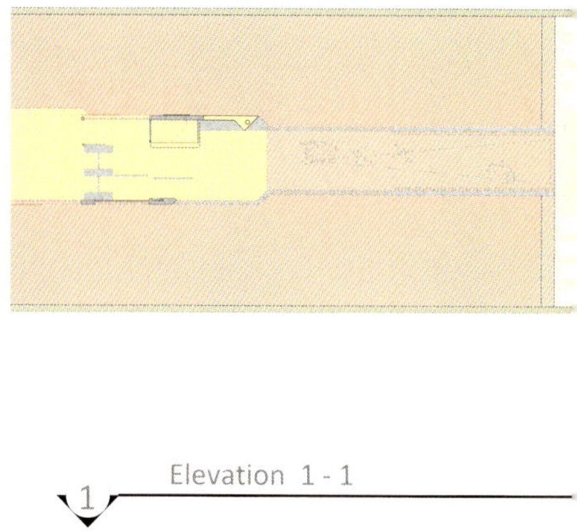

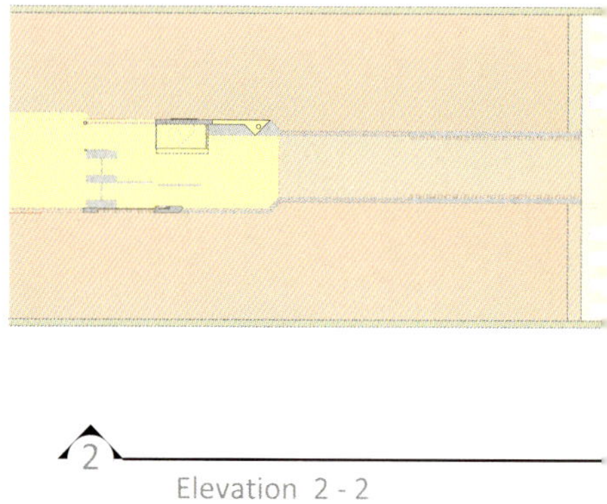

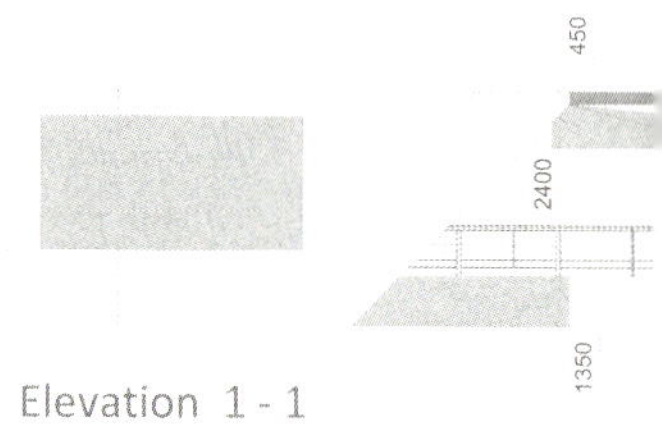

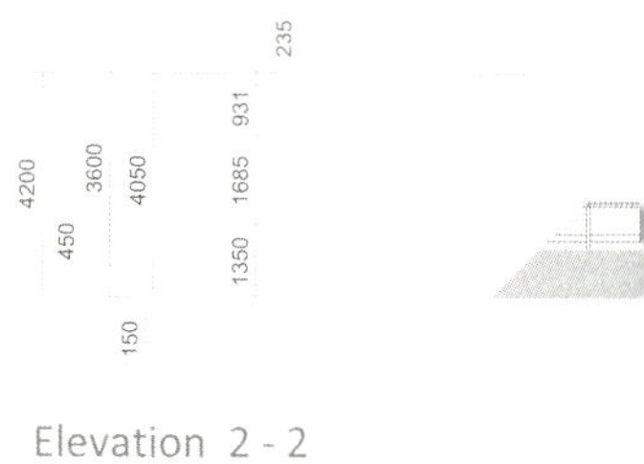

Proposed plans for drivers' facility

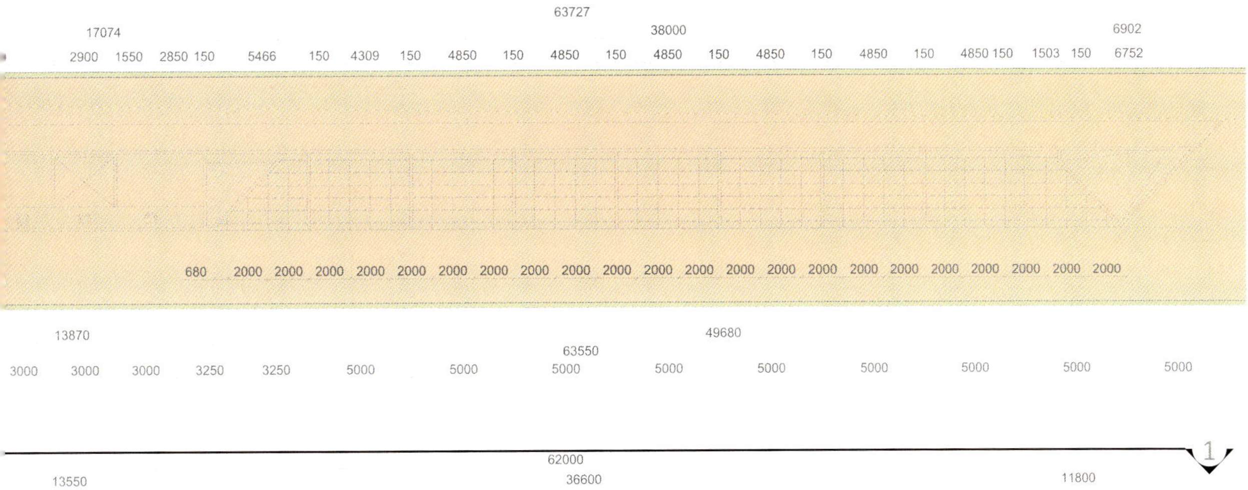
1

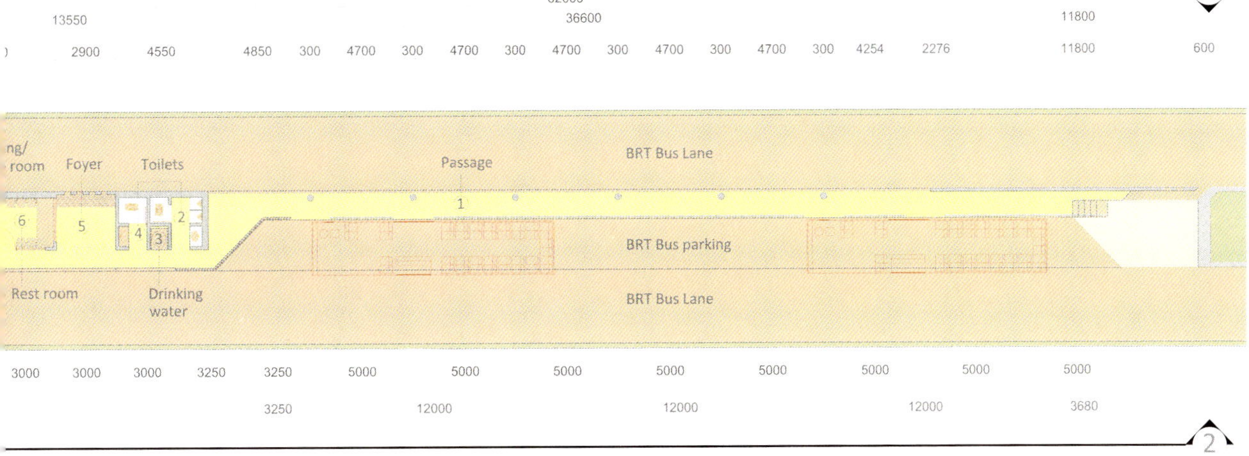
ng/
room
Foyer
Toilets
Passage
BRT Bus Lane
BRT Bus parking
BRT Bus Lane
Rest room
Drinking
water
2

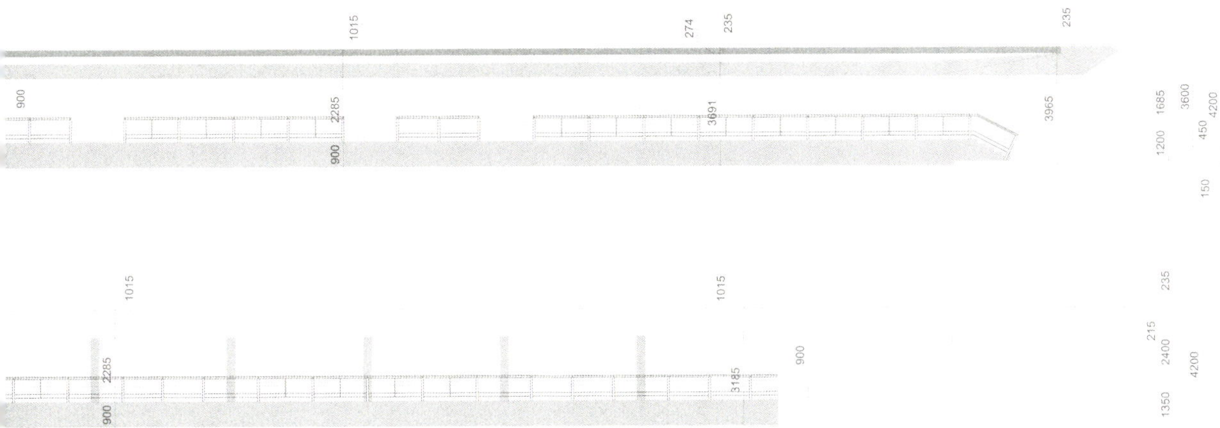

Interchange with Terminal

These interchanges are foreseen on the city periphery where Janmarg, GSRTC and feeder systems converge. Hence, facilities such as parking of buses and private vehicles, activity areas and pedestrian overbridges are envisaged as crucial design features. The interchanges would be located where local public transport offers connection to the regional/city bus services and there is adequate space for all supporting facilities. Instead of planning off-road facilities, the interchange is located in the centre of the road, with other traffic flowing on either side.

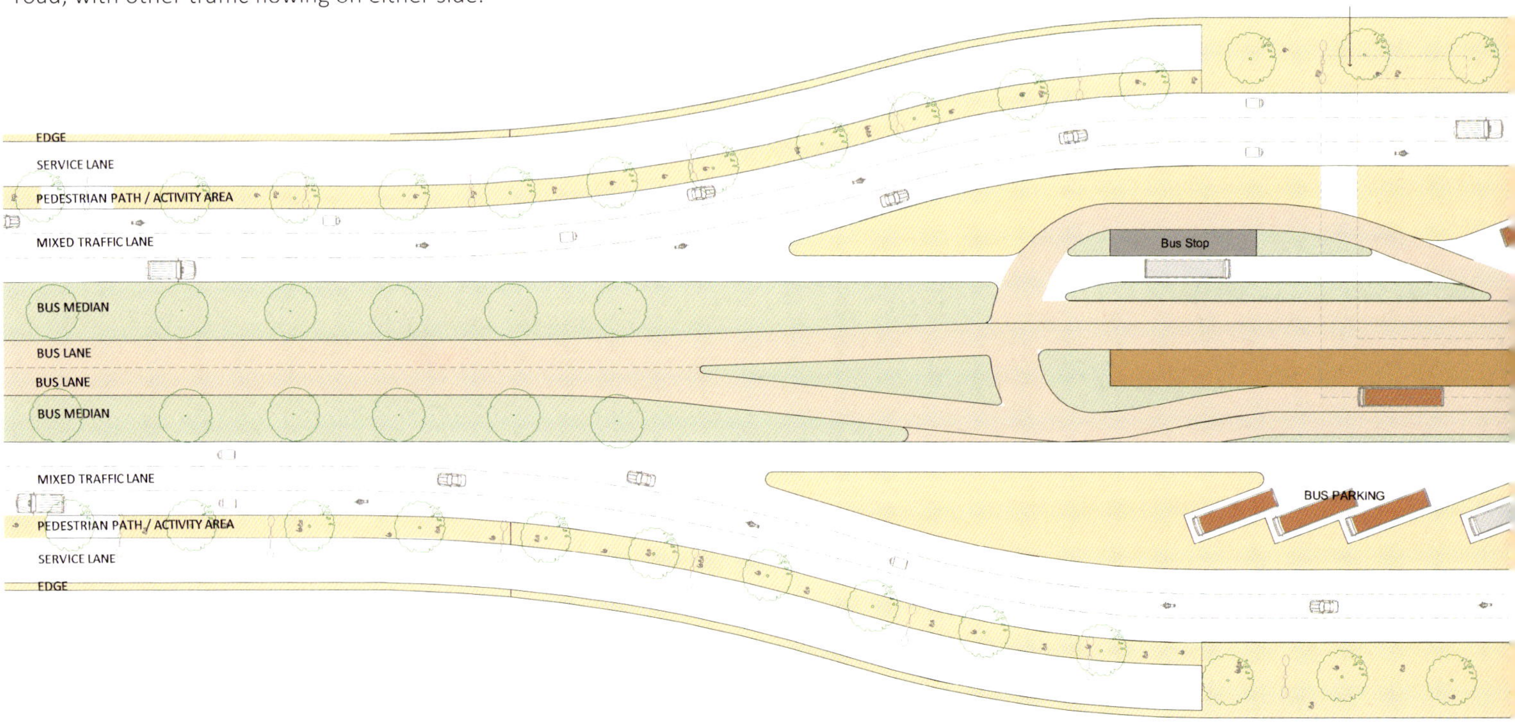

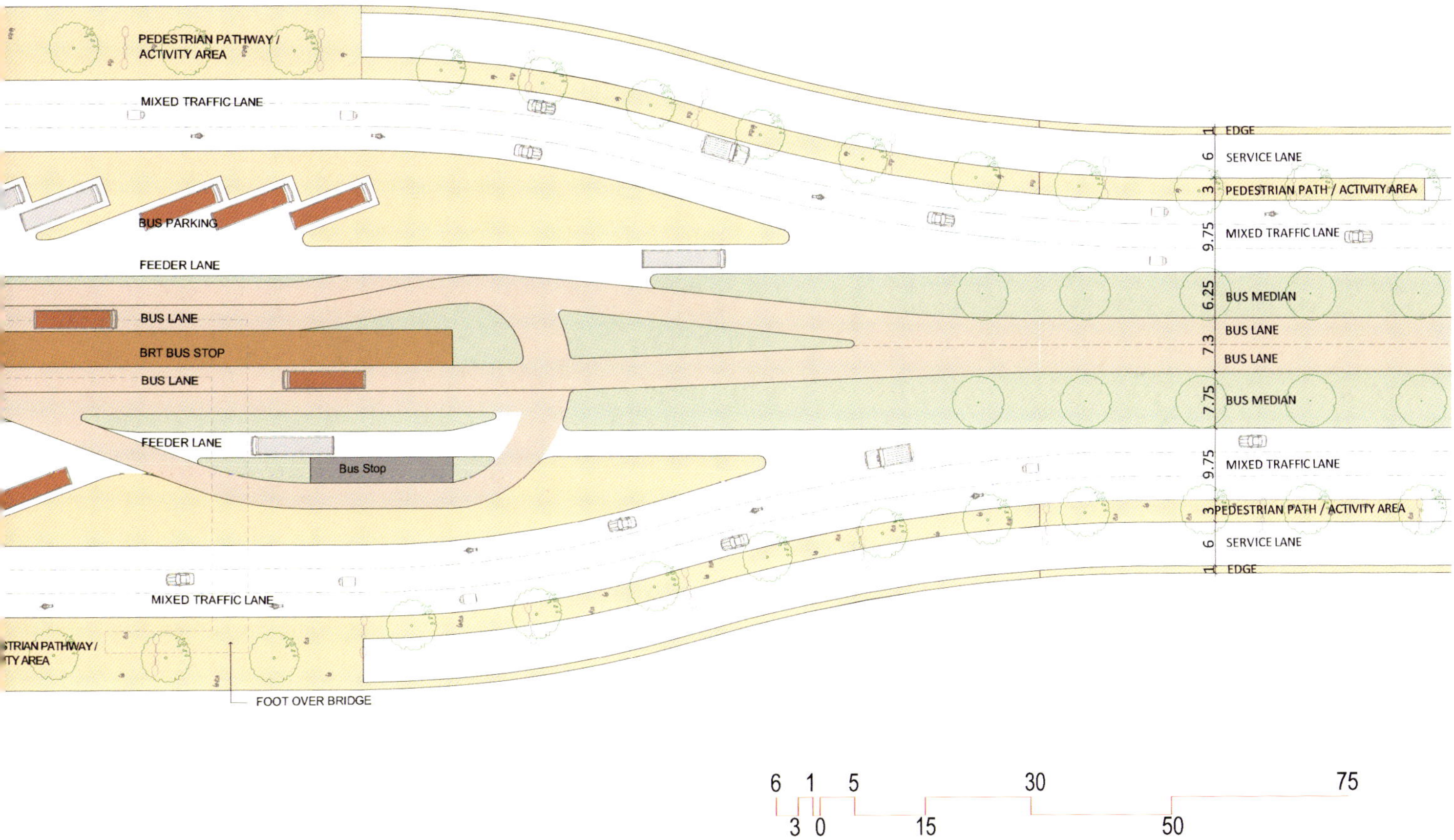

Proposed plan for on-road interchange

Elevated Turnaround

The provision of a turnaround on the BRTS corridor allows for termination of route runs either at the end of the corridor or at specific points en route, based on demand. Currently, en route termination is possible only where space for turning is available, mostly at junctions such as Narol, Nehrunagar and Anjali crossroads, which offer a large area at roundabouts. Therefore, at present, the location of turnarounds does not correspond to passenger demand in sections. This reduces flexibility in route planning and results in extra operation costs due to operation of buses in low-demand sections, especially in off-peak hours. In order to rationalise this, elevated turnarounds are proposed at some key locations, which include Viratnagar, Anjali crossroads and Dani Limda.

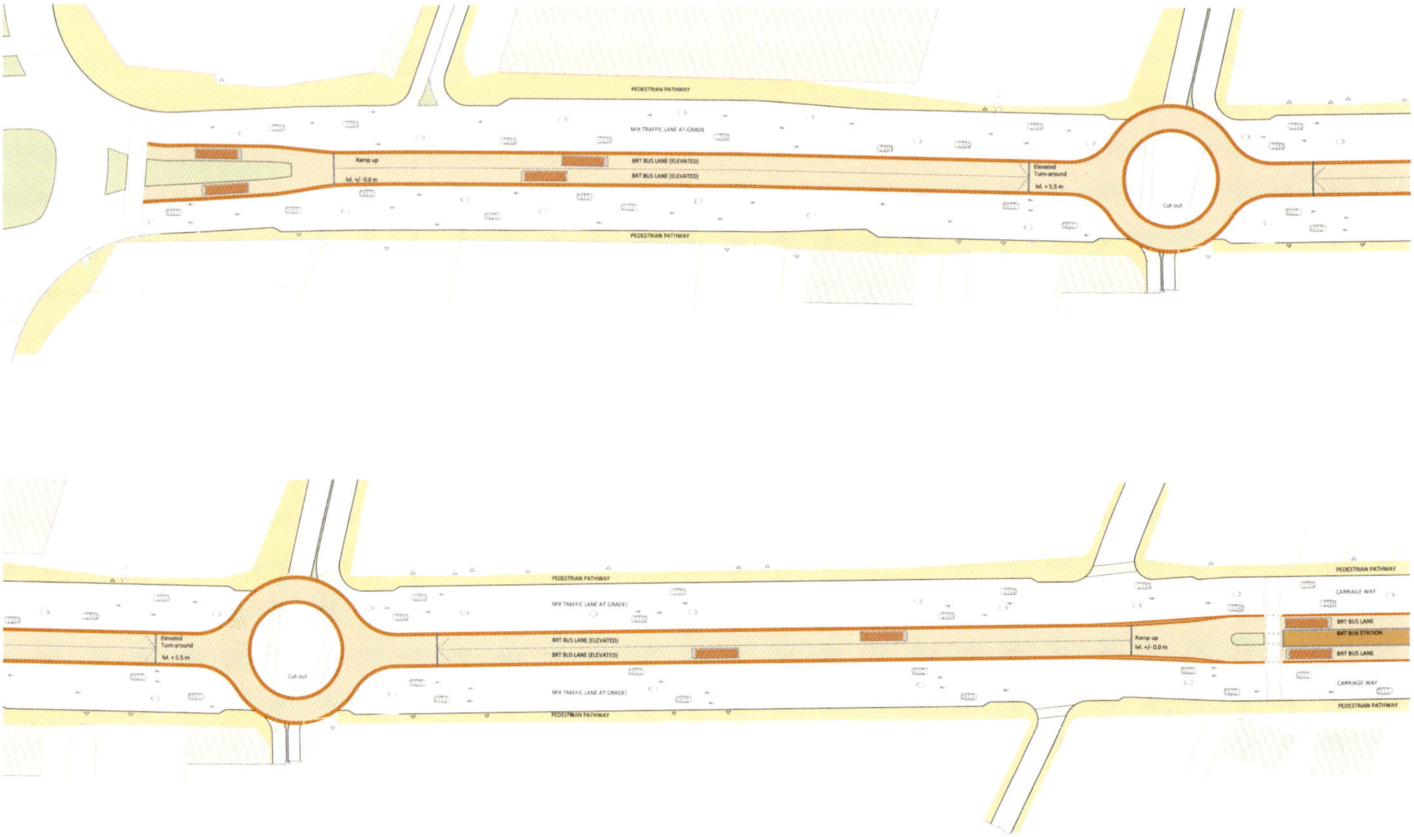

Proposed plan for elevated turnaround

All set for a BRTS ride

A system for all

'Janmarg' – the people's way

Conclusion

When the Ahmedabad BRT system was conceptualised, there were no case studies or templates in India to guide its design. The Indian Roads Congress (IRC), which prescribes design standards for urban roads, does not have any codes or standards on how BRT systems should be designed. In fact, if IRC were to be the template on which BRTS is designed, it would be impossible to have segregated lanes, different configurations of lane widths for other traffic, bus stations in the middle of the road and other BRTS infrastructure. Yet, Ahmedabad built a successful and widely acknowledged system—a system which other cities in India come to study and from which they take back lessons.

Ahmedabad realised very early in the design process that bus lanes are not the only components of a BRT system. Other components such as MV lanes, cycle tracks, parking, footpaths, workshops, depots and terminals are equally important. A robust Integrated Transportation Management System (ITMS) is essential to hold these components together.

Certain components are non-negotiable. For example, buses need to run on segregated corridors and site constraints should lead to innovation that manages segregation. It may mean one-way bus lanes, elevated corridors or bus plus pedestrian-only corridors. If segregation is not achieved, the system will pay a heavy price in terms of rapidity and reliability.

Bus stations cannot be avoided in any situation. They are places where the user enters the system. Simply adding bus lanes without providing bus stations at regular intervals will not add passengers. Similarly, priority at intersections is critical. Buses cannot be kept waiting at the tail of the queue for the signal. The design must place them at the head of the queue. Low cost should not mean compromise on quality. In some cases, higher specifications may mean higher capital costs, but will be beneficial in the long term with lower maintenance costs.

The biggest lesson from the Ahmedabad experience is the need to evolve and innovate constantly. Cities should be ready to go back to the drawing board and modify design elements that will enhance the system. Janmarg's success can be attributed to its willingness to continually explore new ideas. It deviated from standard practices and it worked.

The present document demonstrates how flexibility can be achieved without compromising on core values to achieve desired outcomes. It provides ideas and examples which other cities may wish to further investigate; it demonstrates the value of thinking 'out of the box'. However, it is not intended to be used as a 'standard' for BRTS design. Cities need to evolve their own design and be prepared to move away from standard practices without compromising on core values.

Bibliography

Ahmedabad Bus Rapid Transit System: Phase I, Detailed Project Report, Centre of Excellence in Urban Transport, CEPT University, February 2006.

Ahmedabad Bus Rapid Transit System: Phase II, Detailed Project Report, Centre of Excellence in Urban Transport, CEPT University, August 2008.

Ahmedabad Bus Rapid Transit System: Phase III, Detailed Project Report, Centre of Excellence in Urban Transport, CEPT University, March 2013.

Bus Rapid Transit Planning Guide. Institute for Transportation and Development Policy: 2007.

Berger, Louis. *Integrated Public Transit Study*. Gujarat Infrastructure Development Board: 2000.

Working paper on 'Bus Stop Design and Location', Centre of Excellence in Urban Transport, CEPT University, May 2006.

Working paper on 'Environmental Impact Assessment', Centre of Excellence in Urban Transport, CEPT University, July 2006.

Working paper on 'Fare Collection and Fixation', Centre of Excellence in Urban Transport, CEPT University, November 2006.

Working paper on 'Institutional Aspects', Centre of Excellence in Urban Transport, CEPT University, November 2006.

Working paper on 'Land Use Restructuring', Centre of Excellence in Urban Transport, CEPT University, April 2007.

Working paper on 'Pavement Design', Centre of Excellence in Urban Transport, CEPT University, July 2006.

Working paper on 'Road Utilities', Centre of Excellence in Urban Transport, CEPT University, November 2007.

Working paper on 'Traffic Volume Characteristics and Junction Management', Centre of Excellence in Urban Transport, CEPT University, December 2006.

Working paper on 'Vehicle Technology', Centre of Excellence in Urban Transport, CEPT University, November 2006.

About the Authors

I. P. Gautam

I. P. Gautam began his career with the Indian Revenue Service as an Assistant Commissioner of Income Tax and joined Indian Administrative Service in 1986. He has served as Secretary and Principal Secretary, Government of Gujarat, in various departments like Industries, Energy & Petrochemicals, Narmada, Ports & Transport, and Urban Development & Urban Housing, etc. He has also served as Director (Finance) of Sardar Sarovar Narmada Project for five years and as the Municipal Commissioner of Rajkot and Ahmedabad.

Gautam spearheaded the implementation of Bus Rapid Transit System (BRTS) in Ahmedabad, one of the first in the country. His major contributions include power sector reforms, conversion of thousands of auto rickshaws to CNG, implementing PPP arrangements for the city bus service and BRTS, effective rehabilitation and resettlement of projects-affected people, housing for the urban poor and many innovations in civic management and project financing.

During his tenure as Municipal Commissioner and Chairman of Sabarmati Riverfront Development body and Ahmedabad Janmarg Ltd., nationally famous projects like the Ahmedabad BRTS, Kankaria Lakefront Development and Sabarmati Riverfront Development were completed and the civic body received many international and national awards for its work.

Prof. H. M. Shivanand Swamy

Prof. Shivanand Swamy, an economist and urban and regional planner, has been an educator, researcher, policy advisor and consultant on development planning, specifically on integrated land use–transport planning and design and urban development management. As an academic, he has been involved in teaching at CEPT University since 1986, and his teaching and research interests are in land use–transport planning, transportation economics and finance.

Prof. Swamy has assisted the cities of Surat and Ahmedabad in evolving their city mobility plans. He has been instrumental in planning and operationalising the Bus Rapid Transit System (BRTS) in Ahmedabad and Surat, and lent his expertise to the Union Ministry of Urban Development in evolving planning and design guidelines for BRTS as well as in scaling bus-based services in various cities of India. Besides Ahmadabad and Surat, he is involved with developing the BRT System in Bhubaneswar, Hubli–Dharwad and Vadodara.

Abhijit Lokre

Abhijit Lokre is an urban planner with over thirteen years of work experience. His key interest areas are urban transport and planning, street design, transit oriented development, transit infrastructure and transport policies. He leads the design team for BRTS Projects in Ahmedabad, Surat, Indore, Vadodara and Hubli–Dharwad. The scope of work includes detailed design for the BRTS, quality control for site work, coordinating with local authorities for preparing the institutional structure, business plan and transit policies.

At the Centre of Excellence in Urban Transport, he is involved in research on BRTS projects in India and parking policies. He has been trained by Sustainable Urban Transport Program (SUTP) and GTZ as a trainer in urban transport and mass transit systems. He is also trained to lead training programs for mid-level professionals by the World Bank.

Vijay Arya

Vijay Arya, a graduate of the School of Architecture, Ahmedabad, with post-graduation from Helsinki University of Technology, founded Arya Architects with partner Meghal Arya. The firm started in 1999 and has since established itself as a practice that engages with the challenges of the contemporary ethos of India as a growing economy, along with an acknowledgement of its valuable traditions.

His portfolio in architecture for transit is extensive, focussing on the infrastructure design for various BRT systems across the country. Every project designed and realized in his practice strives to create benchmarks in design, response to environment and functional efficiency. Described as one of the brightest emerging architectural practices in India by *Wallpaper**, UK, it is seen as a value-based practice, contributing towards raising benchmarks in design in the country. In the short span of a decade, his work has sustained its quality output through a process of research, analysis and finally timely deliverables.

Support Team:

Shefali Borikar-Shurpali
(Architect, Urban Designer)

Sandeep Paul
(Architect, Urban Designer)

Halak Bhatt
(Architect, Environment Planner)

Aanan Sutaria
(Architect, Transport Planner)

Sohel Mansur
(Architect, Urban Designer)

Dixita Patel

Vishal Gariyal

Dhvani Pandya

About Centre of Excellence in Urban Transport, CEPT University

The Centre of Excellence in Urban Transport, CEPT University, established in 2009, is an initiative of the Ministry of Urban Development (MoUD), Government of India. It is supported by Ahmedabad Municipal Corporation. CoE-UT, CEPT, has been envisaged as a resource centre for dealing with issues in urban transport planning and management. The overall objective of this nationally recognised Centre is to become a think tank and resource centre for research, education and training in planning and management of urban transport. It has a mandate to cover three aspects of capacity building in urban transport – human resource development, knowledge management and technical assistance and advice.

The Centre set up a Masters specialisation programme in Urban Transport Planning and Management in 2009. It also introduced the 'Leaders Programme in Urban Transport Planning and Management' – a certificate course for in-service urban transport professionals in July 2012, in collaboration with the World Bank and the MoUD.

CoE-UT, CEPT, has organised several national level workshops and seminars on BRTS planning and design, Comprehensive Mobility Plans, etc. It also took a lead in organising the first Asia BRTS Conference in September 2012 which attracted more than 250 delegates from India and abroad.

The Centre has signed a Memorandum of Understanding with the Institute for Transport Studies, University of Leeds—a leading transport institute in Europe—for academic and research cooperation in urban transport.

The Centre is also involved in several research works, developing a manual on design of footpaths in urban areas and a guideline document on planning and design of bus stations, research on land use transport integration and road safety levels in Ahmedabad etc. Apart from these, the Centre has also been providing technical assistance to the MoUD on urban bus specifications and has been contributing to numerous national committees, working groups and government-led missions/ projects related to urban development and urban transport in varying capacities.

Team Leader
Prof. H. M. Shivanand Swamy

Core Team
Abhijit Lokre
Shalini Sinha
Nitika Bhakuni
Sandeep Paul
Kunal Parikh
Shefali Borikar-Shurpali
Chintan Daftardar
Aanan Sutaria

Architectural Consultant: Arya Architects
Vijay Arya
Meghal Arya

Road Engineering: LEA Associates
Dr. M. P. Raju
Pradeep Kumar
Sagar Deshmukh

Structural & Utility Consultant: Multi Media Consultants Pvt. Ltd.
Apurva Parikh

ITS Consultant: VBSoft India Ltd.
Vivek Ogra

Procurement Consultant: Coordinates Infrastructure Consulting
Gautam Patel
Hiren Joshi
Nirav Joshi

Institutional Expert
K. Mukundan

Electrical Consultant: JIT Engineering Services Consultants
Jital Jhaveri

BRTS Team 2005–2014

Aashka Shah
Adarsh Vishwam
Adnan Gandevia
Akash Mahale
Ami Rathod
Anjana Menon
Ankur Dadheech
Anup Murdia
Anusha Vaid
Archna Goswami
Arjun Joshi
Arunika Karmakar
Ashish Pant
Ashok Vaghela
Astha
Avinash Yadav
Bhavesh Mistry
Bindi Shastri
Birva Shah
Boski Shah
Charul Patel
Chetna Jain
Chintan Patel
Chirag Shah
Darshana Nair
Darshit Shah
Dashrath Rathod
Devang Deshmukh
Dhaval Dixit
Dhruma Bhavsar
Dhvani Pandya
Dhwani Shah
Divyank Patel
Divyaraj Zala
Dixit Prajapati
Dixita Patel
Faiz Shaikh
Fenil Aariwala
Gambheer Singh
Garvit Rathod
Gaurangi Karnik
Gauri Jumde
Halak Bhatt
Harshal Gandhi
Himali Gajjar
Hiral Patel
Hiren Mistry
Jainal Shah
Jaydeep Kalaria
Jigeeshu Joshi
Jignasha Bhamrah
Jignesh Barot
Kaivalya Pathak
Kartik Raman
Kaushik Chodvadia
Khelan Modi
Kiran Dixit
Kruti Multani
Krutika Gandhi
Laghu Parashar
Mallika Jain
Malti Rani
Manjiri Akalkotkar
Manoj Ajudia
Mansi Doshi
Maulik Shah
Mehul Rana
Mitesh Patel
Neha Soni
Nehali Bhatt
Nidhi Shah
Nikhil Sharma
Nirav Patel
Nirav Vidwans
Nishant Sheth
Nishtha Makhwana
Nitin Warrier
Nivesh Chaudhary
Pankaj Sharma
Pankaj Suthar
Paresh Shah
Parthiv Soni
Parul Tripathi
Pooja Sanghani
Pranati Avasti
Prashant Parekh
Prashant Vardhan
Pratik Dave
Pratik Suryavanshi
Pritesh Suthar
Priti Saini
Priya Thavani
Priyanka Bajariya
Priyanka Pawar
Priyanka Tinekar
Prutha Shah
Querie Sakhiya
Rajal Dave
Rajesh Asathi
Rajesinh Chand
Rajkumar Mishra
Reema Prajapati
Rejeet Mathews
Ritesh Patil
Romil Patel
Ronak Nagpuria
Ruchin Pandit
Ruchita Shah
Rujul Joshi
Rutul Joshi
Rutika Bhatt
Sagar Setia
Sahana Ganesh
Sandeep Chhatrola
Sandeep Ojha
Sandip Patil
Sanket Bhatt
Saurav Dhar
Savitri Patil
Sayan Roy
Shashi Tindwani
Shelly Kulshrestha
Shraddha Jain
Shreyansh Shah
Shrutika Parihar
Shweta Moon
Sneha Rapur
Sneha Sharma
Sohel Mansur
Sohel Shaikh
Souvik Nath
Srujan Gupta
Sugandha Rana
Sujal Pandya
Sungdi Imchen
Sunil Tite
Suparna Maiti
Surbhi Gupta
Swapna Wilson
Swapnil Joshi
Swarnima Chauhan
Tuhin Subra Maparu
Tushar Deepak
Umesh Ninama
Uvika Gupta
Vaibhavi Mehta
Vijal Desai
Viniket Kalaria
Vishal Gariyal
Viyush Patel
Vineet Wanchoo
Yogesh Sharma

BRTS route map, Ahmedabad

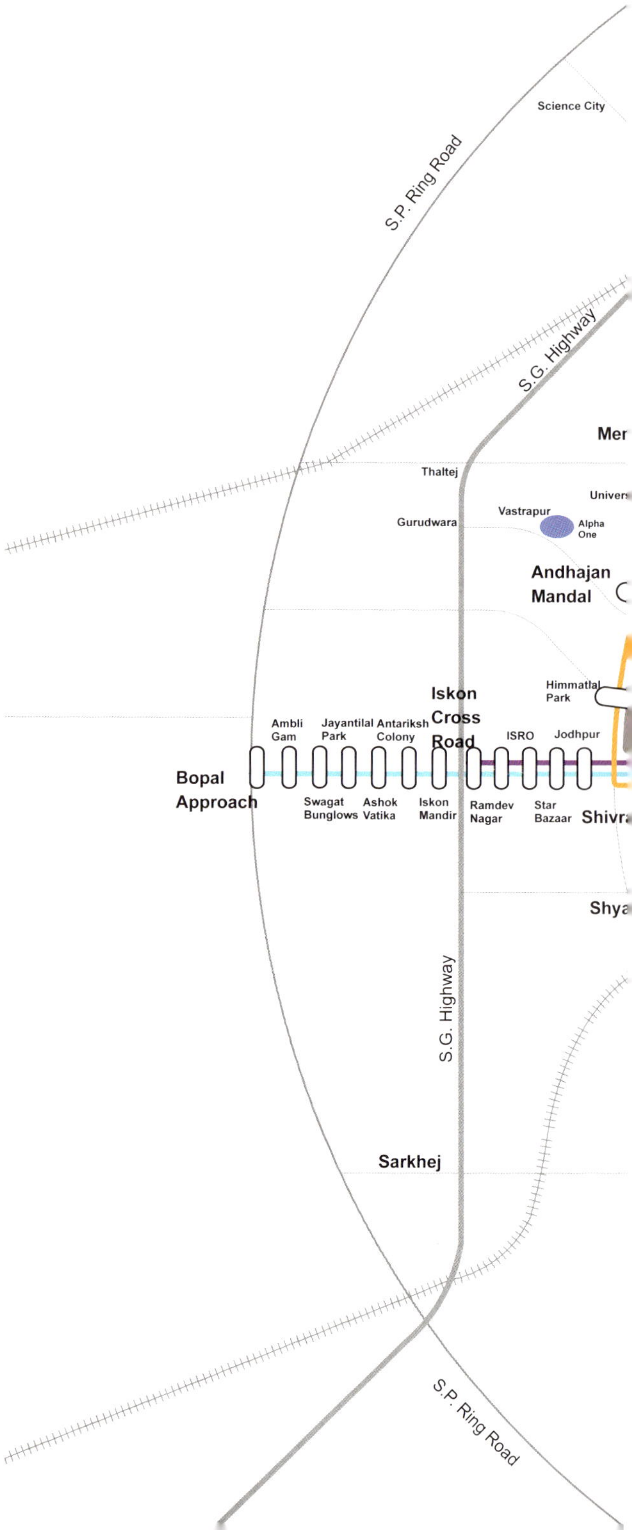

Legends

- BRTS Bus Station
- Interchange
- Chandkheda–L.D. Engineering
- RTO–Maninagar
- Bopal–Maninagar
- Iskon–L.D.–Naroda
- Anjali–Naroda
- Science City Approach–Odhav Fire Station
- Circular East (Naroda–Narol–Naroda)
- Circular West (RTO–Kalupur–RTO)
- L.D. Engineering–Odhav
- Visat–Kalupur–Maninagar

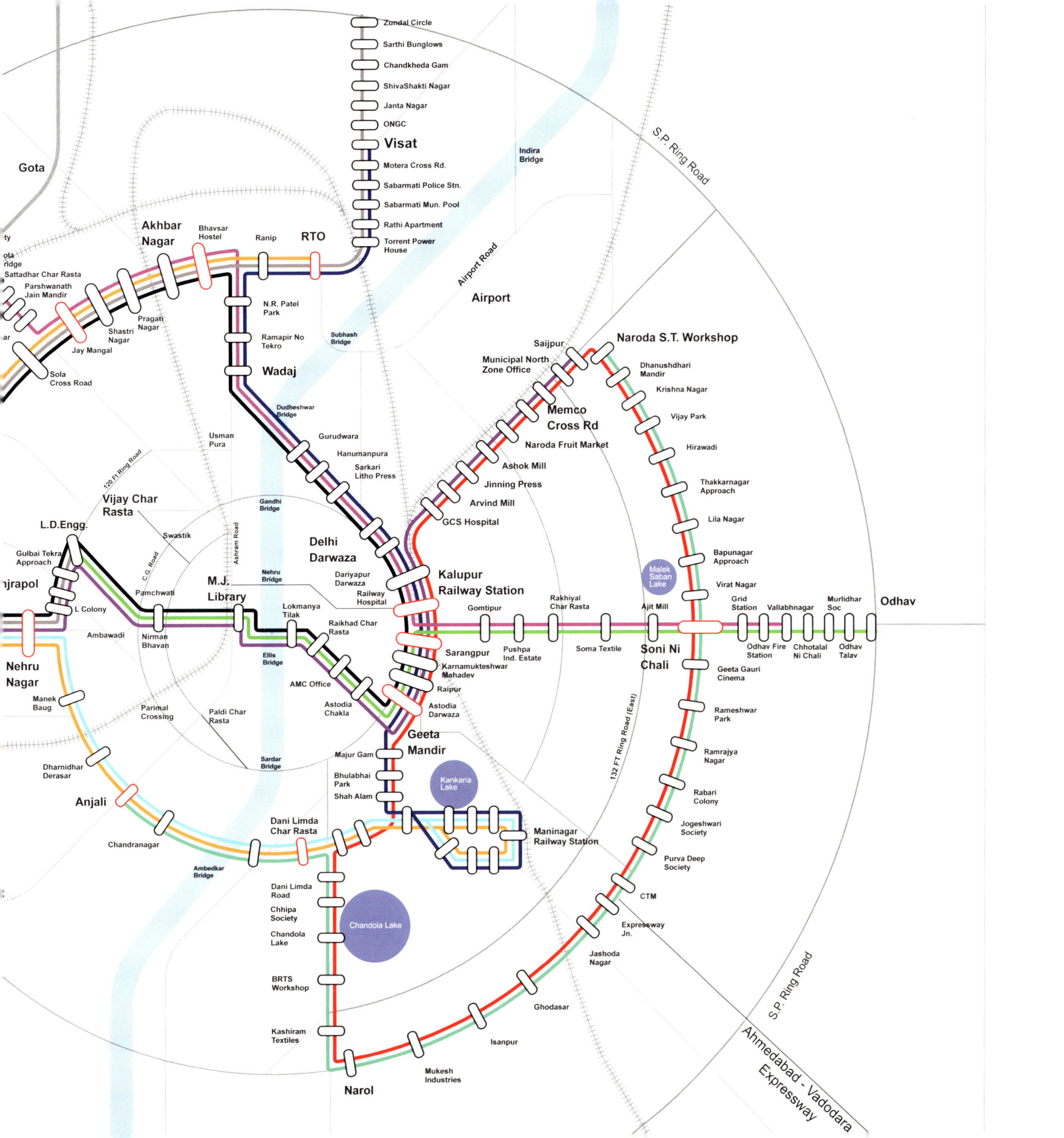

Zundal Circle
Sarthi Bunglows
Chandkheda Gam
ShivaShakti Nagar
Janta Nagar
ONGC
Visat
Motera Cross Rd.
Sabarmati Police Stn.
Sabarmati Mun. Pool
Rathi Apartment
Torrent Power House
Gota
S.P. Ring Road
Indira Bridge
Akhbar Nagar
Bhavsar Hostel
Ranip
RTO
Sattadhar Char Rasta
Parshwanath Jain Mandir
Pragati Nagar
Shastri Nagar
Jay Mangal
Sola Cross Road
N.R. Patel Park
Ramapir No Tekro
Wadaj
Subhash Bridge
Airport Road
Airport
Saijpur
Municipal North Zone Office
Naroda S.T. Workshop
Dhanushdhari Mandir
Krishna Nagar
Vijay Park
Memco Cross Rd
Naroda Fruit Market
Hirawadi
Ashok Mill
Jinning Press
Arvind Mill
GCS Hospital
Thakkarnagar Approach
Lila Nagar
Dudheshwar Bridge
Gurudwara
Hanumanpura
Sarkari Litho Press
Usman Pura
120 Ft Ring Road
Vijay Char Rasta
L.D.Engg.
Swastik
Gandhi Bridge
Delhi Darwaza
Gulbai Tekra Approach
C.G. Road
Ashram Road
Pamchwati
M.J. Library
Nehru Bridge
Dariyapur Darwaza
Railway Hospital
Kalupur Railway Station
Bapunagar Approach
Malek Saban Lake
Virat Nagar
L Colony
Lokmanya Tilak
Gomtipur
Rakhiyal Char Rasta
Ajit Mill
Grid Station
Vallabhnagar
Murlidhar Soc
Odhav
Ambawadi
Nirman Bhavan
Raikhad Char Rasta
Ellis Bridge
Sarangpur
Pushpa Ind. Estate
Soma Textile
Soni Ni Chali
Odhav Fire Station
Chhotalal Ni Chali
Odhav Talav
Karnamukteshwar Mahadev
Geeta Gauri Cinema
Nehru Nagar
AMC Office
Raipur
Manek Baug
Astodia Chakla
Astodia Darwaza
Parimal Crossing
Paldi Char Rasta
Rameshwar Park
Geeta Mandir
132 FT Ring Road (East)
Majur Gam
Sardar Bridge
Ramrajya Nagar
Dharnidhar Derasar
Bhulabhai Park
Kankaria Lake
Shah Alam
Rabari Colony
Anjali
Dani Limda Char Rasta
Maninagar Railway Station
Jogeshwari Society
Chandranagar
Purva Deep Society
Ambedkar Bridge
Dani Limda Road
CTM
Chhipa Society
Chandola Lake
Expressway Jn.
Chandola Lake
Jashoda Nagar
BRTS Workshop
Ghodasar
S.P. Ring Road
Kashiram Textiles
Isanpur
Mukesh Industries
Narol
Ahmedabad - Vadodara Expressway